Meetings with Remarkable Women

Meetings with Remarkable Women

BUDDHIST TEACHERS IN AMERICA

Revised and Updated Edition

Lenore Friedman

SHAMBHALA
Boston & London
2000

Shambhala Publications, Inc.
Horticultural Hall
300 Massachusetts Avenue
Boston, Massachusetts 02115
www.shambhala.com

Printed in the United States of America
☉ This edition is printed on acid-free paper that meets the
American National Standards Institute z39.48 Standard.
Distributed in the United States by Random House, Inc.,
and in Canada by Random House of Canada Ltd

Library of Congress Cataloging-in-Publication Data
Friedman, Lenore.
Meetings with remarkable women: Buddhist teachers in
America / Lenore Friedman.—Rev. and updated ed.
p. cm.
ISBN 1-57062-474-7
1. Women Buddhist priests—United States—Interviews. I. Title.
BQ738.F75 2000
294.3′092′273—dc21
[B]
00-021722

BVG 01

This time, for Jane

Contents

Preface to the Revised Edition

On a stormy Sunday afternoon in mid February 2000, Linda Ruth Cutts became the second abbess of San Francisco Zen Center in a centuries-old ritual known as the Mountain Seat Ceremony. It took place in the Buddha Hall at the San Francisco Zen Center and was attended by a few hundred people who sat quietly on cushions and chairs as the elaborate, stylized sequences unfolded.

This event seems emblematic to me of the many changes that have occurred in the world of women and American Buddhism in the years since the first edition of this book was published in 1987. I thought then that we were on the crest of a wave. Now it's clear how naive and shortsighted that idea was. The number of new women leaders and teachers alone (at every level and in all traditions) is staggering.*

> In one hand Linda holds a tall wooden staff and in the other a horse-hair whisk. At repeated junctures she waves the whisk first to the right, then to the left, and then down in front of her with a bow. Throughout, she moves with gravity, spontaneous authority, and deep humanness, as well as an occasional mischievous smile.
>
> The ceremony seems to demand the bolt-upright attention of every cell and synapse in her body, and a simultaneous surrender to that ever-present, ever-elusive intelligence beyond her personal self. Six sangha members, in dark-colored robes, ask her questions in a kind of ritual dharma combat. Her an-

*For a more detailed account of these developments, see the epilogue.

swers are strong, spontaneous, humorous. Once she remains silent, then beckons the questioner to come closer. She then steps forward herself and embraces him.

Earlier in the ceremony Linda had referred to her husband, Steve, as her "life dharma companion," likening the two of them to yoked oxen plodding through the mud. Now Steve and their teenage daughter, Sarah, speak of the qualities of mind she will bring to her new role as abbess, as well as those that have graced and fertilized their intimate family life. Her husband pauses many times as he speaks, his voice choked with tears.

Within the stark formality of the ceremony, Linda's feminine nature is apparent. Her words are sometimes startling, always direct, and unabashedly loving. She addresses Bodhidharma by saying "Big water buffalo, I drink your dharma milk, empty, nothing holy." To Suzuki Roshi, "founder of these temples," she says, "You gave everything to us. This little sprout vows to not let the teaching be cut off." And later, "May we care for each other with big, joyful motherly-fatherly mind. Watching over the plants and animals and our beautiful earth."

In other Buddhist institutions as well, from coast to coast, the emergence of feminist values like inclusiveness, welcoming families into sanghas, honoring diversity, social awareness, and activity, and the democritization of structures are all evident to one degree or another. Daily services have been altered to acknowledge female as well as male forebears. At San Francisco Zen Center, the morning chant now honors "all women teachers, known and unknown." Female figures Tara and Kwan Yin now stand or sit in meditation halls alongside male Buddhas. These changes have occurred gradually, and from the ground, perhaps, they have been hardly noticeable. But as I've explored the breadth and depth of the changing place of women in Buddhism, I have felt increasingly moved.

. . .

The opportunity to reconnect with the remarkable women teachers I interviewed for the first edition of this book has been a true pleasure. Yet there has also been an undercurrent of pain. Four of the original seventeen have died since the book came out in

1987. These are Venerable Gesshin Prabhasa Dharma; Roshi Jiyu Kennett; Ayya Khema; and Maurine Stuart, Roshi. Gesshin died only a few weeks before this manuscript was completed, so I had talked with her in depth several times, and we had been in touch by mail until close to her death. In each of the other cases, I was able to contact three close informants—students, associates, dharma heirs—for details about the later life and accomplishments as well as the death of their teacher and friend.

The richest part of this process has probably been the freshness and immediacy of my renewed appreciation for each woman's uniqueness, her particular style of transmitting (or simply *being*) the dharma, by which I mean the essential nature of reality. One is always grateful for reminders to wake up, to loosen our attachments to separative ideas and conditioning. These reminders and shakings up occurred with every teacher I talked to (or talked about, in the case of the three who had already died). Sometimes they came not only from the words that were spoken but from the spirit of the particular person, which came shining through unmistakably between the words (with Joko, for example, and with Karuna and Ruth Denison and Bobby Rhodes). Sometimes the subject matter of the interview was especially compelling to me at the moment (as it was with Lama Tsering). Sometimes the issues we talked about were inescapable and difficult, like illness and death, which came up more often than I would have anticipated.

A few other themes struck me. Several people have been dealing with the pros and cons of expansion and higher visibility (for example, Pema, Gesshin, and Colleen), and quite a few have branched out into new realms and venues for disseminating the teachings (Sharon, Pema, Jacqueline, and Gesshin). A number have specifically addressed the urgent hunger for meditation instruction in our prisons (Colleen, Karuna, and Sharon).

I thank all of you for being there so fully, once more.

Finally, in addition to those people interviewed and named in the text, I want to thank others who generously gave of their time and attention, including Jyokuko and Kyogen Carlson, Arida Emrys, Trudy Goodman, and Sabine Volchok.

May we all meet again.

March 11, 2000

Acknowledgments

There is a fire trail much frequented by runners and dogs that winds up through canyon, creek, and deep woods five minutes from the heart of Berkeley. While walking on this trail I conceived the idea for this book, made the decision actually to begin it, and sketched chapter openings and first drafts in my imagination. It may have been the heady morning air, but even before much of substance had been committed to paper, I would catch myself in midstride composing lyrical acknowledgments to one and all, including my dog. Embarrassed, I'd stop, but not without wondering if I'd ever, in the real world, get that far. Now, having scaled the mountain, my first acknowledgment must go to that familiar piece of protected wildness, to the morning air, the sun and shadows, the birds, the trees.

To all the teachers I've written about, who gave me their time, welcomed me to their centers and often to their homes as well, how can I say thank you? Had this book never been published, I would still have felt more than rewarded by the opportunity of meeting and talking to these seventeen remarkable women. The whole experience unquestionably changed my life. I can only hope that what I have written truthfully conveys something of the essence of their teaching and their lives. To say thank you is hopelessly inadequate. Still, I say it. Thank you, Toni. Thank you, Maurine. Thank you, Joko. Thank you, Pema. Thank you, Gesshin. Thank you, Karuna. Thank you, Roshi Kennett. Thank you, Sharon. Thank you, Ruth. Thank you, Bobby. Thank you, Joanna. Thank you, Yvonne. Thank you, Sonja. Thank you, Tsering. Thank you, Jacqueline. Thank you, Colleen. Thank you, Ayya.

Acknowledgments

To supplement my necessarily time-limited contacts with many of these teachers, I spoke as well with quite a number of their long-time students. They provided me with acute and deeply felt impressions and anecdotes that helped flesh out my own, more limited experience. For their generosity and candor I would like to thank Myushin, Jikan, and Egyoku from the Zen Center of Los Angeles; Brenda Beck and Elizabeth Hamilton from the San Diego Zen Center; Carole Rankin, Wade Hancock, Sheila LaFarge, and Marlane Habraken from the Cambridge Buddhist Association (a special thank-you to Marlane for exceptional hospitality in an hour of need); Heidi Renteria and Rodney Smith from the Insight Meditation Society; Suzie Bowman and Sol Sandperl from the Providence Zen Center; Sally, Chris, Kevin, Joyce, Stewart, Wayne, and Sam from Genesee Valley Zen Center (now Springwater Center); Julie Wester, Rhea, Jain Heim, and Jeff Daniels, who talked or wrote to me about Ruth Denison; Jane Hooper and Judy Rose from the International Zen Institute of America; Michael Searle and Frances Vaughan, who talked to me about Sonja Margulis; Marilyn Hayes, who talked to me about Bhikshuni Pema Chodron; and Revs. Meiten, Ando, Komei, and Meian from Shasta Abbey.

I would like to especially acknowledge the support that the Berkeley Zen Center women's group has given this book from the start, even before I was a bona fide member. On my first interviewing trip I took along with me a list of questions asked by group members. It helped steady me when I was wobbly, walking a new path.

Many thanks also to Miriam Queen for a long and thoughtful response from Osaka to my request for impressions about women Buddhists in Japan; to Gary Snyder, whose information and ideas may have to go into a sequel to this book; to Charlene Spretnak, who wouldn't let me get away with representing only one vipassana lineage in this country; to Marian and Dow Votaw, at whose wonderful house near the ocean I was able to write a major portion of the manuscript; to Leonard Schwarzburd and Kent Johnson for refusing to believe I couldn't learn to operate a computer; to Barbara Gates and Wes Nisker for their informed enthusiasm at a time I needed it and for publishing a skillfully edited excerpt in the *Inquiring Mind;* to Deborah Hopkinson and Lisa Campbell of the Diamond Sangha for their warm response and excellent excerpting of a chapter for *Kahawai;* to Kristin Penn for consistent interest and attentive editing of several excerpts for *Karuna;* to Mariquita Platov for her early and continuing encouragement for the whole project and for dropping the seminal Blyth quotation into one of her letters; to Fran Tribe for generous help with transcription; to my editor, Emily Hilburn Sell, for immediately grasping my intention and for a response to the completed manuscript that made me jump for joy; to Grace Abad for heroic typing and transcribing accompanied by irrepressible good humor; and to Gregory Friedman for his interest in all of it with the perfect glint of amusement in his eye.

Finally (yes, dear M, here it is), I wish to thank my closest friends, mostly for their very being: Jessica Barshay for a thousand things, including, before the beginning, saying *she'd* want to read the book if I wrote it, and later giving it the benefit of her clear, cool eye; Loie Rosenkrantz for being there and being there even when I wasn't, and for reading everything with delight and just the right amount of skepticism; Marion Tripp for also (inimitably) being there, for flagging all the exclamation points, and for loving sections closest to my heart; Carolyn North for telling me *of course* to finish it when I almost didn't; Rosalind Grossman for truly listening and truly leaping; Anna Douglas for fertile walks and talks; Christine Federici for beautiful soup and neck rubs in the nick of time; and Sharon Lebell for early excitement and support as well as ongoing peerless advice. To all of you—my pearls, my sisters, my sweet sangha, my friends—much love. It couldn't have happened and wouldn't have mattered without you.

Meetings with Remarkable Women

Introduction to the First Edition

I

The least admirable part of Buddhism is its attitude to sex. The Buddha accepted women into the Sangha with the utmost unwillingness, and indeed prophesied that they would be the ruin of his system. . . . When we look back over the history of Zen, we find not so much an antipathy to sex or a perversion of it such as we see in (monastic) Christianity, but rather a sublime indifference to it. Women do not appear in the anecdotes of the *Hekiganroku* or the *Mumonkan*. A book entitled *Zen for Women* has yet to be published.

—R. H. Blyth (1960) [1]

Bless your maverick spirit, Mr. Blyth, and your penetrating eye. The present book may not precisely answer your challenge, but it has been energized by it. It would surely delight you to know that recent translations have brought to light a number of women in the very Zen collections you cite. To be sure, these women are neither named nor fully fleshed, but shadowy figures who appear momentarily to speak their often trenchant lines and then depart without a trace.

It is true that Buddhism has neglected women. It is true that the Buddha resisted admitting them into his monastic order and, when he finally did, laid down rules that seem shocking today. His equivocation and discriminatory strictures have been explained as a response to the social norms of the time, which, to protect the new order, he chose not to flout. The fact is that, ex-

3

cept for remnants in Mahayana countries, the female order was in decline by the third century C.E. and by the ninth had disappeared almost completely. Although it is showing significant signs of renewed life in our time, historically monastic Buddhists have overwhelmingly been men.

It is true that women are egregiously absent among the huge bulk of Zen teaching stories. And to be sure, all the patriarchs, masters, and sages have been men. Even so recent a book as Rick Fields's *How the Swans Came to the Lake: A Narrative History of Buddhism in America,*[2] an exemplary work in almost all respects, is virtually devoid of women.

But—and I don't want to exaggerate—the picture is changing. A number of years ago the poet Gary Snyder said that "the single most revolutionary aspect of Buddhist practice in the United States is the fact that women are participating in it. From the beginning, women essentially had been excluded. But in America, fully fifty percent of the followers everywhere are women. What that will do to some of these inherited teaching methods and attitudes is going to be quite interesting."[3] Snyder said nothing at all about female *teachers* because, at the time of his remark, they weren't there. The current wonderful flowering, which this book chronicles, is a phenomenon of the past few years only.

As recently as 1980 Rita Gross, in a paper presented at a conference called "East-West Religions in Encounter: Buddhist-Christian Renewal and the Future of Humanity," said that our generation of Buddhist women practitioners has "no lineage heroines or major contemporary teachers to imitate and emulate." When I first started my research in 1983, I knew of only three women teachers. Now I can cite a dozen of the first rank, with others coming up right behind them.

Women are "coming up" in many places, of course: in Western religious institutions, in business, in politics. Buddhism is not alone in having feared and suppressed women's minds and aspirations. But suppress them it did, for twenty centuries. There have been exceptions, of course—shining and spirited beings like the early disciples Dhammadina and Khema, like Lion Yawn and Queen Srimala and Myoshin and the Japanese "tea ladies." But let's begin at the beginning.

II

From the time of the Buddha's earliest teaching, women have been actively participating in Buddhism. According to I. B. Horner, author of the pioneering early work *Women under Primitive Buddhism* (1930),[4] the first women lay disciples were converted soon after the Buddha's initial sermon in the Deer Park at Isipatana. They were the mother and former wife of Yasa, "the noble youth," who had already achieved full enlightenment, and whose father too had become a lay disciple. "To these women Gotama spoke of exactly the same matters in exactly the same terms as when he was speaking to Yasa and his father," Horner writes.

The extent to which the Buddha truly accepted women as equals will never be known with certainty, of course. All evidence rests with the written versions of the story recorded long after the fact by fallible monks. To me the most convincing speculation, based on the spirit of most of the teachings as well as information about social conditions in India at the time, is that the Buddha did accept women as spiritual equals but, being human, he was not immune to the ingrained prejudices of his time and place.

How fierce and deep-seated some of these prejudices were can be glimpsed in some passages from early Buddhist texts. The prototype of woman as evil is found in the Theravadin scriptures known as the Pali canon. But according to Diana Y. Paul, in her fascinating scholarly work *Women in Buddhism*,[5] hell was populated with grotesquely formed, elderly, repulsive women in both Theravadin and Mahayanist literature. In "The Tale of King Udayana of Vatsa," from *The Collection of Jewels,* an anthology dating from roughly 100 C.E., women are given "tremendous power," says Paul (who translated it into English for the first time). Two stanzas read:

> The dead snake and dog
> Are detestable
> But women are even more
> Detestable than they are.

Women are fishermen.
Their flattery is a net.
Men are like fish
Caught in the net.

And from the *Mahaparinibbana Sutta* comes the following dialogue between the Buddha and his beloved disciple Ananda, who later proved to be an eloquent advocate of women's rights.

Ananda: How are we to conduct ourselves, Lord, with regard to womankind?

Buddha: As not seeing them, Ananda.

Ananda: But if we should see them, what are we to do?

Buddha: Not talking, Ananda.

Ananda: But if they should speak to us, Lord, what are we to do?

Buddha: Keep wide awake, Ananda.[6]

Traditional Buddhist attitudes toward women as inferior "reflect a view of woman as temptress or evil incarnate," writes Diana Paul. "She has an animalistic nature associated with innate sexual drives not found in the nature of the male." She is biologically determined to be sexually uncontrollable. Only by despising her own nature can she "perhaps deny her biological destiny of depravity."

Paul explains this monkish misogyny as a consequence, in part, of the fact that monks were dependent on housewives for alms. Their feelings of being "manipulated and dependent would result in self-hatred projected upon women." They likened each woman to a microcosmic power capable, in her negative aspect, of wreaking havoc. *Samsara* was identified as the feminine and had to be overcome. The prevailing dualities were male/spirit/*nirvana* versus female/body/*samsara*.

Moreover, to these early Buddhists, mothers represented "sufferers and perpetual givers of life in pain, almost as if it were a natural law for women to suffer." The texts that refer to women as religious beings almost never refer to motherhood, which is equated with suffering, bondage, and dependency. And the religious aim of Mahāyāna is to be liberated from these conditions.

The only means by which mothers could receive recognition was through giving birth to sons. Early Buddhist texts tell of women being ridiculed and humiliated by society in general until they produced a male child. Paul cites the interesting inevitability by which the Buddha's mother had to die seven days after giving birth to him "in order to preclude any sexual intercourse after such a marvelous event." Apparently all mothers of buddhas were destined to suffer this fate.

The story of the original order of Buddhist *bhikkhuni* (nuns) is an intriguing one, despite its ambiguities. The traditional account is "probably a monastic invention," according to Frances Wilson, who recently retranslated the story, since there is evidence that mythmaking has already intruded.[7] One example is the important role of Mahaprajapati, the Buddha's aunt and stepmother. It is echoed in the history of the nun's order in Jainism (which briefly preceded the Buddhist order in India) by the similar role of the aunt of Mahavira, founder of the Jain religion.

Today we are seeing new vitality in the women's monastic order worldwide, but the bhikkhuni community did not survive as a vital force in either early or Mahayana Buddhism. Although theoretically viable, the bhikkhuni path was doomed from the outset, Paul believes, because of the deeply felt threat to society and religion posed by women leaving their families.

The Buddha evidently had grave doubts himself. As the story goes, five years after he started preaching, he was approached in Negrodha Park by a large company of women dressed in yellow robes and led by Mahaprajapati. They were travel-stained, their feet swollen from long walking. They wanted to leave the world and lead an ascetic life, and came to beg for his consent. Three times they asked and three times they were refused. Weeping but undaunted, Mahaprajapati and her followers cut off their hair as a sign of renunciation and followed the Buddha on foot to Vesali. There they were met by the Buddha's closest disciple, "the gentle Ananda, who, shocked to see them in this doleful plight, but deeply impressed by their zeal and determination, undertook to plead their cause for them with Gotama."

He asked three times, to no avail. (We can hear the repetitive rhythm of folktales here; and, as with folktales everywhere, versions differ.) Finally Ananda appealed to the Buddha's sense of justice and truth; were not women as capable as men of leading a contemplative life and treading the path of enlightenment? The Buddha admitted that they were, and that there was no natural impediment to their attaining nirvana. He must have been moved by the sight of these "delicately nurtured women who always traveled in carriages, but who were come across the North Indian plains on foot to him at Vesali," writes Horner. She also notes that this is the only recorded instance of his being "overpersuaded" in argument.

But shortly thereafter he uttered his famous dictum regarding the end of the Buddhist order. "It is couched in no measured terms, and seems *at first sight* to be instinct with dejection and mourning over shattered hopes," in Horner's view. What he reportedly said was: "If, Ananda, women had not received permission to go out from the household life and enter the homeless state, under the doctrine and discipline proclaimed by the Tathagata [i.e., the Buddha], then would the pure religion, Ananda, have lasted long, the good law would have stood fast for a thousand years. But since, Ananda, women have now received that permission the pure religion, Ananda, will not last so long, the good law will now stand fast for only five hundred years."

Although this statement is usually felt to express the Buddha's grudging acceptance of the women's order, Horner points first to the probable effects of monks' editing here (they would "naturally" minimize the importance given to women) and second to the absence of any other indications of his reluctance. Ultimately, Horner concludes that the length in years that the orders lasted was less important to the Buddha than opening them to as many people as possible, that "half the number of years (five hundred) under the conditions now presenting themselves might be more valuable than twice the number (one thousand) under the old."

This view is shared by Sulak Sivaraksa writing in the journal *Kahawai*.[8] He believes not only that the Buddha's statement is usually wrongly interpreted, but that this might have contributed to the discontinuation of the Holy Order of Almswomen. He also concludes that "it is better to point the way to Nirvana to as many earnest seekers as possible, than wait until the opportunity has passed, perhaps beyond recall, and even the demands have diminished, perhaps to the vanishing point."

But in Frances Wilson's translation of the passage under discussion, there seems little doubt of the Buddha's expectations:

> Just this, O Ananda, if women go forth under the rule of the Dharma, this rule of the Dharma will not be long enduring. It is as if, O Ananda, in a big field belonging to a householder, a quantity of thunderbolts with great flashes of lightning fell to the extent that the field was destroyed, ruined, and brought to nought. Just thus, O Ananda, the rule of the Dharma—if women go forth from a homelife—will not continue for long. Suppose, Ananda, there were a sugar cane field belonging to a householder. Upon it fell a blight by the name of Crimson disease until the sugar cane was destroyed, ruined, and brought to nought. Just in this way, when women go forth, the rule of the Dharma is not long maintained.

At that point in Wilson's account, the Buddha expounded the famous Eight Chief Rules for the women's order, likening them to a causeway built at the mouth of a river or canal in order to dam the waters. Horner says, "He had knowledge of the world, he had belonged to it, and could imagine the havoc its slanderous tongue might create in the order if chances for scandal-mongering were not cut out. Therefore . . . he pruned his system accordingly."

The major thrust of the rules is to place the women's order beneath the higher status and authority of the monks. The bhikkhunis were to be dependent on their male counterparts for important ceremonies and observances and were to defer to them at all times, however junior the monk or seasoned themselves. The first rule (or eighth, depending on the source) reads: "An alms-woman, even if a hundred years standing, shall make Salutation to, shall rise up in the presence of, shall bow down before, and shall perform all proper duties towards an almsman, if only just initiated."

Given the social norms of the day, perhaps the most interesting narrative detail is that Mahaprajapati later asked the Buddha, through the advocacy of Ananda, whether the same rule of seniority should not hold for both orders, and depend on status rather than sex. What Horner calls these "feministic instincts" were clearly ahead of their time—and were naturally rebuffed.

The women's disciplinary rules also reinforced the prevailing attitude that women were more "passionate" than men by prescribing, for women only, an additional probationary period for the purpose of cooling, if not eliminating, their passions.

But when Mahaprajapati heard the news that acceptance of these rules would constitute her initiation, she is reported to have compared them to a garland of jasmine flowers that a young woman might with both hands place on her head after bathing. "Even so do I, Ananda, take upon myself these Eight Rules never to be transgressed my life long."

Thus the Bhikkhuni Sangha, or Nuns' Order, was established. Ayya Khema, who is a major force in reviving the order today, and about whom more will be said later, writes that women flocked from all classes of society to embrace the new life open to them. "The barriers which had existed for centuries were broken. Slowly they emerged from the grooves in which they had been so long immured. Widows came forth from their enforced seclusion, bereaved mothers and childless women found consolation in the practice. Maidens escaped the humiliation of being sold to the suitor who bid the highest, slavegirls sought freedom from their masters, dancing girls and courtesans were accepted and strove to live exemplary lives."[9]

The Buddhist Sisterhood is likened to India's first "women's space" by J. Hughes in a provocative booklet entitled *Buddhist Feminism*.[10] It gave women the opportunity for "a life separate from, if somewhat subordinate to, monks; wandering, studying and meditating in the company of other women, free from the restrictions of children and family."

Initially, then, the order flourished, and many of the women attained the highest realization. Some of them were counted among the Buddha's ablest disciples. We know their names and stories from sutras and from the *Therigatha,* a collection of enlightenment poems of the *theris,* as the earliest bhikkhunis were called. Dhammadina was described as "greatly wise," and Khema was ranked foremost for her insight. Punnika Theri, a former slave, is said to have admonished a brahmin: "O ignorant of the ignorant! Who has said that one is freed from evil karma by water baptism? If this is so, all turtles, frogs, serpents, and crocodiles will go to heaven!"[11]

And here are three poems from the *Therigatha,* in new renderings by Susan Murcott and John Tarrant.[12] Their universality and fresh immediacy seem to transcend space and time (2,500 years).

MUTTA

Free I am free
I am free from the three
crooked things
mortar, pestle and
my crooked husband.

I am free from birth
and death and all
that dragged me back.

VIMALA (an ex-prostitute)

Young
intoxicated by my skin
my figure   my good looks
and famous too
I despised my sisters

Dressed to kill
at the whorehouse door
a hunter spread her snare
for fools
I laughed as I teased them

Inside
it all came off

Head shaved,
robed, alms wanderer
I   my same self

sit at the tree's foot
No reason

All ties untied
I have cut men and gods
out of my life

Annihilated
I am cool, quenched

CITTA

Though I am thin, sick
and lean on a stick
I have climbed up Vulture Peak

Robe thrown down
Bowl turned over
Leaned on a rock
then great darkness opened

During the reign of India's great Buddhist king, Asoka (269–232 B.C.E.), it was claimed that 96,000 bhikkhunis once gathered at Jambudipa. Although the claim was probably exaggerated, clearly the order still thrived. King Asoka's daughter, Sanghamitta, was ordained at age eighteen and was later sent by her father on a mission to establish the order in Sri Lanka. She carried with her a branch of the sacred Bodhi Tree from Gaya. "It was ceremoniously planted at the Mahamegha garden at Anuradhapura, where it exists up to the present day—the oldest historical tree in the world," according to Ayya Khema.

For several centuries the order flourished in Sri Lanka and spread as well to countries of Southeast Asia. It was also established in China during the fifth century C.E. by a mission of bhikkhunis from Sri Lanka. However, this fully ordained line died out completely between 900 and 1,000 years ago in all Theravadin countries (Burma, Thailand, Cambodia, and Sri Lanka).

"It is difficult to account for the complete disappearance of an Order so well established," writes Ayya Khema. "It is possible that the bhikkhus (monks) themselves opposed any effort to re-establish it. That they only tolerated the presence of the bhik-khunis is plain, for at the first Great Council [following the Buddha's death], Ven. Ananda was made to beg pardon of the Assembly for having persuaded the Buddha to grant ordination to women."[13]

It is Ayya's great hope to revive the fully ordained order in Sri Lanka today. She has already established an International Buddhist Women's Center in Colombo (for laywomen as well) and the Parappuduwa Nun's Island on an inland lake (on land donated by the Sri Lankan government). She is also devoted to increasing the prestige of bhikkhunis in that country by providing excellent education and training. In general, monastic women suffer extremely low status throughout Southeast Asia.*

In the introduction to *Women in Buddhism,* Diana Paul writes that, like Judaism and Christianity, "Buddhism is an overwhelmingly male-created institution dominated by a patriarchal power structure. . . . the feminine is frequently associated with the secular, powerless, profane and imperfect." In Mahayana texts generally she has found a complex, destructive set of images denying women fulfillment within the Buddhist religion. One has to remember that these texts were the approved doctrinal statements of the monastic elite and that the most popular and influential of them were generally less biased. But women's association with nature and sexuality—an association that may be polluting and deadly for the male—runs throughout. It was interesting to me that, like the biblical myth of Genesis, in which woman is the cause of the Fall, a sutra in the Pali canon associates the origin of sexuality with the fall of humanity; several other early Buddhist texts accuse women of responsibility for this fall as well.

But the picture has another face. A second theme runs through this literature, one that sees the feminine as wise, nurturing, creative, gentle, and compassionate. And although women as religious figures are almost always depicted as counterparts to men, there are exceptions. My favorite is Lion Yawn.

*An important historical event occurred in February 1987—the First International Conference of Buddhist Nuns in Bodh Gaya, India, at which Ayya Khema was a principal speaker.

She appears in a sutra with a beautiful name: *The Harmony of the Young Sapling Sutra* (written about six hundred years after the Buddha's death). Frances Wilson provides the first English translation.[14] In it a merchant's son, Sudhana, is on a pilgrimage. He comes to a great park named Sun-Bright filled with trees by the name of Moonrise that shine with light for a mile in all directions. There are trees the color of lapis lazuli, trees raining multicolored flowers, fruit trees, jewel trees, music trees, perfume trees. There are fountains, lakes, pools, and lotus ponds surrounded by jeweled benches anointed with sandal paste. All this was the work of the nun-bodhisattva, Lion Yawn.

When Sudhana caught sight of her, she was seated on "numerous great lion thrones" under the trees, surrounded by great retinues. "She was like a tranquil lake, like a wish gem yielding all desires." She was like a lotus, a lion, a great mountain, an enchanting perfume. She was like cool sandalwood, and like a great brahmin unpossessed by greed, hatred, or delusion. She was like tranquil water refreshing the hearts of all beings. And she was proclaiming the dharma to many assemblies, composed of different types of seekers at different stages of realization. "For them in this garden Sudhana saw the nun Lion Yawn teaching the Dharma to each who had come and been seated. She taught each according to disposition, resolute intention, and faith so that all became destined to Supreme, Perfect Enlightenment."

An illumined being and perfect teacher was this nun-bodhisattva Lion Yawn. Perhaps the only other woman to surpass her in Buddhist tradition is Queen Srimala, who possessed the "lion's roar" of eloquence, and whom Diana Paul postulates as a female buddha.

Regarding a woman's capacity for full realization, the Mahayana sutras present three major views: (1) a woman must await a male birth to become a bodhisattva or buddha, (2) an exceptional woman can undergo "sex change" in this lifetime, and (3) women are accepted as bodhisattvas and potential buddhas. The first view is consonant with the sense of the female body as defiled and therefore incapable of perceiving the true dharma. (Women are like "soil saturated with salt where one cannot grow either corn or common herbs," according to the *Abhidharma-*

Kosa, a late-fourth-century metaphysical treatise.) In the second view, a spontaneous sex transformation from female to male symbolizes a change from the sensual state to the desireless state of enlightenment. As the Buddha declares in the *Sutra on Changing the Female Sex,* "If women awaken to the thought of enlightenment, then they will have the great and good person's state of mind, or man's state of mind, a sage's state of mind. . . . They will be forever separate from the female sex and become sons."[15]

In the *Sutra of the Dialogue of the Girl Candrottara,* probably composed in the third or fourth century C.E. and first translated into English by Diana Paul, an extraordinary young woman— whose name means "on top of the moon" because whatever touched her body would shine brilliantly—shows many signs of precocious realization and later eloquently explains the most profound dimensions of the dharma. She also, almost as an aside, lets fall a brief statement about the irrelevance of sexual transformation from the perspective of Emptiness—and then blithely changes her sex upon hearing the Buddha predict that she is about to become a buddha. When she heard these words, Candrottara was "ecstatic, leaping in the air countless times to the height of seven Tala trees. Resting on the seventh tree, the girl changed her female body, transforming into a boy."

The most liberal and egalitarian portraits of women—as advanced-state bodhisattvas—are found in an extremely small number of sutras, some of which, however, are among the most influential and popular texts in Mahayana scripture (e.g., the *Vimalakirtinirdesa* and the *Sutra of Queen Srimala Who Had the Lion's Roar*). Here we find metaphysical statements on the conditioned and the unconditioned. For example: If all phenomena are impermanent and insubstantial, there is no male and no female. Such distinctions are illusion. The dharma and the path are neither male nor female. As the *Diamond Sutra* states, in the unconditioned realm there is no dichotomy between the male and the female. And enlightenment is sexless and ageless, according to a commentary on the *Lotus Sutra,* the *Fa-hua i-shu.*

In the *Vimalakirtinirdesa Sutra* there is an enlivening dialogue between Sariputra and a goddess whom he asks (in Diana Paul's translation):

Sariputra: Why don't you change your female sex?

Goddess: I have been here twelve years and have looked for the innate characteristics of the female sex and haven't been able to find them. How can I change them? Just as a magician creates an illusion of a woman, if someone asks why don't you change your female sex, what is he asking?

Sariputra: But an illusion is without any determinate characteristics, so how could it be changed?

Goddess: All things are also without any determinate characteristics, so how can you ask, "Why don't you change your female sex?"?

Then the goddess, by supernatural power, changed Sariputra into a likeness of herself and changed herself into a likeness of Sariputra and asked: "Why don't you change your female sex?"

Sariputra, in the form of a goddess, answered: "I do not know how I changed nor how I changed into a female form."

The goddess replies: "Sariputra, if you can change into a female form, then all women [in mental state] can also change. Just as you are not really a woman but appear to be female in form, all women also only appear to be female in form but are not really women. Therefore, the Buddha said all are not really men or women."

Queen Srimala, who had the lion's roar of a buddha, was "very much her own person," according to Diana Paul. The precise date of the sutra that bears her name is not certain, but many commentaries on it were written between 400 and 600 C.E. The sutra relates that, having achieved realization herself (despite controversy among commentators regarding the stage of her bodhisattvahood—to claim the eighth stage, as some do, is to give the feminine remarkable status), Srimala proceeded to convert first all the women of the city, then her husband, and finally the other men. She addresses her followers as "good sons and daughters" equally. There is no suggestion of hierarchy or division of labor according to sex. And the entire tone of the sutra suggests female imagery, says Paul. Queen Srimala herself, she feels, closely approaches the image of a female buddha.

The *Sutra of Queen Srimala* was a popular inspiration to court women in India, China, and Japan, Paul suggests, because it portrayed woman both as compassionate and as struggling to exist and understand the world in freedom.

It is necessary to mention—but briefly, because she has been so fully studied elsewhere—the widely revered female celestial bodhisattva Kuan Yin, as she is known in China and Southeast Asia, or Kannon (or Kanzeon), her name in Japan. She was a later incarnation of Avalokiteshvara, the Indian male bodhisattva who, with absolute compassion, perceives the suffering of the world. The origin of the female form of Kuan Yin is usually associated with the introduction of Tantric Buddhist texts into China during the Tang dynasty, and a subsequent fusion of the bodhisattva with White Tara, originally a female consort to Avalokiteshvara. Diana Paul fleshes out the transformation in greater detail. See also John Blofeld's book *Bodhisattva of Compassion*.[16]

Throughout the Mahayana teachings, sexuality is considered antithetical to the enlightened state. But in Tantric Buddhism, androgyny—a unity of the best attributes of both sexes—is seen as a state of perfection. With the joining of Buddhist teachings with Tantric teachings, the feminine took on a profoundly more important role than it had in primitive Buddhism. In Tantra, female and male principles are understood as currents running through the bodies of both men and women, which the practices activate and integrate. Female images emerge that are sexual *and* spiritual, ecstatic *and* intelligent, wrathful *and* peaceful. "How refreshing," Tsultrim Allione writes in the introduction to her book *Women of Wisdom,* "not to have to be chaste and peaceful with downcast eyes in order to be spiritual!"[17]

Tibetans consider the male principle to be dynamism (interestingly enough, associated with the moon) and the female principle to be perfect wisdom (associated with the sun). Integrating the two is profoundly important to Tibetan Buddhist practice.

As a comic footnote, here is a commentary (made by a male Zen student in San Francisco, reported by Susan Murcott in *Kahawai,* Fall 1981) on the feminine principle as "emptiness" and the masculine principle as "great action." His words: "That means that the women clear the table and the men sit around smoking cigars."

One final example of an evolved Buddhist woman who shows her mettle comes from the literature of Zen. Her name was Myoshin and she was a disciple of Zen master Kyozan. Her story is told in the *Raihai Tokuzui,* part of Zen philosopher and teacher Dogen Zenji's masterwork, *Shobogenzo.* In this story Kyozan perceives that Myoshin possesses the spirit of a great warrior, and he appoints her to be head of the temple office. One evening seventeen monks arrive from Szechwan. They are on pilgrimage, seeking the Way from different masters, and hope to talk with Kyozan. Taking shelter in the temple office at nightfall, they engage in conversation with each other, debating the famous wind-and-flag story of the Sixth Patriarch. Though each monk speaks in turn, none of them grasps the essential point. From the other side of the wall, Myoshin hears their deliberations and exclaims: "Oh lamentable blind donkeys! How many straw sandals have they wasted. They do not see the Buddha Dharma even in their dreams."

When the seventeen monks hear her comment, they feel ashamed, set their robes in order, and, burning incense and paying homage, ask Myoshin for teaching. "This is not the wind that moves; it is not the flag that moves; it is not the mind that moves." Hearing her express the dharma in this way, the monks look inside their authentic selves and, bowing with gratitude, become her disciples. And without waiting to talk with Kyozan, they return directly to Szechwan.

"Truly, this is not matched by the three wisdoms and the ten holinesses; it is an act of one who directly transmits the Dharma from the Buddha and teachers," concludes Dogen.[18] For its time (1240 C.E.) Dogen's *Raihai Tokuzui* is a radically positive statement on the equality of women, particularly for anyone who "takes the Dharma seriously," in Dogen's phrase. (Discovering it in Japan was an important event in Roshi Jiyu Kennett's life; see Chapter 7.)

At best, then, Buddhism historically encompasses a grand ambivalence toward women. The dharma itself is beyond ambivalence, resting nowhere, shattering concepts. The *teaching* of the dharma is another matter, since it arises from minds and from language conditioned by history and personal experience. This is true of all religions—how could it be otherwise? The more they become "solid," the more they betray their original transcendent inspiration or mystical core. This produces such ambiguities as Buddhists feeling closer to the spiritual heart of Christianity, say, than to certain manifestations of Buddhism. It explains why Meister Eckhart, Martin Buber, Mother Teresa, the unknown author of *The Cloud of Unknowing,* Hildegard von Bingen, and Gerald Red Elk speak to some of us as directly as some of the great Buddhist sages.

But for many women practicing today, one of the greatest obstacles remains the absence of clear female role models and foremothers in Buddhist literature and scripture. It is still a truism that all major teachers, lineage holders, and masters down the ages have been men. When, a few years ago, the Diamond Sangha in Hawaii changed the wording of one of their daily chants, substituting the term "founding teachers" for "patriarchs," it remained inescapable that the actual forebears in question were still all male. Happily, sangha members applied some energy and imagination to the situation, and with the help of translator Thomas Cleary and their teacher, Robert Aitken, Roshi, they began to publish (in their journal *Kahawai*) a series of heretofore unknown stories of obscure women in Zen history which have come to be known as the "Kahawai Koans."[19] We meet some remarkable and feisty realized women who engage in spirited dharma combat with monks and masters as equals. Usually such women are invisible, hidden away in huts and teahouses, where those who seek them out or stumble upon them are given a rousing dose of dharma. I was intrigued by these "tea ladies." There seemed to be a thread of continuity between them and some of the Tibetan Buddhist women mystics described by Tsultrim Allione in *Women of Wisdom.* I wondered if this sort of unaffiliated and untitled "invisible" position was a more natural one for women, or was it a societal construct—or both? I also wondered if one of the women still to be interviewed for this book might turn out to be a tea lady (see Chapter 11).

Lately I seem to be noticing tea ladies in all sorts of places. A friend whom I've known for twenty years turns out to be a tea lady in disguise. In a charming book called *A Journey in Ladakh* by Andrew Harvey, one meets Moneesha, a crusty lady who delights in poking holes in spiritual pretensions. About her late teacher, Thuksey Rinpoche, she says:

> He's an attentive, simple, tender, funny old man, and that is why I love him. He's too busy attending to the world around him to have time to tell everyone about his *experiences*. And even if he had time he wouldn't want to. You are looking; he has found what he has been looking for. That is the difference, and that is why you are always worrying, talking, analyzing, comparing. It's enough to drive anyone to chocolates—all this chatter about the Buddha and Nirvana from a lot of neurotics obsessed with their own sensibilities and reactions! You should scrub latrines or something, do something useful.

The voice is right in the old tradition. (If you think about it, you probably know a few tea ladies yourself.)

III

In recent years, as the secret has gotten out that there are more and more women practicing in all branches of Buddhism in the United States, we have been reaching out to each other in various ways—wanting to know each other's experience, wanting to sort out, in the particular safety of each other's presence, some of the difficulties and paradoxes of women practicing within a patriarchal tradition.

One of the earliest responses to this need was the publication, by the Diamond Sangha in Honolulu, of *Kahawai: A Journal of Women and Zen*. Since 1979 it has published articles and translations, letters and dialogues, and for a long time it was the only channel any of us had for news of each other.

Then, in the summer of 1981, the first conference on Women and Buddhism took place at Naropa Institute in Boulder, Colorado. It was a gathering of women practitioners from all three major traditions in this country—Tibetan, Zen, and Theravadin. A second conference was held there the following year as well. Women from all over the country attended lectures and workshops, shared their practices, hopes, and concerns. At the end, they felt they were "all one sangha."

That women may wish to practice intensively together, separately from men (not necessarily all the time, but *some* of the time), is gradually becoming recognized here. Although this is a relatively new occurrence in the United States, it may be less unusual in other parts of the world. In London, for example, Friends of the Western Buddhist Order have been conducting women-only retreats for years. Ruth Denison was probably the first in the United States to start leading retreats for women in the seventies. More recently they have been held on the East and West Coasts by Maurine Stuart (formerly known as Maurine Freedgood), Jacqueline Mandell, Christina Feldman, Michelle McDonald, Julie Wester, and Anna Douglas. Anna Douglas feels they provide a place of safety where heart and intuition are heard more clearly and the deepest spiritual issues can be explored without fear in a context of individual and collective healing.

Along these lines, a group of lay and monastic women in Washington, D.C., have been looking for a suitable location for a Women's Dharma Monastery, an ecumenical community and meditation center for women of all Buddhist traditions. They write that "it would be devoted solely to women's spiritual life," and they hope to protect the integrity of each tradition "while encouraging the growth of wisdom and compassion in the midst of diversity." This spirit of inclusiveness and nonsectarianism (despite two thousand years of entrenched ideological schisms) is a clear expression of essential values of both Buddhism and feminism.

Some of the women involved in the creation of this center are ordained bhikkunis. While it has been possible in the Mahayana traditions for women to be fully ordained (though sometimes with great difficulty: see Roshi Kennett's story in Chapter 7), in the Theravada and Vajrayana traditions the full ordination ceremony had been lost for a thousand years. In 1980, however, at the urging of the venerable Tibetan Buddhist leader His Holiness the Gyalwa Karmapa, Ane Pema Chodron, an American bhikkhuni in the Tibetan tradition, searched out and found a written version of the ancient ceremony that was still being performed in

Hong Kong. The story of her ordination there is told in Chapter 3. This teacher is now abbess of a monastery in Nova Scotia. She was the first American woman in the Tibetan tradition to undergo the ritual, but now several more Western women have followed her. When there are ten such women, it should be possible to perform the ceremony in the West.

At last, here and there, women teachers were beginning to appear. To commemorate this fact, in June 1983, Providence Zen Center hosted a one-day conference with Maurine (Freedgood) Stuart, Jacqueline Schwartz Mandell, and Bobby Rhodes, teachers from the Japanese Zen, vipassana, and Korean Zen traditions, respectively. The response was so enthusiastic that in 1984 they invited six women teachers to a weekend conference that attracted over a hundred participants (mostly women with a sprinkling of men). In March 1987, the first women's conference was held on the West Coast. Over 150 women came together in Berkeley, California, for a Celebration of Women Practicing Buddhism that represented all traditions (including unaffiliated practitioners) and was completely nonhierarchical in structure. The response was beyond expectations—fifty women had to be turned away—and so much energy was generated that plans for a second conference six months later were under way before the first one ended.

By the time of the earlier conferences, however, signs of pain and unrest had been surfacing in a number of sanghas around the country. As intimacy developed during the meetings, some potentially explosive and sensitive issues came into the open. "One of these was the issue of sexual relations between teachers and students," Deborah Hopkinson reported in *Kahawai*. "This issue was charged with so much emotion and intensity that we decided to treat our discussion of it as unrecorded oral history, and so we turned off the tape recorders for the only time in the conference." This report came out of the second Boulder conference, but the subject remained alive at the Providence conferences as well.

Today these issues have come completely out of the closet and are being discussed (some might say overdiscussed) frankly and fully. The key issue for feminists is the inherent abuse of power in such teacher-student affairs. But once opened, the situation is a

Pandora's box of paradox and pain. Lives have been fractured. Mature and immature women practitioners have left Buddhism behind, appalled and disillusioned.

Most of us recognize that this is not a "Buddhist" problem. From a feminist perspective it can be seen clearly as a problem intrinsic to patriarchy itself. Buddhist institutions have unquestionably been strongly patriarchal, here and elsewhere. But right now, in America, the ground just perceptibly is beginning to shift.

Buddhism in the United States may in fact be at a crossroads. The emergence of influential women seems to be coinciding with what might be termed American Buddhism's incipient coming of age. It is now almost a hundred years since Shoyen Shaku became the first Zen master to visit the United States in 1893. It is just eighty years since he returned from Japan to begin teaching a few Americans the practice of Zen. It is only thirty-five years since several other Japanese masters, including Nakagawa Soen Roshi and Yasutani Roshi, began to visit regularly, to instruct students and conduct *sesshins*. It is roughly twenty-five years since major centers were established in New York City, San Francisco, and Los Angeles, with resident Japanese roshis and rigorous training programs. It is roughly twenty years since first-generation *American* roshis Philip Kapleau and Robert Aitken established centers of their own in Rochester and Hawaii, closely patterned after Japanese models. It is fifteen years since two major Tibetan teachers, Tarthang Tulku and Chögyam Trungpa, established centers in California and Colorado, respectively. It is also roughly fifteen years since a Korean and a Vietnamese Zen master, Seung Sahn and Thich Thien-an, each established a following and a teaching center—one in Providence and one in Los Angeles. And it is just over ten years since three young Americans—one woman and two men—after studying for years in Southeast Asia, brought the *vipassana* tradition to the United States, establishing a center in Barre, Massachusetts.

So Buddhism has been transplanted to American soil. It has been watered and fertilized by rich, ancient Asian traditions that have helped strengthen its roots and young stems. But the terrain and climate here are different, and different nourishment seems needed now. For Buddhism to become truly established in America, it will need to move away from reliance on inherited forms and to look instead at the very ground on which it is growing. In other words, who are *we,* the current generation of Buddhist practitioners? What do *we* most need to deepen our understanding? In what unique and perfect form would the Dharma flourish *here, now?* In some places there has already been a shaking-free from Asian forms and a collective searching for more authentic, indigenous ones. But this is in no sense an accomplished fact. Asian teachers are still frequently in authority. And even if not, Asian forms are still strictly followed. After all, one might ask, isn't that Buddhism?

Some people are pondering that question quite carefully. What, in fact, is Buddhism? What is the dharma? What is the ground of our being? And what is the best means to seek it? Traditional Buddhists devised the most skillful means at their disposal, and for centuries, in India, China, Japan, Southeast Asia, and Tibet, these have been honed and perfected. As Buddhism moved from country to country, its methods and character changed considerably. Doubtless, in the beginning, the old ways were copied closely. But the most skillful means in one culture are not necessarily the most skillful means in another. And as time went on, each country developed a distinctive form of Buddhism with its own flavor and particularities.

Fifteen years ago, Thich Nhat Hanh, a Vietnamese Zen master and poet who has visited the United States several times, wrote in his book *Zen Keys,* "One cannot become a practitioner of Zen by imitating the way of eating, sitting, or dressing of the Japanese or Chinese practitioners. *Zen is life; Zen does not imitate.* If Zen one day becomes a reality in the West, it will acquire a Western form, considerably different from Oriental Zen."[20]

This is the stage we have arrived at now. American Buddhism is in the process of finding its own nature. It must be said that the process is a tumultuous one. Upheaval and disarray seem endemic in many Buddhist communities across the United States. One by one, a number of illustrious male teachers have fallen from pedestals that, wittingly or unwittingly, they helped to erect. It is a striking fact that three of the teachers interviewed for this book have broken with the masters from whom they received transmission. Another has severed her ties with a brother roshi in her lineage. Another, embroiled in a situation of painful ferment within her community, has left for an extended period of evaluation in a different state. One woman practiced for years in Southeast Asia, was ordained twice in the Theravada tradition, and became one of the recognized teachers of vipassana meditation in this country. When I interviewed her in late 1983, she had just resigned her teaching position at the center she had helped to establish and has now gone her independent way. "I could no longer stand before women and say that I represent a tradition which does not recognize a woman as an equal being," she said. (See Chapter 11.)

So structures are being shaken. While the greatest turmoil seems to be within Zen Buddhism (by far the longest-established tradition in this country), reverberations plainly cross boundaries everywhere. Everything is up for questioning, from ceremonial procedures to the role of monasticism. One of the more dramatic occurrences was the splitting down the middle of the Rochester Zen Center in 1980 (see Chapter 1), when half the sangha, led by Toni Packer, left behind all but the bare-bones forms of their practice. Some have described this as Quaker Zen. But Toni Packer and her sangha are still evolving, are recently questioning even the term *Zen*. Other centers have been less radical, but are gradually letting go of other things: prostrations, chants, robes. The Diamond Sangha in Hawaii, led by Robert Aitken, Roshi, has for years worked on feminizing political and decision-making processes as well as retranslation of sutras, excising sexist language that had been transmitted unaltered down the centuries.

The trend seems to be toward more open, fluid, feminist structures and away from rigid, patriarchal ones; toward democratic consensus processes and away from hierarchy and authoritarianism, toward secular communities of great diversity, centered on practice in the world, in families, in relationships, and concerned with the traditional female values of caring and nurturance.

In many respects, Buddhism and feminism reflect similar values and perceptions. They are both deeply experiential and intuitive. They both sense the fundamental interconnectedness and relatedness of all beings. They both instinctively *include* rather than exclude. So, to many, their interpenetration seems wholly natural, wholly auspicious. Although most of the women teachers described in this book do not technically consider themselves feminists, it will be seen that their inclinations and basic teaching are entirely consonant with feminist values. As these women inevitably grow in stature and influence (and they almost certainly represent the growing edge of American Buddhism today), they will surely be molding the look and feel of Buddhist practice in the West for years to come.

If most of the teachers discussed in this book do not particularly call themselves feminists, we need to ask why they do not. My understanding, from talking and listening carefully, is that basically their stance reflects an underlying vision of nonduality—a disinclination to polarize, exclude, proclaim enemies, or solidify around any fixed idea. I would like to acknowledge, accept, and include this perspective, and at the same time try to extend our dialogue somewhat further.

Part of the problem, I believe, is that we're not clearly discriminating between different levels of reality. We're stumbling into the thorny thickets of nirvana and samsara, absolute and relative, unconditioned and conditioned, transcendent and temporal. It's not so easy to find our way. But it is, ineluctably, in the conditioned realm that we live our lives and have our practice. It is *phenomena* we are taught to observe carefully. We learn to be mindful, to pay attention, to leave out nothing, to know where we're standing— *in this world*—that the only way beyond our limited experience is *through* it. But what if we've been conditioned not to see certain things? What if we have trained ourselves not to know how we feel in certain situations? What if we need some extra light to illuminate the dark places?

I'm suggesting that feminism, in part, is that light. More than ten years ago Elise Boulding wrote a book called *The Underside of History* about the unrecorded role of women since the Stone Age.[21] By now scores of other books have appeared, documenting the contributions of women to every conceivable sphere of life. These books have been necessary to help us know the whole story, rather than the partial one that for aeons has been considered "truth." This book in a sense is in that lineage. Because our world has for so long been constituted along patriarchal lines, our perceptions and expectations and very language reflect partial truth.

William Blake said, "Deny nothing." Our practice is about denying nothing, about perceiving without judgment, or seeing without knowing, as Toni Packer says. If the problem with feminism for some of our teachers is that it becomes hardened and fixated with judgments and "knowing," then that's something to keep in mind. Certainly these patterns have been known to occur. But they are not the nature of the beast. By all means let's stay awake. But our awakeness is to *this* world, to samsara, which is the same as nirvana, to the stones and garbage and sunshine and decay, to the hate (including self-hate) and the love. Even when I understand it, the "absolute" or "transcendent" position can at times feel uncomfortably arid and elitist. (We're sliding here into paradox again, of course. There's no "position." Knowing where we stand means knowing there's no place to stand.) But none of these teachers is guilty of arid elitism—they don't exclude the real world at all, in any of its manifestations. But if by denying feminism, they are disallowing a means for illuminating shadows in many of our lives, then I am suggesting another look.

After all, isn't Buddhism itself such a phenomenon—another "ism" capable of casting great light and also of hardening into a solid, immutable structure? Let us by all means question feminism as well as Buddhism, letting go of dead accretions, while carefully guarding their skillful means for seeing.

IV

One is always at the beginning. . . . Religion survives by redefining itself.

—Iris Murdoch[22]

Some of the women teachers I write about have maintained close ties with their inherited traditions, while at the same time infusing them with a warmth and softness closer to their natures. Others have sloughed off inherited forms, altogether or in part, and are exploring new ways of practicing and transmitting the dharma that are more consonant with Western experience. Perhaps the most challenging development has been the willingness of some to go beyond the category of Buddhism itself. Toni Packer has left Buddhism behind. Joko Beck includes it along with other traditions that are useful. (She still believes, however, that among all religions, Buddhism probably offers the clearest mode of practice.) That this may not be a revolutionary development in our time is suggested in a quotation from Bankei (1622–1693):

> I don't talk about Buddhism, and I don't talk about Zen. There's really no need to talk about these things. Since I can manage perfectly just by dealing with people's own selves as they are right here today, there's no need for me to talk about Buddhism or Zen either.[23]

If women are helping to change the face of Buddhism in this country, what are some of their particular concerns? How, in fact, are women teachers different from male teachers? One dominant theme echoed by almost all of them is the primacy of our daily, embodied lives as the realm for practice. Christina Feldman, a vipassana teacher (who lives in England but comes to the United States frequently to lead retreats, most recently retreats for women and in women's spirituality), spoke in an informal interview about a lack of balance in the way Buddhism is usually presented. She described "this path of striving and of erasure of the self" as being a one-sided path that totally neglects another whole dimension of spirituality.

> In traditional teachings the world is generally seen as something which you get out of as quickly as possible. There is a whole value system in which things like relationship, connection with nature, and social activism are presented as being inferior to a fully dedicated spiritual life. And inwardly, things such as your body, your feelings, your emotions are things to get over, to be transcended. Basically one is to aspire towards seeing them as empty.

But the fact of many people's lives, particularly many women's, is that they've spent a lot of time establishing a relationship of integrity with the world, they've spent a lot of time getting over negative conditioning around their bodies, they've spent a lot of time really recognizing the impact and the importance of their feelings in their lives. I feel a balanced approach to spirituality is not one of just getting over things or getting out of things, but also of nurturing those very things which make up our lives as vehicles for understanding. Basically our total life experience is a vehicle for understanding if it is used skillfully, if it is used in the way of love and compassion. That approach seems to be more conducive to actually giving to the world. It breeds a sense of connectedness with life rather than a divorce.[24]

Tsultrim Allione agrees:

Women need to become aware of what practices actually work for us, what practices are adapted to our energies and our life situations. We cannot be satisfied with just doing something because it is supposed to lead to enlightenment or blindly obeying the edicts of male teachers and administrators. We need to observe what actually works. Women need upaya (skillful means) as much as men need to balance their energies with prajna (profound knowing) and emptiness (sunyata).

I have found that many Buddhists are anxious to leap to the absolute point of view and consider any discussion of possible differences in the spiritual paths of men and women as useless dualistic fixation caused by a lack of understanding of the true nature of mind. But . . . *both* the absolute *and* the relative truth must be considered.[25]

She goes on to describe the many ways in which the actualities of women's lives—especially motherhood—provide ground for spiritual development, and urges women who are spiritually awake to make connections between their lives and the teachings. Her perception of the tremendous spiritual potential of motherhood as a spiritual path is echoed by Carol Ochs in her *Woman and Spirituality:*

The de-centering of self achieved through asceticism can be accomplished as well through true devotion, which is first and

29

foremost physical caring. In caring for their infants, mothers don't seek to mortify their sensitivities—they simply know that babies need to be diapered and infants who spit up need to be cleaned. They count their action as no great spiritual accomplishment. By merely doing what must be done, their spiritual development proceeds without pride and without strain—it gracefully unfolds.[26]

To mother is to learn to love and to let go, she says—in other words, to decenter the ego. In place of the question "What is God?" she substitutes "Where is God?" and answers: "In and through all our experiences . . . and ultimately inexhaustible." The experience of mothering is full of these "quiet revelations." We perceive that we are only the conduit for love, it is not under our control, it is greater than we are, and it transforms us. "We consent in letting another's life touch us at the deepest core of our being, forever. We consent to letting the process of raising the child transform us as it forms the child."[27]

In recent years there have been rumblings and reevaluations constellating among female adherents of Western spiritual traditions as well. Responding to similar strains of male-centeredness and misogyny in Christianity and Judaism, groups of women have been creating new forms of expression for their spiritual life. Some have turned to Goddess worship, others to indigenous traditional forms—Native American, African, Hawaiian—more consonant with their values and instincts, while still others are creating a new women's spirituality. Another response has been to remain affiliated with the original tradition while attempting to change it from within.

"For some," write Carol Christ and Judith Plaskow, "the vision of transcendence within tradition is seen as an authentic core of revelation pointing towards freedom from oppression, a freedom that they believe is articulated more clearly and consistently within tradition than without. Others believe that the pre-biblical past or modern experience provide more authentic sources for feminist theology and vision."[28] For example, women in the Catholic Church, including many nuns, have for years been militating for ordination of women priests. More recently a second group, rejecting priesthood as a manifestation of patriarchy, have abandoned this ambition and instead are creating their own forms within the structure of the church. Their new forms are nonhierarchical and ecumenical in spirit, such as rituals of baptism and communion based on the circle, open to all. And they are incorporating elements from other traditions, for example the sharing of bread and wine of the Jewish Sabbath. No longer "going along," no longer battling, they call themselves Women-church, and their influence is growing.[29]

"That patriarchical religion is unhealthy for women is rather obvious," writes Charlene Spretnak, a long-time vipassana practitioner and editor of the groundbreaking anthology *The Politics of Women's Spirituality*. "To survive and evolve as free women, we must maintain unity and draw on our inner resources." On an intellectual level, she says, it was always clear to her that all time (and all space) was of one essence—was *now*. But, she says,

> I never *felt* that knowledge as an experiential truth until I encountered women's spirituality and discovered that temporal boundaries can be rather simply dissolved by the female mind's propensity for empathetic comprehension and bonding. Through ritual moments and countless meditations, through absorbing the sacred myths of our prepatriarchal foremothers and passing them on to my daughter, through experiencing in my own daughter/mother mind and body the mysteries celebrated in the ancient rites, I have come to know, to *feel* oneness with all the millions of women who have lived, who live, and who will live.[30]

More and more these days, for men as well as for women, these considerations are neither irrelevant nor alien. Here again, for example, is R. H. Blyth:

> What claim can Zen possibly have to universality when it ignores one half of humanity, and assumes sexlessness, that is halflessness, in the other? Religion has always omitted women, as it has omitted nature, and human nature, but the result has been that religion has omitted itself.[31]

And Jack Kornfield, a vipassana teacher and cofounder of the Insight Meditation Society, recently stated:

Some of the most important changes in Buddhism in our time will be the positive result of reintroducing the feminine. Specifically I mean a return to the heart, the validation of feelings and emotion, receptivity, and connection to the earth. Till now, Buddhism has been preserved in a fundamentally masculine context, with stress on knowing rather than on heart and feeling. And it's gotten out of balance. Bringing spirituality back into the body and the feelings and the heart is needed to heal both Buddhism and the earth.[32]

Finally, here is Robert Aitken, one of the most respected Zen teachers in America, writing in *Parabola*:

> Vajrayāna people are fond of criticizing Zen students for their black robes, black cushions, and solemn faces, implying that we tend to shut ourselves from our natural being. They are right in some respects. Dark, unpatterned clothing and black cushions help to minimize distractions in the dōjō, and encourage the deep-dream dimensions of *makyō* [visionary and other altered states occurring during zazen], but solemn faces and the overemphasis on "great determination" and endurance reflect our samurai inheritance, an accretion on the Buddha Dharma that should be wiped away. For "samurai," read "male." In Far Eastern culture, the female virtues in women and in men tend to be covered over. In wiping the samurai from Zen practice, we expose gentle human nature that nurtures our own aspirations and those of all beings.[33]

That women are different from men—despite the ways we are the same—is verified by common sense and everyday experience. But in recent years this perception has been confirmed by research in many branches of science, from developmental and social psychology to neurophysiology. Women's bodies and brains are different from men's. And it has been noted that our earliest and most crucial formative experience—our relationship with our mothers—is, for women, with a person of the same sex as ourselves. For men, of course, it is the opposite, requiring opposite developmental tasks. All this makes for differences, subtle and incomparable, in the way we perceive the comings and goings of the universe.

Introduction

This morning, walking along the ocean, I wanted to shout out loud, "Form is beautiful!" The ocean speaks the dharma to me more clearly than any dharma talk—an experience that is perhaps more common among women than men. Before the ocean, we feel the dharma in our bodies: the ache of the undertow, the silence (just caught) beneath the crash and roar of waters, the shock of givenness—and goneness.

So often one hears that women "get it" faster than men, are the quicker students (of Zen, of vipassana, of Vajrayana—it is repeated in all traditions). And the questions inevitably recur: Why, then, have women not been teachers before? Why do they so often leave practice after many years? Is our particular mode of knowing not consonant with the way practice centers and teaching methods are designed? When I was growing up, my father praised me whenever I thought "like a man"—that is, logically and rationally. The rest of my experience was tolerated or patronized (or never revealed). Perhaps, despite the Buddhist insight that truth is beyond rationality, our structures still too often demand that we think "like a man."

Or perhaps the problem lies with structure altogether, with anything that becomes fixed and impregnated with tired projections. If it's the truth we're after, it is certain to elude our monuments and sanctified forms. On the other hand, don't some women and men still find these inspiring and empowering? We're of so many sizes and shapes, and answers don't come ready-to-wear. There are only these prickly questions. But don't we need to sit with them, let them "turn over," as Joko Beck says? Aren't questions our very life? Answers are the past. Ane Pema Chodron once said, in effect: The past is behind us. This is *now*. Let's get on with it.

V

Can any generalizations be made about the women teachers in this book? Actually, very few. If anything, it is their diversity that has struck me most. Some of them knew as children that there was a reality beyond the world of the senses. Others were jostled into awareness much later. Almost all of them live in the world, with children and families. In some cases, the husbands have practices of their own; in others not. Some of the children practice, others don't. All these teachers are insistent that everyday life is our essential spiritual arena.

An unusual number have played or performed music. One is a poet and painter. Two of the women who have been ordained speak in almost identical language about how their lives were changed by the taking of vows. Teaching styles range from the most traditional to the most fluid and open. In several cases, where radical shifts occurred, I have chronicled this process of change.

About the heart of the matter—the heart of the dharma—they all speak with one voice: in different accents, with different emphases, in different settings. But the overarching fact is that for the first time in history, the teachings are being transmitted by a significant number of women. It would be difficult to exaggerate the importance of this fact. Again and again on my travels, women told me about the first time they heard the dharma from the mouth and mind of a woman teacher. In every case the experience was powerful and affirming—and the memory of it frequently brought tears.

I would like to say explicitly that this book, however solid and whole it may appear to the reader, is sure to be incomplete. Although I did my best, only by a miracle could there *not* be women I don't know about who should have been included. Had there been more time and space, I would certainly have included at least one more teacher from the Tibetan tradition.[34] It was my original intention to interview two additional teachers: Jan Chozen Soule, Sensei, previously at the Zen Center of Los Angeles, but currently not formally teaching; and Rina Sircar, Burmese teacher of vipassana meditation in the United States, who had entered a period of mourning for her recently deceased teacher, the Venerable Taungpulu Sayadaw, in the time remaining for her interview. To anyone I've overlooked, I extend my apologies—and express my delight that you are there.

It should not be assumed, by the way, that women given full chapters are necessarily more important in my mind than those treated more briefly. In some cases the decision had more to do with external events and timing than assessments of stature or seniority. Moreover, at several points along the way, I knew the book would be out of date before it was finished. I've tried to update material where possible, but one does have to stop somewhere. Let us simply assume, as the dharma teaches us, that everything I've recorded is still changing, and that the most this book represents is a moment, or a series of moments, in time.

Finally, for whatever interest it may have in relation to the rest of the book, here in brief is my own dharma story.

Like so many others over the years, I first learned about Buddhism and Zen from Alan Watts—not from his books but from a weekly radio program he was conducting during the early fifties in Berkeley, California (where, a transplanted New Yorker, I was completing my B.A. in anthropology). In his engaging way, he engaged me utterly, and though later, during my "pure" and snobbish years, I derided him as a showman and popularizer, I now feel deeply grateful for his ability to express the genuine spirit of the dharma in language we could all understand. As a result I read D. T. Suzuki's books and, in the mid-fifties, did graduate work at Columbia University in Japanese literature. In the evening I attended a seminar with D. T. Suzuki himself. (Much later I learned that around the table with me sat such luminaries as John Cage and Karen Horney.)

Not until the late sixties, however, having moved back to California, did I read Philip Kapleau's *Three Pillars of Zen*[35] and therein discover that there was a practice called *zazen*. Very soon I was sitting at the Berkeley and San Francisco Zen centers, and spent part of a summer at Tassajara Zen Mountain Center, where I had some precious time with Shunryu Suzuki-roshi before he died.

But then something shifted. (Perhaps I'd been denying it before.) I began to feel increasingly alienated and disaffected. There seemed an impenetrable coldness in the *zendo* that I wasn't able to comprehend or dispel. Today I relate this experience (or part of it) to some of the issues I've discussed above. Might the outcome have been different had the atmosphere and structure of the center been different?

In any case, I left practice—or at least I tried. For years I went back and forth, exploring other possibilities and endlessly returning to Buddhism. Each time I returned, it felt like coming home. But like a teenager, I seemed to need to keep leaving. Then, in 1975, I heard a lecture by Joseph Goldstein and was soon attending my first ten-day vipassana retreat in Toledo, Washington. At the front of the meditation hall, both a male and a female teacher sat facing us. Both gave interviews and dharma talks. For whatever complex of reasons, this practice felt wholly congruent, wholly without impediment at the time. And, with enormous relief, I returned home again, and for seven years developed roots and community.

Still, when the idea for writing this book came to me in the early eighties, I realized that part of my motivation might be that I'd never had the experience of working closely, over time, with a teacher, and that unconsciously I might be looking for one. We all know the maxim that when the student is ready the teacher arrives. But maybe, I thought, sometimes the student has to get up and *go*. Perhaps *going* might contribute to "getting ready." Today I think there was truth in that. Certainly the remarkable outcome is that I've found two teachers with whom I now practice intensively (as well as a third with whom I sit whenever I can), who complement each other beautifully. That they're all in the Zen tradition may well have some karmic significance. The spiral has circled back on itself, and these days I sit happily at the Berkeley *zendo* where I am a practicing member. Many things have changed there. We have frequent open meetings, a lively and active women's group, and a regular discussion group led by students on issues related to our daily lives and practice. There are women in all leadership positions (except roshi), and women have been directors of the board for years.

Perhaps the most gratifying result of my work on this book so far is that two teachers, Maurine Stuart and Toni Packer, are now coming regularly from the East Coast to the San Francisco Bay area to lead retreats (some for women only) once or twice a year. A nucleus of people has formed around the ongoing creation of these retreats, and they now constitute a growing small sangha with a life of its own. And a network has begun to form among local practitioners of Zen Buddhism, vipassana, and Tibetan Buddhism interested in sitting together without regard for old entrenchments or divisions.

In this regard it is good to know about the Buddhist Sangha Council of Southern California, which coordinates activities encompassing the Theravada, Mahayana, and Vajrayana traditions, representing many nationalities and ethnic communities as well. Furthermore, in different parts of the country, many more opportunities are being created in recent years for ecumenical and Buddhist-Christian dialogue. My hunch—and hope—is that as time goes on, American Buddhism will be making room for this kind of development, fostering the emergence of forms that more closely express the true heart of the dharma.

I

Toni Packer

Think it through for yourselves. . . . Human beings throughout history, interested in a religious life, have tried to kill the self, or fight the self, have invented systems for ego attrition. But it's a plain fact that the self cannot kill the self. Because what's left is still self: the victor, the one who has overcome . . . which is a new image! So what is one going to do in the light of this understanding?

Can energy gather in not knowing what to do?

—Toni Packer

In Rochester, New York, just up the road from Mount Hope Cemetery, there is a large stone house set back from the street behind a wall of stones you can see were placed by hand. There is no obvious sign, but this is the Genesee Valley Zen Center. Quiet now, it was the focus five years ago of events that split Rochester's Zen Buddhist community down the middle. The storms and shakings produced are still being absorbed, not only in Rochester but in Buddhist communities around the country.

What happened, in brief, is that Toni Packer, then chosen successor to Philip Kapleau (venerable roshi of Rochester Zen Center), after painful and patient self-questioning, severed her ties with traditional Buddhism and began teaching Zen work in a fresh, unbeholden way. There have been other dramatic events in other Zen communities in recent years. But this one was probably the most seminal, most prophetic. Without implying a simple cause and effect, one senses a connection between what happened in Rochester and the fact that, in other centers across the country, the question of what Zen should look and feel like in America today is being asked and pondered out loud for the first time.

I had heard sketchily of the events in Rochester and had listened to a number of Toni's lectures on tape. Her voice is powerful, resonant. I had the impression of a brilliant mind and a commanding personality. In the fall of 1983 I visited Rochester and was looking forward to meeting her with anticipation, and not a little awe.

It is already dark and the ground and hedges are wet with recent rain, the evening I arrive at GVZC. There are no lights in the windows of the big stone house, and no one answers my knock after I haul my valise up the front steps. Then I notice a sign directing me around to the side door. Halfway there, I see two people walking up the drive. The tall one, a young man, introduces himself as Kevin. "And this is Toni," he says. I automatically say, "Hi, Toni," and then stop. "You mean *Toni* Toni?"

We all laugh. I have been taken aback because Toni of the powerful voice is just a person: in a knitted cap and down jacket, face pink from outdoors, smile welcoming me, eyes blue and very bright, short silver hair just showing under the cap.

Just a person. I recognize the voice, but the kindness in it now touches me. I am tired and my head is aching. In the kitchen we sit down at a long wooden table in the middle of the warm, spacious room, and soon someone is making tea. Then Toni's assistant, Sally, appears—a pleasant-looking woman about thirty, very direct in manner—and shows me where I'll sleep upstairs.

My room is tiny with heavy wooden shutters reaching almost to the ceiling. As we walk back down the handsome broad staircase, I confess my head is hurting badly. "I'll give it a rub if you'd like," Sally offers.

Back in the kitchen I sit down in the corner chair at the table, and Sally places her hands on my shoulders. I close my eyes, breathing deeply, almost wanting to cry. Her fingers now gently touching my head, she says, "This *is* a bad one, isn't it?" She has a slight British accent, which I later learn is Australian. Someone sits down opposite us on the other side of the table. Through flickering lids I see it's Toni. She has a cup of tea and sits there, very quietly. Sally's fingers are moving gently over my head. She begins to concentrate on the right side where the worst pain is, though I haven't said a word. As my body relaxes, I feel Toni's presence quite palpably. Utter stillness. Nonintrusive being-there. Over the next few days, and in subsequent encounters elsewhere, I learn that Toni brings these qualities with her, into whatever room or situation.

Before meditation practice that evening, there is just enough time to have a hot tub with Sally. This is a small tank in the downstairs bathroom, with barely enough room for two people. In a wooden barrel alongside is a cold plunge for one person at a time. Sally tells me Kevin conceived and put together the whole thing.

The meditation hall turns out to be an attractive room, very simple, with polished wooden floor and paneling, nicely exposed ceiling beams, and a beautiful, large, leaded glass window. There is room for about twenty sitting cushions and pads. An adjoining room holds perhaps twelve more. On Sundays when Toni gives her weekly talks, the place gets crowded and people sit in the halls and upstairs as well. For the talk, everyone joins together in the meditation hall, filling in the empty spaces quietly and efficiently.

On Sundays and during workshops and retreats, an alcove opposite the zendo is piled with extra cushions. There are not only *zafus* and *zabutons*—the traditional sitting cushions and mats—but small rectangular pillows for placing under zafus for extra height if needed, and still smaller ones filled with buckwheat hulls that can be placed under knees. The physical rigors of sitting are not stoically endured at GVZC. One feels a caring attention to details there. Toni often uses the words "loving care."

The next day we sat on cushions on the floor of her bright, pleasant room on the upper floor of the center for our first extended talk. I asked about some of the changes that had been made in the way Zen was practiced and taught here now. For example, *dokusan,* the traditional interview between teacher and student, is now called simply a "meeting." Students who want to talk with Toni call up in advance and are scheduled for sometime during the week. There is no rushing to be ahead of someone else as is the tradition in some other centers. People who don't have jobs, and who can therefore get there early, are not privileged over those whose jobs make them late. Almost always, everyone gets in. If there are fewer people, the meetings can be longer. If someone has a special need that might require more time, Toni will suggest a special appointment.

I asked about the way they use koans. Some people don't work on them at all, Toni said. Others do. Some work on simple attending, or on the breath. Some people come up with a question that moves *them*, like "What is love?" One man, for instance, had had many relationships but had never been truly related to anyone. "What is love, really?" became his koan.

Lenore: Then you don't assign koans anymore?

Toni: Not unless people want them.

Lenore: Let's say someone wants to work on koans. How do you introduce Mu, or do you? Is that the first koan?

Toni: As a first koan people work usually on Mu or "Who?" Strictly speaking, "Who?" is not a koan. It's an inquiry—"Who am I?" or "What is it?"

Lenore: You give people the option?

Toni: Yes. I ask if there is a special affinity for one of them, or whether one of these has come up by itself. Very often a question has come up even before the person ever heard of Zen.

Lenore: May I ask you something more about Mu? [I had only very recently begun to work with it. See Chapter 2.] When I speak Mu to myself as I'm sitting, the experience is that it penetrates all the way down—as far down as it can go in my pelvis. My breathing really deepens, and it feels as if my concentration . . . it gets *darker* is how I perceive it. But what is this Mu I'm saying? Is it a sound? It's not a mantra, I can tell it's not a mantra. And I think I'm a little scared. Of some blackness, maybe—it feels as if it could be very black, in this Mu. It's going to some new place in me.

Toni: Let me speak to what you've said. The way I verbalize it to people is that Mu is the expression of not-knowing. This is the most satisfactory way of putting it. Because it's not a mantra, it's not a word. It's not-knowing. Mu is just the tip of this whole vast not-knowing. And that's dark. Whatever comes up, like fear, is also Mu, because you don't know what it is. You leave aside all your psychoanalytic and other knowledge about what fear is, and face it directly, in the Mu. Facing—not "I" face "that"—but the fear, whatever it is, the churning intestines and the queasy stomach and the constricted throat and the whole thing: let all of that merge in this not-knowing. And there is this complete readiness to die. You're not going to die physically. If terror comes up, where is it?

In the *Tibetan Book of the Dead* the lama whispers in the ear of the dying, "Whatever comes up, the buddhas, the devils, it's all the production of your own mind. Don't be afraid." But it really has to be this not-knowing. And then, when you get up from your sitting, maybe here or there you really don't know what something is, and therefore you see it. If you don't know, don't quickly have a name, an explanation, a description—it doesn't mean you're going to be disoriented. When you need to think, you will.

Perception without knowing—that's Mu. It's this questioning without knowing—really dark, deep. If fear comes up, you may already have thought, "Where is that going to take me?" That thought has already slipped through the mind, it has triggered that fear. "What's going to happen to me? What is this?"

Lenore: I think sometimes the fear is just *there.*

Toni: Yes. But doesn't it need to be touched? And don't be too quick to say it isn't connected to a thought. Because what else would it be? A thought can slip by so quickly. "Death." "Dying." The thought is already gone, but what it triggered throughout the organism is there.

Lenore: So you're saying, if fear is there, what *is* it?

Toni: What *is* it! Some people work on that. They find it more effective or more meaningful than Mu.

Lenore: I like Mu because . . .

Toni: It's not associated . . .

Lenore: Yes. I have no association with it at all.

Toni: That's why people pick it, particularly these days. And then this openness of listening, of attending, not knowing . . .

Toni was born in Berlin in 1927, her childhood darkened by the horrors of Hitler and Nazism. She was only six years old when Hitler came to power. Since her mother was Jewish, there was considerable fear within the family, and in order to protect the children, Toni and her older sister and her stepbrother were baptized. Toni remembers the Lutheran minister coming to the house and sprinkling water on them. She also remembers the real religious fervor that came up later, a yearning for something beyond herself. She was haunted by questions about the war and the persecution of the Jews. Her parents were very careful, afraid to speak freely in front of the children lest they repeat something outside that could be dangerous to them. Friends and schoolmates were wearing the uniform of the youth movement. Toni envied them. She would have felt more secure wearing the tie and leather knot, although what it all meant was unclear. Then came the bombing and the nightmare of terror and destruction. How, Toni wondered, was this compatible with the notion of a loving God looking after his children and protecting them? It didn't make sense.

She was also troubled by a feeling of guilt that never left her. If Jesus died on the cross to take on himself the sins of the world, why did she still feel guilty? Why hadn't he taken away *her* guilt? Gathering her courage one day, she asked the minister about these things. But with a curt remark, he withdrew. He didn't want to deal with Toni's questions at all.

Often, at home, her mother was sad. Toni wondered if she was in some way responsible. Her brother did poorly in school and often provoked their mother's rage. Each time this happened, Toni suffered with him. "What happened to him happened to me." She often wished it really would, so that she wouldn't have to go through the agony of seeing it happen to him. Even when he was very small, she remembers fearing he would take his life. And then, a few years ago, he did.

As I talk with Toni, I feel her pain. The tragedy of her brother's life is present in the room.

She smiles. "But Christmas was a happy time. It was different. A lot of relatives and friends would come. And there was this tremendous relief. At that time there was no guilt."

Another thing she remembers is the first bombing attack. She and her sister were sick in bed with diarrhea. But when the raid began, they jumped out of bed, diarrhea gone, weakness gone. "There was tremendous energy and right action. You knew just what you needed to do." They helped put out the fires. But later, when it was all over, the thoughts flooded back in. "Oh, my God, what happened? What could have happened?" Tremendous depression set in, and then, very powerfully, the question arose: *What is the meaning of life?* It didn't let go. It was with her all the time, nagging her, goading her. What was the meaning of this life which was so utterly nonsensical, incomprehensible, cruel? Where could she find out why we do the things we do?

Later the family moved to Switzerland, and it was there that Toni met a young American student named Kyle Packer. They were married in 1950 and came to the United States the following year. They settled in upstate New York, and Kyle encouraged Toni to attend college at the University of Buffalo. Afterward she did some graduate work in psychology as well. But the department was behavioristic, emphasizing testing and learning experiments with rats. Toni's interests lay elsewhere, and she left rather soon. On her own she read Freud and Jung and Joseph Campbell, especially Campbell's four-volume *Masks of God*.

"I think that in these books I made my peace with the whole problem of the feminine—partly by seeing that it is also a cultural thing, and that there were times when female goddesses reigned high. That was before the warriors and charioteers and horseback riders came and conquered with superior power and imposed a more masculine and very often suppressive religious system. This whole problem lost its sting for me. I saw that it was a relative and conditioned thing, who was in power and who suppressed whom. There was rivalry on both sides, and fear of one another. The male fear of the feminine, and women's fear of suppression by a man. But it could shift at any time."

It was during this period that she first encountered Buddhism. And, exactly as it had been for me and many others of our generation, it was through the work of Alan Watts. She read all his books, then D. T. Suzuki's and many more. At the point of her saturation with Buddhist philosophy, Kyle brought home Philip Kapleau's *Three Pillars of Zen*. She recalls leafing through it half-heartedly, like someone presented with an extra dessert after an overrich meal. She checked idly for references to Alan Watts, found they were all negative, and then noticed the first instructions she'd ever seen about meditation. She sat upright. Here was something she could actually *do*.

Before long she was sitting *zazen* regularly at home. Then, nine months later, Kapleau's book came out in paperback, and on the back cover Toni read that he had established a center in Rochester, New York. This was in 1967, and she and Kyle and their adopted son were living in North Tonawanda, New York, a small town between Buffalo and Niagara Falls. Rochester was an hour and a half away. They drove in, took the six introductory classes, and joined the center.

Toni remembers her first impression vividly. As a child she had been accustomed to visiting German cathedrals whenever the family went touring. They had seemed impressive and mysterious, with the smell of incense and areas corded off where no one could go. What was beyond the red velvet cord? In Rochester, after an introductory lecture in the dining room, everyone was invited into the sitting room. Here, to be sure, there was incense, and a Buddha figure—but no cording off. You could be right there with it all. You could have an altar in your own home, with a Buddha figure of your own. And he was not a god, but someone like yourself, and there was a practice and a discipline open to anyone, without distinction. No boundaries.

Very soon Toni was attending sesshins and working on koans with Kapleau-roshi. Their relationship grew in mutual respect and affection. In a very early dokusan he told her that if she ever taught, she would not have to teach the way he did. She was startled. At the time the thought of teaching was furthest from her mind, but she remembered what he said. Years later, his words took on greater meaning, and he never withdrew them, though the consequences caused him pain. There was special poignance in the situation because not long before he said these words to Toni, Kapleau-roshi had himself with a heavy heart broken with his own revered Japanese master, Yasutani-roshi. Yasutani had irrevocably opposed changes that Kapleau felt were necessary in transplanting Zen to this new country.

For Toni, finding Zen practice was like finding food she had been hungry for without quite knowing it. She plunged in with her whole mind and body. She worked hard, with freshness and intensity, finding energy to spare. Her intelligence was challenged as never before. Her deepest questions could be held and plumbed until only questioning remained. The discipline supported her. For a long time the forms did not oppress her. They provided a structure to work within.

Most Buddhist scriptures, however, she found too elaborate, dry, unpalatable. Could she experience what they were talking about, for herself? That was the only thing that made sense to her. Finally, in a book by W. Y. Evans-Wentz called *Tibetan Yoga and Secret Doctrines,* she found a few passages that spoke to her directly. They concerned a number of practices for relating to thoughts during meditation, such as cutting them off, following a thought to its end, or letting thoughts roam freely. Then the practitioner is likened to someone sitting on the bank of a stream, letting thoughts just stream by. But even here, thought processes are still being employed; one is still thinking. One is *using thought to detect thought*. Seeing this is the first step.

"I can't tell you how often I read this," Toni told me, "and what joy there was in understanding something—not verbally, but the words leading you to understanding something directly. Being able to see for myself how this mind works. So that one is not trapped by it, doesn't deceive oneself, and doesn't deceive others. Which happens easily enough. Without attention or awareness, that's how it works!"

In the early 1970s she was being asked to counsel students about personal concerns or psychological problems coming up in practice, and then to give public talks on Zen at universities and other places. Each step of the way she felt pushed a bit beyond herself. More a private than a public person, she would not have sought these activities. But it had been part of her training that when your teacher asked you to do something, you said yes. So when Roshi asked, she complied.

At the same time, her perspective began to widen. With her contacts outside the center, with new students, and with old students whose concerns she was listening to, she was no longer focused only on her own work. She began to perceive some of the traditional forms in a new way. Bowing, for instance.

She had learned that bowing can come from a place of self-lessness. Prostrating before the altar or before Roshi in dokusan could happen out of emptiness. But now, when students came to her and bowed to *her*, were they seeing her clearly or putting her above them as an image? And could she be sure that she was not feeling herself thus raised up? What images were being created in both their minds? Even though she was wary of—aware of—these things, students might not be.

And what of chanting? There were many chants, and they were long and often repeated rapidly several times in succession. What was the purpose of this? If the meaning was important, wouldn't speaking the words more slowly avoid the pitfall of speaking them mechanically, by rote?

Toni was also seriously questioning the harsh and often merciless use of the *keisaku* (hitting stick), with which meditating students were whacked on the shoulders to arouse their energies. She was deeply concerned about what the hitting was doing to the minds and bodies of the people being hit. Likewise, what was it doing to those who were wielding the stick? The use of the stick was reverentially referred to as an act of compassion. But did stick-wielding really arise from compassion? And didn't energy awaken naturally in the course of questioning? (Later on, at her new center, the practice of using the stick would be abandoned altogether.)

Honed by years of practice, Toni's mind could allow such questions to arise and be looked at. She did not need to react or to act in any way. She paid attention. She considered. She took her time. She knew Roshi trusted her, and she trusted herself. She could not carry out practices that felt wrong to her. She consulted with a few older students. And gradually she began to make a small formal change here and there.

This was at a time when she and Roshi were teaching in tandem. He would be gone for months at a time, vacationing as well as traveling to other centers in this country and abroad, and Toni had been asked to take charge in his absence. During one of his periods in Rochester in 1975, he had called Toni into his office and told her that he was thinking about retirement, possibly in five years. He would probably move to a warmer climate with a small number of disciples. And he wanted her to take over the Rochester center entirely when this happened. Would she be willing?

Toni was thunderstruck. She remembers driving home with a sinking heart to tell Kyle. Though it would not take place for several years, the prospect lay heavily on her, like a stone. She didn't know how to take such a responsibility. She couldn't continue doing things the way they were being done; she knew that clearly by this time. But was she capable of doing them differently?

Still, she told Roshi yes. Her training left her no alternative.

It was sometime during this period, in a book that Roshi himself had loaned her (Jacob Needleman's *The New Religions*), that she came across the teachings of Krishnamurti for the first time. The effect was catalytic. All her misgivings were reinforced; all her questions were stretched further. Krishnamurti says: shun all systems, all authority, all images. End your particular attachment, *now*. The mind must be free of all authorities. And, echoing the Buddha's last words to his disciples: be a light to yourself. He also said, in a discourse on love, "It may mean complete upheaval; it may break up the family . . . you may have to shatter the house you have built; you may never go back to the temple." Whether or not Toni read those particular words, they speak uncannily of the upheaval that was to follow.

At the beginning of 1981, Kapleau-roshi left for a year's sabbatical and Toni was put in charge of the center. She was still trying at this time to find a way to be true to her own inner direction and at the same time remain loyal to her teacher and the tradition precious to him. She wrote down all the little things she felt needed changing, like the wording of certain vows and sutras, the pace of chanting, special seating and other zendo etiquette that denoted hierarchy. When she spoke to Roshi about them, he was disconcerted. Why did she want to go so fast? He acceded to the slower chanting, but wanted her to leave other things the way they were. Under Harada-roshi (one of his own masters), he said, a new teacher would not have dreamed of changing anything. That would have been outright impudence. What you do in dokusan, he said to her, is up to you. But the forms were another matter. "We've created something here."

Toni realized how strongly he felt that it was his center, and how much he didn't want it changed—at least not quickly. And to the latter, at that point, she agreed.

She wanted it to work. She struggled to make it work, to find an accommodation that would harmonize this conflict. According to some of her students, they were in favor of her leaving the situation long before she was. They described acute division at the center at the time, turbulent meetings during which Toni's actions were criticized. And all the while she knew they were seeing only the ripples of a much deeper shift within her.

"I began to question this *whole thing* I was doing," she told me. "Belonging to a group, and the identification with it. But I tried to rationalize it away. I didn't want to tackle it. I was part and parcel of it."

Problems were bound to arise. For example, there was the incident of the *rakusu*. For many zen students, the rakusu symbolizes attainment of a new stage in their practice. In certain traditions it signifies completion of a certain number of koans. In others it comes with the taking of vows and ordination. At the Rochester Zen Center in the 1970s, it was given to students who had completed their first koan and the "miscellaneous" koans, and who were ready to begin working on the *Mumon-kan,* a collection of koans assigned to students at advanced stages.

The rakusu is a kind of loose vest worn over one's robes or even over ordinary clothing. It is constructed elaborately of a traditional number of rectangles of fabric that are sewn together in a prescribed way. In some traditions the vest is sewn by the student who is to wear it, the sewing itself being a kind of meditation. A mantra is said with each stitch, totalling over half a million. In Rochester, the rakusus were made by others and presented to the students who had attained them, as a badge of their attainment.

Of course this practice made for hierarchy, for division. How could it not? And to anyone whose mind was questioning these things—and Toni was questioning everything—the rakusu must have felt onerous. In a setting where ego and pride—distinctions of any kind—were to be seen through, how could the rakusu have a place?

Toni took hers off and never put it on again. She must have known this would not go unnoticed. Yet this and the other changes that she had already instituted were actually far behind the current reaches of her mind. So the depth of some people's opposition shocked and disheartened her. If there had been any other path, she would have taken it. Conflict and confrontation were painful and exhausting to her, raising specters from her childhood. But she could not go backward, or sideways either. To see through delusion, you cannot promote delusion. Rakusus, prostrations, special seats in the zendo—all meant separation. However many times she looked at it, she had to go forward.

A significant meeting took place when Roshi returned to Rochester from Santa Fe in June 1981. People had been writing and talking to him, complaining about the changes that had been taking place. In a roomful of indignant people, Toni was permitted to have only two staff members with her. Accusations were leveled at all three. By the end of the meeting (and even after the earnest intervention of a long-time member in a discussion that lasted until 2:30 in the morning), she knew that ultimately, if not immediately, she would have to leave—despite the heartache it would cause, despite the division. There were couples, for example, one of whom was her student and the other Roshi's. What would they do? How would they negotiate separate allegiances? These questions would have to be faced. It would be painful. It would take time. But first the separation would have to take place.

Toni was aware that the whole situation had also been sapping her health. "Some people would love this type of thing, thrive on it. Whereas for me, having grown up in Hitler's Germany, this really touched off a lot of old fears—of being accused, of being denounced."

And the much deeper issue—was she still a Buddhist?—had not even yet been raised. She knew that sooner or later she would have to raise it, but she hadn't yet faced it completely. She still could not just abandon the whole thing. So when Roshi said the next day, "If you stay, you can do anything you want. I give you complete freedom to work in your own way," she agreed to stay.

Toni: He said "All right. Do what you need to do." But before long I knew he couldn't give me that "complete" freedom, because I wasn't going to carry on with Buddhism anymore.

Lenore: How did that become clear?

Toni: Well, I myself was doing all these prostrations, and lighting incense, and bowing, and *gassho*-ing and the whole thing. I realized that I was influencing people, just by the position I was in, the whole setup. I could see it, and I wasn't going to have any part in it anymore.

    Unless you are really set on discovering, if anybody supports you in *not* discovering, you won't do it. Which I find in Zen. The system is very supportive to *not* questioning some things. Even though it claims to question everything. You question everything and you "burn the Buddha," but then you put him back up!

    I examined very carefully: did I have any division while I was bowing? It had always been said, "When you bow, you're not bowing to the Buddha, you're bowing to yourself. And when you're prostrating, everything disappears, you disappear, the Buddha disappears and there's nothing." I tried to look, and it wasn't completely clear. I could see there was often an image, of the bower, or of the person who "has nothing." Often there was a shadow of something, somebody there who was doing it. Or maybe the idea of being *able* to do it emptily!

Lenore: Let me ask you something. Is it okay to bow if you're empty?

Toni: Why do you do it? Why do I do it? Let me ask you this: if you had never come in touch with this particular tradition of bowing, in a moment of deep understanding or profound outpouring of love—would you bow?

Lenore: Well, in a way I've learned to. I've learned this gesture as an expression of respect and gratitude and love. And sometimes it just comes spontaneously to me.

Toni: Do you then teach others to do that? People in the West, whom you've never taught to do this, don't do it spontaneously.

Lenore: So you might convey an empty gesture?

Toni: Yes. Love you cannot teach. It's either in you or it's not, and how it expresses itself, or whether it expresses itself at all in gestures, is irrelevant.

In the end, the pieces began to come together with a kind of inevitability. And despite some of her students' experience of a lengthy process, it all seems to have happened remarkably quickly. Toni had been left in charge of the center on January 1, 1981, when Kapleau-roshi moved to Santa Fe. In June he returned to Rochester for the stormy meeting described above. In November Toni went to visit him in Mexico, where he was vacationing, to tell him she could not go on because she no longer considered herself a Buddhist. "It was very difficult for me to do. If he had wanted me to stay another year, then I would have stayed even within the old framework." But after talking to the trustees, he only asked her to stay till January. So the whole story took place in one year's time.

From another vantage point, however, it still goes on. Wounds are still healing. There is criticism, bitterness, a sense of loss. While many have joined one center or the other, some have remained unaffiliated, wary, even disillusioned. Some deeply want to work toward healing the schism. The very phenomenon of two Zen centers in one city feels discordant, antithetical to notions of harmony and nondivision. Some are examining their own behavior and ways of thinking that contribute to polarization. One student wrote Toni a letter, which she quoted in a Sunday talk, deploring the ways in which "we too have kept alive the division between the two sanghas."

In characteristic fashion, Toni said, "There are not two sanghas. There are only human beings, split and divided within themselves." She is not impatient for peace and harmony. Rather, she wants to know: What *are* peace and harmony? Whether we're talking about two nations, two centers, two individuals, or the inner state of *one* individual, what we're dealing with are thoughts, ideas, imagination. "Do you see that?" She knows that many will find this disconcerting, will fight it with all their being. But growing up in Germany, Toni experienced the travesty of periods of "peace" that were only intervals between wars.

All of us are moved to solve problems in the world, she says, yet we're not in touch with the problem directly. We bring our confusion to the situation. We may have some limited, temporary impact, but not the real answer. For that we would need to enter into the problem and see it fundamentally, in ourselves.

How can we contribute to peace and harmony when there is no peace and harmony in ourselves? And genuine peacefulness and harmony must be differentiated from some idea that one repeats, some "image of oneself as someone who works for peace and harmony." Such images prevent our seeing the disharmony in ourselves, the division, the fragmentation.

So Toni is not in a hurry these days to cover over whatever raw feelings there still may be, even in the service of peacefulness or love. Division is *real*. Anger and bitterness and self-interest are *real*. Let us not cover them over before looking at them, experiencing them, understanding how they arise.

"What is the source of hatred, violence, war, dissension, division? If one is consumed with this problem—it is destroying the world—where does one start?"

Toni starts with the self. Because as long as there is self-interest, it will collide with another self-interest. And until we come together as no one, there will be no peace.

Again and again she emphasizes the importance of nondefensive listening. And her ability to remain open and friendly toward criticism of every kind can be very disarming. She has based a number of talks on pointed and challenging questions from some of her students. (One asked, "Isn't what you're doing just psychology? What about enlightenment, or becoming a buddha?" Another wrote: "My only fear is for those of your students who are too blinded by your eloquence and beauty of personality to find their own true path.") She has inaugurated a series of discussion periods to address any and all questions that might arise in relation to the changes at the new center.

We need to listen to each other, and to ourselves, without any threat, she says. And this can happen only if there really is no threat—which is no easy matter at all. It takes "tremendous attention, and energy of awareness, not to be pulled into all these tendencies blindly." It is so easy not to look at what is happening in ourselves when we are envious, ambitious, or disparaging of others. Where do these reactions come from? What is the source of disharmony, war, the lack of relationship among human beings? We must look and ask and sit with these questions. Again and again: *what is it?*

What, even, is Buddhism? Who knows? she asks. Who can really know? She recalls again the Buddha's words: Be a lamp unto yourself. Rely on the truth and take refuge in nothing else.

That is what Toni teaches, whether or not she calls herself a Buddhist. She teaches—she *is*—this questioning lamp, casting light on whatever arises or comes her way. "It's possible for a human being to *see*, not just think about it. But you have to sit and let the question sit, and just look and listen internally, without knowing."

Toni teaches by questioning. She questions not only all your beliefs and conditioning, but also the usual framework of teacher-and-student. She is not there to give you anything, nor to impart the truth. There is *something* taking place, but it has nothing to do with a giver and a receiver. Two minds are meeting and, if there is openness, something may move, shift, clarify. "Do you see that?" Toni will say, again and again. Or, "Can there just be listening, without wanting, without preferring this to that?"

Her words are never meant to persuade or convince or even to inspire. Words are not the truth. Truth is direct seeing, and it cannot be taught. "In clear seeing there is neither 'teacher' nor 'student.' There is no division." There are two people, whose minds are much more alike than not, raising questions together, looking at "the whole thing" together, attending, attending, again and again. Sometimes clarification happens. Sometimes not.

While I was in Rochester I talked to Toni personally only twice. But each time I was jolted, gently, into seeing—or beginning to see. What I began to see was the tendency of my mind to operate out of ideas and images charged with feeling, and therefore experienced as "true." The dialogue that follows illustrates directly how Toni functions as "teacher."

We had been talking about some of the changes that had been made at GVZC, things that had been dropped, like bowing. And I had commented on my strong impression of the center as, nevertheless, a "Zen place." When asked what I meant by that, I replied:

Lenore: A place where practice of a certain kind, of a deep questioning, is made possible in a certain formal set-ting—the formal setting of the cushions and the mats—you don't call them zafus or zabutons any-more, but they're there. There are bells, there is a cer-tain *way* in which things are done, with a certain . . . I was going to say "aim" in mind, but aim is probably wrong . . . with a certain process in mind. A process which has to do with letting go of conditioning, with not accepting anything at face value, with not wanting to attain, not wanting to attain any *thing*. And there's a *rigor* here, of everybody reinforcing everybody else's work. The rigor of the form and of the stick* . . . a kind of honoring of these things that feels like Zen to me.

Toni: I don't know whether I would say that I am honoring it, because who am I to honor what? But we're doing it in this form because it has been found to be helpful. Anytime something feels not helpful, or something else seems more helpful, we would try that. We would experiment with it. We have eliminated a number of bells. You noticed that there are two, and sitting down we don't give another three bells. We found that it's a much smoother transition to sitting from walking when you just go right on, and you're not bowing to cushions.

Lenore: Tell me, I used the word "honoring," and that has meaning for me, but your answer was very simple, let-ting go of any extra . . .

Toni: Yes, Because if there is no extra, and there is no me,

---

*The stick is no longer used at the center.

then the actions will not be violent. Therefore there is no need to impose respect. You have to impose respect where there is a fear of possible violence or disrespect. If there's no disrespect, there is no need for respect! And with this idea, "I'm honoring that," is there an image of me honoring something else? Who are the two?

Lenore: Ah . . . I see what you're saying.

Toni: In seeing this tray, is there me and the tray, or is there just the tray? If I'm honoring it, I'm setting myself up as some . . .

Lenore: Just to go all the way with that one—I have felt in practice situations that it wasn't so much *me* honoring *it;* I felt that everybody was supporting this endeavor, deeply, together.

Toni: That's an idea! And it has to be questioned, because the idea has to go. Is there an idea of that which may be very inspirational and arouse a lot of energy?

Lenore: Don't you ever feel, in a simple, unadorned way, supported by the fact that there are twenty other people doing the same thing?

Toni: Supported in what?

Lenore: My practice being helped by the mutuality of our effort. Am I just putting the same thing in different words?

Toni: Which of course, as you're putting it right now, is a thought process. It's not the direct thing.

Lenore: Yes. What if my awareness of the person sitting next to me . . .

Toni: Yes. What is that awareness when there is mutuality, other than love?

Lenore: What *is* it?

Toni: What is it? Or is there still an idea—hey, we're all in this together. This gives me a terrific boost, the idea of it. Ideas do give boosts and energy.

Lenore: Although what about the almost physical sensation . . .

Toni: Of energy? There is such a thing as energy generated in a retreat.

Lenore: You know, you're right. I *was* having an idea!

57

Toni: Watch it and you'll find them everywhere. They drop like chestnuts out of trees! And they're so prickly.

Lenore: It's true.

Toni: And the more that is dropped, the more freedom there is for seeing. So much has been made of the energy generated at a retreat. People who were not there would say, "Oh, I felt the energy of the retreat." Then it occurred to me, actually we should then feel energy all the time, because with all these Zen centers now around the whole world, somebody's doing a retreat every moment! And what about the energy that moves these trees and clouds? And I remembered that one blade of grass can move 450 pounds of soil all by itself. One blade of grass in the springtime, breaking through the soil—boy, is that energy-generating! *Life is energy.* And we're making such a limited thing out of it, what we ourselves are creating. And then we feel pretty good. That we're doing something! [Both laugh.]

That energy is what one Zen teacher once called a firecracker energy. Somebody asked him what is Zen in America, and he said, "A firecracker." That was many years ago. But it's a good expression because there's a tremendous energy that comes from inspiration and ideas, and we're doing this and we're great, aren't we? It makes a big splash on the dark sky, and then—it fizzles. Then we have to get it someplace again. Because we're not in touch with the energy of all of life.

Lenore: Do you think there's no experience of solidarity? No experience of . . . let me see what I mean . . . I wonder if this is getting into devotion? And whether that's an idea?

Toni: Devotion is *packed* with ideas!

Lenore: You know, we're really touching on something important. I never thought about it in terms of ideas, but I know that I have a great capacity for . . . rapture? Well, that will cover a lot.

Toni: Yes. Rapture—sort of a little bit mystical and stuff. Ecstasy.

Lenore: Yes, all that stuff! So in a way, that's hard to give up.

Because it's very juicy and feels wonderful. And on the other hand, you don't *know* how ready I am to give that up! To settle. To live more out of rock bottom.

Toni: What is this rock bottom? [Pause] I don't have the feeling that at the moment this is an idea—but don't let it become one!

Lenore: No.

Toni: You don't have to express it. Let it be a question. The beauty of the question is always that there is no answer, that you *look*. The only function of the question is to prompt the looking, not the answer. Whatever is revealed in it is relatively immaterial.

In May 1983, on the eve of GVZC's first general meeting as an organization, Toni talked about "who and what we are—and what we're not." She said that this organization is important only insofar as it helps each person see into and understand himself or herself without delusion. She emphasized the danger that an organization could become more important than the people it was created to serve. That it could become an object of pride and attachment. That it could promote arrogance and division from others. "What is a center?" she asked. Does it create images of self-importance, status, prestige? These things need to be clarified, continually, "so nothing grows unawares."

She talked about how ideals can blind us to what actually takes place in our hearts, minds, and bodies. We repress and deny our shortcomings, then see them clearly in others! How sensitive relationships are between human beings, she said. They require so much love—and so often it is inadequate. She recalled the first time she confronted her mother with the fact that she had been afraid of her most of her life. Her mother wouldn't hear it, couldn't believe it.

"It was such a revelation. I thought she knew it, but she didn't. And she hadn't *meant* to be that way. She had this 'ideal' of being good and loving! So ideals are worthless, dangerous, blinding, hindering. And we constantly build them up and take our refuge in them."

No organizational form, she said, however rationally conceived, can ensure against dangers. It cannot do Zen work! It's only a set of words, a concept. "*We* have to do the work. If there's not this love, this attention to other people and oneself, how can the rules take care of it?" Each person must become aware of impulses toward domination over others, for example, or for the security that comes from blind obedience.

"This center was not formed to enshrine a creed, or the creed of *no*-creed. Not the idea of anything nor the idea of *nothing*. When there is nothing, there is no need for any belief. 'Nothing' cannot be symbolized. It's the absence of self-centeredness and fear for oneself. Who am I when I have nothing to represent me?"

She went on to affirm that the word "Zen" in the center's name does not imply affiliation of any kind. It is used descriptively—of some of the forms used for the work done there: sitting, retreats, talks, meetings with the teacher. Elsewhere she has written that the word "Zen" is also descriptive of a mind that understands itself clearly and wholly from instant to instant. That it suggests a way of seeing and responding freely, without the limitations of the self. And that it points to a truth that cannot be grasped or explained by thoughts, words, or images of any kind.

She went on, that evening, to say some very interesting things about "enclosures." There is so much in all of us that is unexplored. And it is so deep, so dark. The fear of not-being, for example, the fear of evil, of destructiveness and violence. And there is such a longing for something beyond all these, something beyond the triteness of the everyday, beyond the endless difficulties of relationship. And it seems as if, since time immemorial, *enclosures* have been especially conducive to what assuages these—to projection, propitiation, worship, magic, ceremony. She cited the Cro-Magnon caves at Lascaux, the "temple caves," they have been called, and the Gothic cathedrals of Europe "where everything is drawn upward—the architecture does it for you. You shiver all over." And forget to ask: Where does this come from? Who built this? Who painted the icons? Who wrote the scriptures? And who interprets them?

So one must be very cautious when one builds an enclosure. One must observe what happens within it. Within *this* enclosure too, she added, referring to the enclosure of the self. Until one starts questioning—what *is* this self?—it is not clear that it is an enclosure, that it separates us from others, from nature. One sees and touches and contacts the world through one's past experiences, and these color everything, determine one's whole approach. "I see everything through my tinted glasses. Is it possible to take them off?"

Without walls, she said, there are no enclosures. There is space. There is no inside or outside. If we cling to an organization, if we're attached or dependent upon it, isn't this like the enclosure of the self? Are we seeking protection in the wider enclosure of a Zen center? "To explore this we must step outside, not run away into something else again. Is it possible?"

Toni constantly engages her hearers in this fashion. All her talks approach dialogue. Her questions echo in the mind, setting off responses and questions of one's own. Later in this talk she referred to a poem in the *Mumon-kan* (*The Gateless Gate*) that contains the line: *you must climb a mountain of swords with bare feet*. "So can one walk with great care, aware of dangers, not panicky, but stepping carefully? Relating with care, listening with care, really with care, to oneself and the person right next to you?"

In the journal I kept of my Rochester trip, the first entry reads: "She is like clear, sparkling water. Her eyes see the truth and there she is. Just there. She is utterly, simply kind. No wanting, no expectation."

A later entry reads: "I have no difficulty imagining her holding that fundamental question always. That is how I experience her: in the middle of 'what *is* it?'—always. So nothing else confuses or interferes. Nothing else unbalances. It's not even that the question goes on behind anything else in the foreground. Everything else is permeated by the question, organized by it, illuminated by it.

"And I suppose that would affect the self, the personality. Of *course*—the question does not come from the personality, since even that (especially that?) is being questioned."

Reading this over now, I see how many "ideas" it holds. And how these separate me from Toni, separate me from my own experience. Yet they communicate something, if not truth, and therefore I leave them—especially the clear, sparkling water.

Update: Spring 1986

In the two and a half years since my visit to Genesee Valley Zen Center, a number of significant changes have occurred. The first was the purchase in early 1984 of 284 acres of undeveloped land for a new retreat center in Springwater, New York, an hour's drive south of Rochester. Roads had to be built and housing construction started from scratch, but by the spring of 1985, though much work remained to be done, Toni held her first country retreat there. Since then, the major activity of GVZC gradually shifted to the Springwater site, although a smaller Rochester center has continued to be maintained as well.

Now Toni has announced a radical change in the center's name. For some time she had been concerned that the term "Zen" evoked images that were not consonant with the actual work she and those working with her were doing. In a recent letter to members she wrote: "Although the word 'zen' can be used in a universal sense, to most people it refers to a separate religious tradition. It is associated in people's minds not only with Buddhism, but also with Japanese traditions. Its use is linked with specific training methods and goals, and brings with it the image of the 'zen' person. . . . Being linked with a specific tradition results in compartmentalization, division, and isolation. . . . It would be good to use a name that is simple and direct."

Several suggestions were offered, all retaining the name Genesee Valley, but in the end the choice went beyond them to Springwater Center, the simplest and most direct of all.

Another important development, especially to people on the West Coast, has been Toni's now-annual trip to California. What follows is an account of her first visit, which I was asked to write for the GVZC newsletter.

In early May of 1985 Toni came to California to conduct her first five-day retreat at Olema, an hour's drive up the coast from San Francisco. We were sixteen women and ten men, from a wide variety of practice backgrounds, though many had done Zen practice for years. Only a few of us had met Toni in person before. The setting was beautiful: a Vedanta retreat center on two thousand acres of virgin, green, lovingly tended hillsides and woods.

The room we sat in happened to contain a raised dais with flowers, candles, incense, and three large portraits on the wall above it: Christ, Ramakrishna, and the Buddha. Not the most propitious setting for Toni's teaching, one might have thought. However, in almost no time, all the particulars faded, edges softened, opinions dropped away, and we sat together simply, with beginner's mind, and heard the birds singing. The birds! All day long they sang, layer upon layer into the distance. They woke during our first sitting in the morning, and if we walked outside during the first walking period, we could hear their morning calls as the sun rose. There were deer and jackrabbits too, and cows that snored. Two people saw a badger.

The whole retreat had a quality of gentleness. For some people the fact that sittings were optional was in itself revolutionary. To question everything, even the attitudinal basis behind one's practice (e.g., stoicism toward pain or exhaustion), was by turns exhilarating, scary, resistance-producing, freeing. As each response in turn was met with gentle care and interest, all the activities of the day, all our interactions with each other and the environment and ourselves were experienced more freshly, tenderly. On an almost molecular level, we learned about nonviolence.

Nothing was mandatory (one could bow or not bow, sit facing each other or the wall); the atmosphere was totally respectful of individual needs and rhythms. We felt encouraged to be self-reliant and to question our own motivations for practice, rather than to blindly obey even internalized authority. During morning and afternoon breaks we took long walks in the surrounding woods, followed deer trails over the hills. This unhurried, meditative time close to trees and grass and wind and creatures opened out and deepened the whole experience.

Walking periods took on a life of their own. Since sittings were optional, it seemed natural to assume that walking was too. And after a while during walking periods one could see everything, from moderately paced walking in a circle indoors, to microscopically slow vipassana-style walking on the porch outside, to yoga and stretching on the library floor! But the quality of attention was genuine and sustained, and for more than one person a corner was turned in their practice.

In her talks, Toni spoke about attention, about self, about death. She read long selections from Huang Po. Often she would stop, listen, and mimic the sounds of the birds outside (*whoo, whoo . . . fshsh, fshsh, fshsh*). Many considered these talks especially lucid and impeccably formed. Like the rest of the retreat, the parts came together simply, naturally, Clear water flowing quietly over rocks.

Update: Winter 2000

There is a very different feeling these days at Springwater Center than the one conveyed in my original chapter on Toni. At that time, one still sensed the shadow of the painful split at Rochester Zen Center, which had ended in Toni's departure and the establishing of a new center of her own. Wounds were still healing; the tension and excitement of breaking away and newfound independence were in the air. Today, Springwater is mostly very quiet, settled, rooted in earth and beautiful hills and many years of peaceful, deeply silent retreats. The energy now derives from dedicated internal inquiry rather than external conflict.

In June 1998, I spent almost three weeks there, first on a seven-day retreat and then on a solo retreat for twelve days at an individual retreat cabin built just for that purpose in lovely woods that drop steeply down to a meandering creek. I came for the uninterrupted silence, for meetings with Toni, for the opening out of space and time. Even after the regular retreat ended and life returned to normal for everyone else residing at the center (which I walked to for one meal a day and other necessities), my protected space was never intruded upon. When I filled my water jugs each day, I would find a sweet silence even in the kitchen while people were preparing meals.

Retreats have become more and more simple, along with a few variations in structure. The sitting room is wide open and full of light. Afternoon sittings are untimed, with people arriving and departing quietly as they need to, often sitting uninterruptedly for longer periods than the regular schedule calls for. Comfortable chairs are stacked outside the sitting-room doors and frequently used. Mats are empty at the beginning of retreats, so people can bring to them whatever they prefer for sitting. Nothing on the day's schedule is mandatory, of course, except for one's daily job.

Sometimes, when Toni is teaching in California or Europe, Springwater may schedule a four-day retreat conducted entirely by staff members. There are no timed sittings, and participants are free to give talks or to sign up for meetings with one another. There are also several retreats a year that Toni attends strictly as a participant. She gives no individual meetings or talks—but other retreatants may sign up to present a talk themselves. Each afternoon there is an open group discussion that lasts about an hour and a half. These retreats have become very popular at Springwater. People report that the talks by participants and the daily group meetings can be unusually moving and powerful.

Koan practice has become a thing of the past. Toni remembers that people began to prefer sitting without putting anything into their minds, without having to "bring something to the teacher." And no one, she says, wanted to return to koan practice after they tasted sitting without any "practice" at all.

Old wounds stemming from the events of the early eighties seem to have healed for most of the people involved. Roshi Kapleau has visited Springwater and shown real appreciation and respect for what has been accomplished there. Increasingly, former members of Rochester Zen Center attend Springwater retreats. Many other new people, too, keep arriving from all over the world and from a wide variety of spiritual traditions. They are attracted by the absence of rituals, hierarchy, or prescribed beliefs and practices. What they seem to experience in this atmosphere of complete openness, according to Toni, is "a taste of freedom."

In recent years, I and a number of others have remarked on changes we've observed in Toni's talks and in individual and group meetings as well. Her words are less abstract, warmer, very direct. She is anchored *exactly here,* transparent, without protective veils. Her words seem to come wholly out of the current moment, without any strain of thought or effort. A palpable tenderness can arise, a sense of "big love," as someone recently phrased it. Nothing is "old" or created out of memory. The words spoken are simply, luminously there, brimming up out of presence.

In late 1998, a day before the beginning of the annual winter retreat in California, Toni and I sat at my kitchen table in Berkeley talking about, among other things, love and death. Kyle, Toni's husband of forty-nine years, had been ill with Parkinson's disease and prostate cancer for eight years. For most of that time, he had done remarkably well. Although diagnostic indicators pointed to the spread of cancer in his body, he had been consistently pain-free, traveled frequently with Toni to California and Europe, and continued to enjoy many of the activities at Springwater Center. Recently, however, not only had test results worsened, but his mobility and stamina were diminishing. Toni described watching him pull on his shoes and socks in the morning with agonizing slowness—painstakingly, patiently. She felt an impulse to help but instead chose to be still, to not intervene, while the lovableness of this man and his clumsy movements enveloped her.

She and Kyle had talked about death, neither of them felt afraid of it, and both knew they would meet it fully when the time came. Their major concern now was to have as much time left together as possible and to be open to what was happening in the present without unnecessary thought or speculation. (Toni later wrote me: "It seems natural not to be in conflict with the total situation.") Just to be with the shoes and the oatmeal and the latest medical report and the gravel or the wooden floor under their feet.

We planned that afternoon to go into these matters more deeply in a subsequent interview for this book. But as Kyle's illness progressed, most of Toni's attention and energy were occupied right there. Her wish was not to be drawn away, especially not into concepts and language. So there has been no "subsequent interview." Instead, wanting to bring Toni's voice into these pages, I'm including some brief passages from a few of her recent retreat talks, all of them addressing the conundrum of the "me" or the self or the personality.

In the first excerpt, Toni says: "All of us talk 'I' and 'you' talk.

We think it, write it, read it, and dream it with rarely any pause.
. . . How is one to come upon the truth if separation is taken so
much for granted, feels so commonsense? . . .

"The difficulty is not insurmountable. Wholeness, true being,
is here all the time, like the sun behind the clouds. Daylight is
here in spite of cloud cover."

Later in the talk, she told this story: "I had always had a difficult relationship with my mother. I was very afraid of her. She
was a passionate woman with lots of anger. But also love. Once
[during a visit to Switzerland] I saw her standing in the dining
room facing me. She was just standing there, and for no known
reason or cause, I suddenly saw her without the past. There was
no image of her, and also no idea of what she saw in me. All that
was gone. There was nothing left but pure love for this woman.
Such beauty shone out of her. And our relationship changed;
there was a new closeness. It just happened."

In another talk, she asked: "Can we inquire out of the darkness
of not-knowing? Into the darkness of not-knowing? . . . [Long
pause] The space of not-knowing is open, unoccupied. . . . No
one separate from all this. . . . One vibrant aliveness without
boundaries, an embrace of love."

Finally, in April 1999, Toni took up the theme again, speaking
of the silence within which all the noise takes place (like the sun
behind the clouds) and the shift from listening-to-the-noise to
listening-to-the-silence.

"Why resist anything?" she asked.

"On the surface of the ocean, there are waves and bubbles and
foam. The bubbles are the personality. . . . As long as we dwell in
this personality world, we cannot be in touch with each other or
with the mysterious universe which is life, aliveness. Can we see,
more than intellectually, that as long as we hold onto 'our world,'
we cannot really communicate with each other on a deep level—
beyond the bubbles and the foam and the waves and all the debris
that floats on the surface?

"It's like stepping outside [a building or an enclosure] into the
open air, stepping outside of it altogether, leaving the windows
and walls behind, not seeing the trees through glass, but with
nothing in between. . . .

"Can we begin to live with each other's personalities—I almost want to say 'in a forgiving way,' meaning 'Let it be, let it be,' like the Beatles' song? . . . Are we interested in exploring and wondering and living—at least for moments at a time—vulnerably, without defensiveness, no matter what it may bring?

"Birds are talking, calling."

Kyle Packer died at home, a few miles from Springwater Center, on November 15, 1999.

2

Maurine Stuart

Dogen Zenji said, "If you cannot find a true teacher, it is better not to practice." What did he mean by that? I'm sure there are many interpretations, but what I feel at this moment is that our practice, whatever it is, is our teacher. *Life* is our practice. If we listen deeply to what's going on—if we're involved down to the very bottom with our life situation—*this* is our true teacher, the most venerable teacher. Life-roshi!

—Maurine Stuart, Roshi

Nine women face nine women, legs crossed on black cushions, eyes lowered. Silence fills the long, wood-paneled room. At the far end is a large stone fireplace built into the wall. In front of it, on a wooden table, there is a delicately carved Kwan Yin (female bodhisattva of compassion), a candle, a small vase of flowers. Opposite, facing the two rows of silent women, sits Maurine Stuart, Roshi. She has crossed the country from Massachusetts to conduct this Zen retreat for women in California.

Only hours before, this had been a large living room filled with couches and chairs, lamps and tables, a rug on the floor. Now stripped bare, with only two rows of black mats and cushions on the wooden floor, with the sound of the bell struck three times to begin the first period of zazen, and the deepening stillness, it is beginning to be a zendo.

Out of her traveling clothes and in her robes now—black organdy over white, thus softened to gray—and with her shoulder-length wavy gray hair tied back in a bun, Maurine sits with us this first evening of the sesshin. We come from many different backgrounds and traditions, and in her opening remarks Maurine stresses the importance of our accepting and respecting each other's needs and styles. We are not just individuals but a community of beings, deeply sharing our practice. We need to be sensitive to the whole, blending and accommodating with each other, attuned not only to our inner processes but to the group as well.

This is a spirit new to many of us, and it is central to Maurine's way of teaching. She talks more often of "our being together" than of her teaching or conducting sesshins. As practice deepens, she says, "our hearts open, I see myself in you, you see yourself in me, and we cannot have distance in our attitude to one another."

After zazen that first evening, and each of the four nights thereafter, we chant together the *Heart Sutra,* the Four Vows, and the Three Refuges, and before we go to sleep we bow to each other with our heads on our crossed hands on the polished wooden floor.

"We are warrior women," Maurine says in her first formal talk the next morning. She reads us a story about the nun-teacher Shido, who founded Tokei-ji Monastery. After receiving formal approval to teach by Master Chokei of Peachtree Valley, she was challenged by the head monk to prove her learning. Instead of speaking on the dharma, she merely held up a ten-inch knife. "I am a woman of the warrior line," she said. "What book should I need?" The monk, still unsatisfied, questioned her further. But she only silently closed her eyes. After some time she said, "Do you understand?" Now the monk, in recognition, spoke in poetry: "A wine gourd has been tipped right up in Peachtree Valley. Drunken eyes see ten miles of flowers."

Before she came to be with us, Maurine says, she heard some people were afraid of practicing with a Rinzai teacher. "These Rinzai people are formidable. They would cut off your head without a thought. This cutting off, of course, is not the cutting off of heads, but immediately cutting off our illusions. So as a Rinzai lady, I sit here and strongly urge you from the very first sitting of this wonderful time together to cut off, cut off, cut off. Become plain and simple."

She talks about the true person—the "one, unlimited, true person"—to be found in each of us. "What else are we here to do?" This true person is neither male nor female, student nor teacher, past, present, nor future. It is "all in one, one in all. And when this is realized, there is no more worry about not being perfect." We can move freely. Whatever occurs, we freely respond. "Freely coming, freely going, freely moving, freely speaking, freely acting. The true person in us is here, to awaken to itself."

She cautions us not to become attached to Rinzai, to herself, or to any teacher. "The true teacher is your own zazen." Sitting in this strong, grounded posture allows us to become still, composed. "In this stillness, the deep stillness of this house, this zendo, the difference between inner and outer, motion and rest, is resolved. Alert and present to what is going on, we forget ourselves. Absorbed in just being, we realize that this one mind is not created or owned by anyone's ego. It is a universal wakefulness that every one of us can tap into. As sesshin goes ahead, we feel this more and more. People become more gentle, more alert, more vividly awake. More vividly grateful for such time together."

By the second morning of the retreat, things are beginning to come together. We have sat and chanted and walked slowly and eaten rapidly together numbers of times. Without talking, we are getting to know each other's rhythms and moods. All different, all alike.

In her talk this day Maurine speaks about the *tao,* the path, the way, the *truth* of it. How do we find this *tao?* By truly meeting your*self,* she says—sitting on the cushion, washing the dishes, cleaning the floor, taking a bath. "What transcends words or silence and is working through us in every aspect of our life, every single moment, in everything we are doing?" Nothing keeps us from finding out but ourselves. Meet yourselves directly, she says, without words or silence. Understand *directly,* with your whole being, not just your head.

In this sesshin atmosphere we become more and more open, she goes on. "Everything becomes more exquisite. The color of the sky, the feel of the material of our clothes, the taste of food, the smile on someone's face sitting in front of us. When you come to dokusan and smile—what an exquisite pleasure. We truly greet one another. Without words or silence, with vital contact, we just *look.*"

By the third day of the retreat, the zendo is truly a zendo. Everyone can feel it. We move together as parts of a whole—sensitive, soft, alert. Sitting begins smoothly, walking begins smoothly, we bow in unison, we chant powerfully together. We keep the zendo clean and chop vegetables together. For the third time we sit together as the first light of day appears outside the windows.

This morning Maurine reads from the *Rinzai Roku* (Record of Rinzai). "Bring to rest the thoughts of the ceaselessly seeking mind, and you'll not differ from the patriarch, Buddha. You want to know the patriarch, Buddha? He is none other than you who sit before me listening to my discourses." She also quotes Bodhidharma, who said to make the mind "like trees and rocks."

Facing the wall, we sit and listen, making our minds like trees and rocks.

"What prevents us from seeing clearly? What prevents us from being what we could be? There seems to be something in all of us, connected with our egos, that resists opening up. This obstacle is very close, as close as our own shadow. Some of you may think that if you gave up everything, you would fall into some kind of abyss. And you're afraid of this. Let go. Be genuinely indifferent to what becomes of it all, and you will truly find a wonderful something there. It always has been there. You have never been without it."

We come to this true freedom, this expansion to the whole universe, she says, through the discipline of zazen, which she likens to a fountain. Small holes are bored through rock, and water is forced through the holes. When it comes through the top, it *blooms*. In the same way, out of our strong, formal posture, out of this deep silence, comes a truly free mind. A mind unattached to any form, free to expand, free to experience, free to change. No pretense, no self-consciousness. She quotes a haiku: "When you're both alive and dead" (thoroughly dead to yourself), "how wonderful the smallest pleasure!"

Eight months earlier, I had flown from California to Massachusetts to talk to Maurine and spend some time at the Cambridge Buddhist Association where she is president and teacher.

It was late October. Autumn had burned past its prime in much of New England. Here it still blazed on every side. Down every street, in every alley, trees were splashing extravagant shades of red and gold and orange against an extravagant blue sky.

Between Brattle Street and Huron Avenue, fifteen minutes from Harvard Square, Sparks Street stretches broad and straight and substantial. Number 75 is a tall, dark brown, squarish house behind a brown picket fence. Inside, the ceilings are high, the rooms are gracefully proportioned and spacious, and natural wood shines on all sides. Since 1979 it has been the home of the Cambridge Buddhist Association. Maurine took the helm at that time from Elsie Mitchell, who had purchased and donated the building. Elsie had been the guiding spirit behind the association since 1957 when she, along with D. T. Suzuki and Shinichi Hisamatsu (both then lecturing on Zen at Harvard) drew up its constitution. This document is remarkable for its nonsectarian and ecumenical spirit. It states plainly that the CBA is not for Buddhists alone, certainly not just for Zen Buddhists, but open to people of all faiths without exception. At any time therefore, there may be Catholics, Muslims, and Jews practicing there together.

In 1982, in the most inconspicuous of ceremonies, Maurine was named roshi by Soen Nakagawa-roshi, her beloved Japanese teacher. "Tell everyone I made you roshi," he said. And that was that. Entirely fitting, says Maurine, who cares little about such things. She wears robes for zazen and ceremonies—and she also wears makeup, cooks elegant meals, and plays the piano powerfully, passionately.

But I knew none of this the afternoon I arrived, a little past noon, hauling my suitcase up the front steps just as Maurine pulled into the driveway and waved. Inside the second set of doors I left my shoes and was shown upstairs, past a large, arresting piece of Japanese calligraphy. In a little room at the top of the staircase, Maurine greeted me with a hug and invited me to sit down at a low table, saying she would return momentarily with tea and lunch. Soon she was unpacking an impromptu picnic that she'd assembled for the occasion: carrot salad, tortellini salad, an assortment of cheeses. The tea was fragrant. We talked and talked.

Warmth and generosity filled the room—and they suffuse the house and the practice that takes place there, I was to learn in the days that followed.

"I have the feeling I was a Buddhist in a former life," Maurine said next morning. We were seated again at the low table in her room after early-morning zazen and breakfast. "When I was a very small girl, my mother said, I always needed time to just go and sit and be quiet. Our house was a very lively place, always many people there, visitors from all over, many things going on. She said I used to take a pail of cold pancakes away for the day and go out and *sit* somewhere, quietly. I always seemed to need that. At one point I went and visited a little store and found a tiny Buddha and some incense, and I used to sit in my room with them. I must have been seven or eight. This was always a need in me: the feeling that you had to, every so often, shut down every-thing, just be in touch. . . . I always went outside somewhere, to a hill where there was wind, or to a slough that had tall grasses, and would sit and listen to crickets and listen to birds and shut down all mental activity.

"And my grandfather was a wonderful teacher, just in the way that he conducted his life. He didn't know anything about Bud-dhism, I'm sure. But I really feel he was a Buddhist innately. He behaved in a way that was very respectful of every living thing, of every human being he came in touch with. He never went to church, and he was a professed agnostic. Sometimes when he really got strong about it, he said he was an atheist. But he prac-ticed a wonderful way of life. When people came to his house, he offered them whatever he had. If they needed something and he saw they needed it, he gave, without any thought of return. He treated his animals and everything on his farm with the most wonderful consideration—love, even. He was my first teacher. I often speak about him in my talks."

Her first actual contact with Buddhist thought came when she went to Paris at the age of twenty-three as a music student with a scholarship to study with Nadia Boulanger. Born in Saskatche-wan, Canada, in 1922, and a voracious reader, she had not till then come upon any books on Buddhism. One day in Paris, however, she noticed a book called *An Introduction to Oriental Thought* and was suddenly reading it avidly. "I can still remember it, the feeling of identification. Aha! That's it! I wrote in the margins: 'That's it!'" Finding the book was a turning point. But there was no one to ask, "How do you practice? What is this? How do you *do* this?" Reading about it felt something like eating a menu: no real food. The book seemed to intimate some sort of practice, but gave no specific instruction. As a musician, Maurine knew that her ability to play the piano was entirely dependent on daily practice. How could she ever understand her *whole being* without practicing?

So she went to New York City, hoping to find a teacher. In the fifties, she had "that wonderful experience" of seeing D. T. Suzuki on television and being drawn right in. "I sat right down beside him and had a wonderful communion with him."

During this time she met and married Oscar Freedgood, an artist and businessman, and in addition to an active concert career, began a family. Then one spring morning in 1966, after taking her three children to school in midtown Manhattan, she decided to take a different route home. She was walking down West End Avenue when she noticed, on the side of a building, the words "Zen Study Society." She thought, "That's what I'm looking for," walked in, and asked for the schedule. Two days later she sat down on a zafu for the first time. Three weeks after that she went to her first sesshin. It was in upstate New York with Yasutani-roshi, who had come from Japan. "And that was the beginning."

The sesshin took place in a Theosophical Society retreat center and was "very spooky." There was an old house with little huts in the woods for individuals to sleep in. There was a living room with floral wallpaper, white sheets over the windows to soften the light, and all the furniture had been moved out. There were lots of people who had never sat a sesshin before, so there was a lot of moving about, lots of twitching and itching. But Yasutani-roshi conducted things in his "wonderful strong way" and it became an all-enveloping experience for Maurine. Nevertheless, she remembers that at the end of the first day, she wanted to leave. All the chanting and bowing, people crying, people laughing—"absolute madness," she thought. But by the end of the second day, something had taken hold. At the end of five days, "I was hooked."

Her experience as a musician stood her in good stead. Almost from the time she was a baby, when she started playing the piano, she had become familiar with regular practice. "Endless preparation, every detail polished, never enough of that. Sitting, sitting, sitting, sitting." Every day. Without exception. Then you can play with freedom. You can tell yourself to get out of the way. Something else now plays you. You've prepared the instrument. It is as ready as it can be. Not perfect, perhaps, but as ready as it can be right now. So you let whatever it is come through. It's free because you don't feel *you* are performing. When you can perform in that way it is spontaneous, effortless, strong—whether it's zazen, cooking, playing the piano, or communicating with your friends.

"This is what I am trying to teach people. That this is not some occult, faraway, Eastern, Japanese, Indian, Korean, mystical thing. That this is an essential matter for every human being wherever you live. This is absolutely part of *everyone*. You don't have to think in terms of some other country or place." (Maurine has never been to Japan.)

"One young person came here with my son one day and said he expected to see an Oriental temple. I said, This is New England, so you'll see a New England house. And we practice Zen in a New England house. We don't need an Oriental temple. We sit on flat cushions which happen to come from the Orient because they are comfortable and practical, good for our posture. But we don't choose them because they're Oriental. We have a Buddha statue, but he could just as well have a Western face. In fact, the one in the zendo almost does. It can be any face—you look at it. It depends on who *you* are. I think this is an important aspect of Zen teaching in America. Yes, you can practice as a woman cooking, you can practice as a mother. You don't have to pop away into a monastery."

Lenore: I heard that at the last sesshin here you were doing all the cooking as well as zazen, giving interviews, dharma talks—flowing effortlessly from one thing to another. How I'd love to learn to do that.

Maurine: Well, I think we don't *learn* that, Lenore. I think it *happens*. When you become really filled up with this, it just bubbles over into all these other activities. So the more you take in, whatever it is, the wonderful thing that we're all taking in all the time, the more you give out. And the more you do that, the more energy comes. People were telling me I was doing too much, that I'd get tired. Not at all. One feeds the other. At the end of sesshin, I did not feel tired. I was happy to go home and get a good night's sleep, but the next morning I felt just as peppy as ever. There's no feeling of conflict. In the zendo, cooking is just as important a teaching as giving a talk.

Lenore: Being filled up, and then letting it go. . . . It's like breathing, isn't it?

Maurine: Exactly. You take it in and you give it out. And you can take in just as much from concentrated cooking. If you're really present with whatever you're doing, it's the same thing. Taking in, giving out.

Lenore: There's some way that efforting comes in here.

Maurine: Well, if you think that you are doing something, then there's a problem. If you get out of the way as much as possible, then there isn't so much problem. If you really feel that, you are letting it do you. This is of course basic to what I practiced as a musician.

Lenore: The effort and the effortlessness. The practice, the discipline, and then the letting go of that. I just had a vision of an instrument—that we're an instrument.

Maurine: Absolutely. *We* are the instrument. The dharma is playing us. Exactly. It's playing everybody. Maybe some of us are out of tune, but as soon as you get the strings not too tight, not too loose, then it makes good music.

Lenore: It's interesting that three of the women teachers I've interviewed are musicians: you, and Joko, and Kennett-roshi.

Maurine: It's just a very basic matter. Your body must be finely tuned in order to express something with it. And

you have to do this every day, every, every, every day.
No exceptions or you feel it.

During the sixties and early seventies Maurine did a great deal
of intensive training at Dai Bosatsu monastery in the Catskills
with Eido-roshi (although later she broke with him over the ex-
clusion and mistreatment of women), and years of sesshins in
New York City, with Yasutani-roshi or Soen Nakagawa-roshi, one
of whom would come each year from Japan. For a wife and
mother, this meant a good deal of juggling. Fortunately, for the
most part, her family was cooperative. She also had the good luck
of finding the perfect person to be with her children while she
was away. Sometimes, she spent the first day of sesshin worrying
if they could manage without her, but she very soon learned that
they could, and that was that. Then after four and a half years of
deepening practice and deepening involvement with the Zen
Studies Society, there was the shock of her family having to relocate to Boston. At first she was desolate. Her Buddhist roots and
community were in New York. Boston was foreign ground.
Soen-roshi, who was in New York at the time, reassured her:
"You will have the Boston Museum," he told her, "with the best
Oriental art collection in the world. And there is Elsie Mitchell.
Find her, and you'll be all right."
And so she did. And so she was.

This is the way Maurine remembers Soen: "Everything was
strict, but warm. Always warm. Always compassionate. Everything, absolutely everything, immersed in compassion. There was
nothing that escaped him. Somebody told me about going to
Ryutaku-ji [Soen's temple in Japan] for sesshin. It was a sesshin
just for monks—and this poor man's feet were bleeding from
running back and forth in their rough straw sandals. He was exhausted and quite discouraged. Soen-roshi came and looked at
these sandals with blood on them and in their place he put wonderful soft slippers. Inconspicuous, wonderful attention. He was
so aware of each one of us, always. Turning every situation, however dark, into some wonderful teaching. Keeping the feeling of
embracing the whole sangha when he conducted sesshin. 'You are

not just here for yourself alone, but for the sake of all sentient beings.' I can hear him saying: 'Keep your mind pure, and *warm*.' Just to be doing *that,* just step by step, simply, step by step, with reverence and a grateful heart. This was that wonderful Soen. He turned everything that was parched, for me, into something that was shining and fresh. Once he had a sesshin and somebody became very upset and ran away. It was a painful and difficult thing for all of us. And he turned it into such a compassion for this person. Instead of people being upset for their own egocentric practice—disturbance of their zazen—he turned it into something wonderful. He did extraordinary things in sesshin. He would look out the window and see the moon was shining. 'Up! We're going for a moon walk.' And we would go out and look at stars. He always said, too, 'Don't look to me, don't hang on me as teacher. Don't attach yourself to *me*. Look to the universe. Look at these stars! Look at this moonlight! Look at the sunrise!' At one of his last dokusans, everybody came up the stairs, and there he was, standing on the landing. He turned everybody to the window, and there was the sun rising. He put his hands on the back of our shoulders and we chanted together, looking at the sunrise."

The arresting piece of Japanese calligraphy that I noticed on the wall at the bend in the staircase just after I arrived at Sparks Street was painted and given to Maurine by this great teacher. There are two boldly painted characters, one above the other. The top one is compact, firm, strong. I learned that it signifies "heaven." The lower one is larger, freer, more complex. It seems composed of two parts connected by a whirling line that sets them both dancing. It does, in fact, mean "dance." Together: *heaven dance*. From the stillness of satori, freely moving into life. The letters *S-O-E-N* are printed vertically along the left margin. They call to mind an incident that Maurine described to me in Cambridge.

She was visiting Soen-roshi and he was painting calligraphy, perhaps the very one hanging in Sparks Street. Paul Reps, the well-known writer, was also present, and he was painting as well. Soen asked Maurine to sing while they worked, and she sang his favorite, Beethoven's Ninth Symphony. If she stopped, he would say, "More! More!" Paul was singing too, and Soen was exclaiming, "Ho! Ho! Beautiful!" Paul finished a painting and signed it with a large *REPS*. Soen finished his and put a tiny *Soen* in the corner. "You see, Paul? You see?"

He was tiny himself, only four feet eight inches high. Yet someone meeting him for the first time once exclaimed, "What a mountain of a man!" He died in Japan in March 1984, but the imprint of his spirit is still vivid in Cambridge today.

At Sparks Street, daily zazen, monthly sesshins, and ceremonies are conducted in traditional style, with traditional Japanese bowing and chanting, bells, gongs, and *keisaku*. At the same time, one notices little things, such as zazen taking place at different times on different days. On Tuesdays, for example, it's in the early afternoon. The schedule is expressly designed to accommodate people with different needs. Almost everyone can find at least one time a week to sit. But it is also understood that those whose schedules still make them late for zazen can quietly sit down in an adjoining zendo, which has its own entrance. People also may join in during *kinhin,* before or after the second period of sitting, morning or evening.

From the moment I arrived at the house I felt welcomed, included. There was a simple graciousness in the way I was invited to take part in the daily schedule, to share a meal, to peruse the library. There was an affectionateness in the atmosphere, in the very walls. When I commented on this to Maurine, she was delighted.

"This is *exactly* what I want to happen here. I really feel this is not something that should scare people. Many places in my experience have been so formidable and so tense. 'You have to do it *this* way! You mustn't bow any way but *this.*' And you lose the spirit! This too comes to me from Soen-roshi. I remember coming once to the door of the dokusan room and I said, 'I've forgotten how the bow should be,' and he said it didn't matter. 'Just bow, that's all.' And I say that to people. 'Don't worry if you've forgotten a form. Just show me your own heartfelt expression of it. Do it from open heart.' This *is* my intention—that people *do* feel included."

I asked why she thought that spirit was so rare in other Buddhist centers. She wouldn't say, except that she believes absolutely that "this is *it*. If I cannot accept you *as you are* . . ."

There are some people who come to the center because they are troubled. Just as they are, they are accepted. And they change. One woman came originally in desperate shape. She had been hospitalized many times, for many years of her life. Initially she ranted and raved, literally beat on Maurine's body. "She was furious. Angry, angry, angry. She would flail about and she would demand, 'Why do you do that? Why do you say that? What do we do this for?' And on and on. And we just accepted her, all of us. We didn't say, 'You can't act this way, you're disturbing the rest of the sangha.' We just let her come. She now has a job, a car, and is in a perfectly sane frame of mind. She comes and sits quietly, with a peaceful expression on her face most of the time. And she feels accepted and cared for. If we just *talk* about Buddhism and don't *do* it . . . !"

Another member of the sangha is a man who recently lost his vision. As the condition progressed, the realization that he was going blind made him angry. "Oh," he said, "I am so angry I cannot tell you." Somebody said to him, "It may be a blessing that you are going blind," and he said that only made him angrier. But he kept on sitting, sitting, sitting through all of it, and one day he came to Maurine and said, "I really begin to understand that I can see with my skin. I have to be so mindful every time I take a step, it's like kinhin. I *have* to feel every step. And now I communicate with people's feelings. I sense them. I'm not defensive about them. I can read them. I can't see them but I know they're there."

Maurine told him he was solving the biggest koan of them all. He was learning how to meet life with his whole being.

Some people at the center call Maurine the ma-roshi. She doesn't cultivate that, but she acknowledges what it implies: that you can be warm and embracing while at the same time maintaining a strong discipline. "Very often I embrace people. Hug them. I warmly kiss them on the cheeks or give them a pat on the back. But I can also stand back, and say no, this is not the time. That's a very subtle matter about which we know as parents, as mothers. Sometimes you're very firm with your child, and sometimes you're bestowing all the love and affection you can. But they know that love is there all the time, no matter how firm the discipline. So I hope what all of us are keeping in our hearts here is pure and warm practice, pure and warm mind. If you coldly remain apart from things, after all, that's not *it*."

One afternoon during my stay in Cambridge, Maurine drove me through Mount Auburn Cemetery, where masses of trees flamed in wild and sculptured profusion. Later, in the townhouse she shares with her husband, she served me tea and played Bach preludes and fugues on her grand piano. The next day she gave me the koan Mu.

We had been talking about practice, and I found myself wanting to ask her about a deep level of doubt that sometimes arises in me. What if this is all a sham and delusion? What if it's all empty form? Or worse, what if I'm doing it that way? What if I'm fooling myself and everyone else? What if it's all going to fall apart, dissolve? And now knowing the answer to that, can I act from that place?

Maurine: You remember that the Buddha said, "Don't take my word for this. Put no head above your own. Have your own experience." Think about what he went through. You know about all the doubts, all the delusions that came and flew around his head. Just as with you and me. Everyone. No one is excluded from this. And shouldn't be. It's an important part of our experience. If you did not question, did not go down to the bottom and say, Is this truly so?, it would be very superficial. Very superficial. We must say: What is this? *What is this?* And say it with absolutely every pore of our being. *What is this?* This is the great doubt we talk about. It is to be answered with your whole being. Not just with your intellect. And the more deeply you feel the doubt, according to some ancient texts, the greater the enlightenment. The more you plumb the depths of this, the more you know. One balances the other. And to be honest is essential. To say, am I really doing this to the depths of my being? Or am I just sitting here?

Lenore: How can I do that without a teacher, by myself?

Maurine: Mu after Mu after Mu after Mu. With your whole being. This is not a technique. It is a way of life.

Lenore: Don't I have to test that, ask "Am I plumbing this? Is my Mu . . .?"

Maurine: No. Don't ask that. Don't ask—*do* it. *Do,* and see what happens.

Lenore: And when doubt comes up about my capacity to . . .

Maurine: It has nothing to do with your capacity, nothing at all. Your capacity is your capacity, and you use this capacity in all kinds of relative situations in your life, but this practice has to do with *absolute* reality, not relative reality. So it has nothing to do with whether you are good, bad, or indifferent. In this respect. It has to do with plumbing the depths of *this* reality, Mu reality, God reality, Buddha-nature reality. And that's in everybody, no matter what you can do physically, mentally, whatever it is. Your spiritual reality is something else. It's in everybody, pure and unadorned. And we hang a lot of *stuff* on it. So: What is this? What *is* this? Why have I clouded it up so much? How do I uncloud it? By being absolutely honest, as you are doing, and saying, Let me strip down to my bare bones and see what's there. There is something wonderful there when you strip down to bare bones. One young woman came to me with this dream. She said I dreamed that you gave me a beautiful pair of shoes, and a photograph album. The album had pictures of me and in all of them I was naked. Wonderful. Just shoes, and naked. So it really is to not be afraid of our weaknesses, our delusions, our illusions, whatever they are. We all have them. But to have this ultimate bottom realization that there is something else there. I think in some curious way I always had that feeling, without making any big bones about it. Whatever was going on around me, if it was extremely difficult or painful

> or tumultuous—and there was a lot of that in my
> life—I always felt there was some quiet inner place
> where everything was all right. Just get there, sit
> down and take a deep breath.

It was interesting to learn that Soen-roshi felt that once you had resolved the koan Mu, once you were thoroughly imbued with it, then you also knew all the rest. "If you really have this one in you," he said, "come to me and I'll give you all the other answers."

Neither Soen nor Yasutani-roshi, Maurine's major teachers, felt that it was necessary to go through the hundreds of koans that many Zen students classically must complete, as a way of deepening and refining their practice. For both of them, and for Maurine, it is a matter of plumbing the essence, the ground of our being. That is what Mu is all about. It has nothing to do with our personal selves. It is something working through all of us, and penetrating that something—through Mu or whatever—is a lifelong process. Practice is endless, requiring many lifetimes even. The "big koan," Maurine says, is finding that Mu reality in our everyday life. "It was a wonderful koan for me to conduct the sesshin, cook the meals, give the talks, do the dokusan, use the stick, do everything, and go from one to the other. *This* was the koan: how do you confront *that?*"

I asked how she used the stick. Only if people request it, she said—by putting their palms together, which she feels causes less disturbance to others than bending over as people do in other zendos. I said it sounded as if she hit both shoulders twice. She said yes, sometimes three times, if someone looks sleepy.

"It can be very refreshing. It shouldn't be painful. After you've had a keisaku from someone whose practice is deep, it is quite different. Soen-roshi's keisaku was not a loud and whacking and big sound like [that of] some of the monks who whack you so hard you're hurting for hours afterwards. His was very strong, but not loud, and just in the right place so that you felt: *Uhhhhh.* There, now I can sit up again!"

(At the retreat in California, Maurine had no stick. Instead, she used her open palms to strike our shoulders, twice—first hard, then soft—in a rhythm that became familiar over the five days. Sometimes she also rubbed our spines, straightening and energizing us.)

Posture, Maurine believes, is absolutely basic to our practice. And posture changes in people all the time. "The reason it changes is that as your practice deepens and your breathing becomes more subtle and more clear and it goes through your whole body, the body changes with each inhalation and exhalation. Posture is extremely important for that reason if for nothing else. Basically, your posture is the expression of your Buddha nature. Absolutely. How clearly, and with what feeling of reverence for your life, you sit up on this cushion! It's a wonderful feeling to just *sit*. And to take a deep breath and feel every pore of you come alive right out to the ends of your hair and your toenails and scalp and cheeks— everything coming alive. It is imperative to have good posture for this experience. Otherwise your breath cannot go through you."

When instructing new people in zazen, Maurine stresses a feeling of firmness, of feeling rooted to the ground. "This is a practice on this earth, not out in space somewhere. You're right here, on this wonderful planet, your knees are solidly planted on the ground. From there you grow. Your spine like the stem of a flower, your head like a blossom on top of it. And everything in wonderful, clear alignment. Then you regulate your breath: let it fill you up, let it slowly out, then let your breath breathe you. Then let your posture do its expression of this. And that changes from day to day, minute to minute. And it should. If we remain some static form, that's not what it's about."

Later, I asked some final questions about Mu.

Lenore: Do you keep the koan in your mind?
Maurine: The koan is filling up your whole body!
Lenore: And the original question: Does a dog have Buddha-nature?
Maurine: That has nothing to do with it. In each koan there are important words. Mu and Buddha-nature. That's what Mu *is*. Buddha-nature. So you are becoming filled up, completely becoming, Mu. You *are* it, but

you are coming to *realize* it. Not thinking: What is
Mu, what is Mu?—no. Got it?
Lenore: Well, as much as I got it, I got it!

There is something of the lion about Maurine. She crackles
with energy. Behind her eyes one sees great reserves of power and
intensity. One feels a huge vitality, a huge embracingness of all of
life. She rarely hesitates. Her rich contralto voice speaks from her
deepest belly to yours. Her laughter comes from there, and her
Mu-u-u-u-u. With a lion's grace, concentration, and dignity she
leads the kinhin line, her broad bare feet firmly, delicately, meeting the earth.

"She is a real Zen master," one of her long-time students told
me. "She expects you to use your abilities." Maurine had told him
a story about her famous French music teacher, Nadia Boulanger.
"Mademoiselle," she had addressed Maurine one day, "you have
great talent. Do you know what that means? It means that you
must work harder than anyone else."

At the Cambridge Buddhist Association, of course, no one is
more "talented" than anyone else, the student made clear. Maurine
is interested in each person individually. But if she senses that
you're dreaming on your zafu, she'll let you know directly.

" 'This is not a tranquilizer,' she will say. 'We're not here just to
calm down and think nice thoughts. This is a dynamic practice.'
And we learn how not to waste our lives," he added, reciting for
emphasis one of the evening chants:

Let me respectfully remind you:
Life and death are of extreme importance.
Do not squander your lives.

The first year or so after Maurine began teaching at Sparks
Street, "it was very loose," another student told me, "almost
frighteningly loose." The schedule of sesshins and sitting hours
was very improvised and things kept changing all the time. For a
while, everyone who came to the center had to practice with the
koan: What *is* this! But over time, Maurine's unique qualities of
traditional Rinzai "strong action" combined with feminine, ma-

ternal caring produced what is now the daily experience at Sparks Street: a powerful, coherent atmosphere for practice.

"Maurine is a very rooted person," another student said. "Have you noticed her feet during kinhin? It's so visual there!" This student has been struck repeatedly by Maurine's devotion to helping people find their unique Zen spirit. "In lectures she says, 'You are your own teacher,' and all her actions reflect that. She has no agenda about what a Zen student should be, as in other Zen centers I've known. Maurine's only agenda is that we learn to express ourselves."

Everyone seemed to agree that Sparks Street is unique, that it is totally human, totally real—an ordinary house inhabited by a strong Zen spirit. Maurine herself shrugs off all roles, moving simply from one moment to the next.

Inevitably, I asked Maurine how important she thought it was that she was a *woman* teacher. "To tell the truth," she said, "I don't really think about it at all. I think it's important to *some* people that I am a woman—women and men who have had great difficulty with women as authority figures in their lives. It helps them to work with someone who has a nurturing womanly aspect." At the Women in Buddhism conference at Providence Zen Center in 1983, she had had the experience that women practicing together reinforced one another, *warmed* one another. It is strengthening to know about other women practicing and teaching elsewhere. But she doesn't want to engender feelings of separation, and in her talk at the conference she said:

"Here we are, happily, men and women together. Manhood and womanhood inextricably bound together forever. In the growing independence and fulfillment of ourselves as women, we must not forget that we have been seen as the transformer, the mediator, the maintainer and sustainer, and should be proud of this. What we choose to do will relate to our being women. I am speaking, of course, as a woman. This does not exclude you men, ever. I adore you. We are not here to imitate one another. One of the frightening things I see sometimes is that people are destroying differences. What a pity. To reduce everything to a sameness in the cause of equality is foolish. Exploring our diversity, our differences together, we go beyond our differences and come to understand and show concern for one another. We go beyond our differences to our deepest level of communication, which is not merely communication, but communion.

"My dear friends, we are already one, but we imagine that we are not. We set up barriers. What we have to recover is our original unity, and we do this by being absolutely who we are."

She commented on the accusation that Zen training, in its strenuousness and rigor, is masculine, tough. "But this is also an essential part of being a woman—to be strong, to have this gentleness, but this strength coming from a really solid inner discipline that our practice gives us."

But the root of all our discipline, morality, meditation, and wisdom must be love and compassion, she said, or all the rest becomes cold and lifeless. "If not for the realization of this compassion toward *all* sentient beings in this world, of what use is our practice?"

She closed by quoting the Dalai Lama, who said when visiting the United States, "My purpose is really only to make some small contribution to the field of love, kindness, and unity among people. It is worthwhile to practice kindness, love, and compassion whether one is a politician, a believer, or a nonbeliever. The key point is love."

"That's it," said Maurine.

Lenore: Are there likely to be more women teachers coming along now?

Maurine: I hope so. But it's not something that can be forced. I think that all teachers are teachers not by choice but by something that comes through them, not because they decide to become a teacher. It's like my friend Elsie Mitchell, who has no designation as a teacher, but by her very life shows the teaching. And *this* is the important way to teach. As women, to show by our lives.

Lenore: Do you think this will have an effect on the way Buddhism evolves in this country?

Maurine: Probably. I think Buddhism will evolve. I suppose there's no doubt about that. In its evolution in each country it always has taken on the aspect of that country. Because it is a nondogmatic, nonfixed kind of tradition, it has taken on the flavor of the country to which it comes. So here, since women are now very strongly practicing, it can't help but be affected, just by virtue of that.

Lenore: So it will change some of the forms?

Maurine: Well, already I think it has changed the forms. In this house, for example, it's my tradition, very strong. I was trained in a very strong way. And our form is correct, in that sense, but not rigid. You said you felt that. Already, it's changed. Always changing, constantly moving on. This is one of the premises of Buddhism. Nothing fixed.

I'm really not into the women's movement in a militant kind of way, as some people are. It's not my way. I don't feel that I have been put upon in my life. I feel that I have had every opportunity as a woman. I've been extremely fortunate. Even in the case of Eido-roshi and Dai Bosatsu, where women *were* mistreated, I was not put upon. But again, if I see that other women are treated unfairly or have been violated, then I cannot—simply because I haven't had that experience—stand by. If I feel my kinship with other women, I must defend them. Not *against* men, but with the idea of making us understand one another better.

The essential matter has nothing to do with male, female, Japanese, Korean, whatever. Those texts that say it's so difficult for a woman to become enlightened, well that was some man who wrote that! This is not gospel truth. If you want to become conditioned by that, then you can spoil your own possibilities.

Lenore: There certainly haven't been many women teachers before now. I've heard it said that women "get it" faster than men, but they either don't take it seriously, don't take off with it, or don't tend to see themselves as teachers. What's your sense of that?

Maurine: Oh, I think what happens is what happens with women in all kinds of places. That women are nourishers, are the carers-for, and so on, and use up their energy. Unless they continue all the time to re-nourish and rekindle this and keep it burning, they will burn out. Because the men—I don't mean this in the sense of an inflammatory speech—but most men, in whatever profession, don't do the house-work. We women do our profession, the housework, raise the children, do the shopping. So there is not for some women the intensity of practice possible to keep it going.

Lenore: Would you be willing to talk about the issue of sexu-ality in the teacher-student relationship?

Maurine: I think that the most important thing that has come out of this, wherever it's happened, is that it makes people—not just the women involved, but everyone who is disillusioned by it, upset by it—understand that they must not hang their practice on a man—*or* a woman. That this is beyond individual matters. And when someone misbehaves in that way, it does not disillusion you about Zen practice; it makes you sit *more* strongly, more independently, and under-stand for your*self,* in the true Buddhist way, what this is about. It is regrettable that so many of these people have become a bit power-struck and have felt that teachers could do whatever they wanted to do. There were fragile-minded young women who were easily swayed to think this could be an essential part of gaining enlightenment. And this was manipula-tive. This is false and untrue and confusing people. It's very sad. The part that disturbs me most is not sexuality, which is a healthy and normal thing, but the misuse of it.

Lenore: It is disturbing that someone who is enlightened, or at least well on the way, could be that unconscious.

Maurine: So it gives you some pause about what it means to be enlightened.

Lenore: It's not a once-and-for-all thing?

Maurine: Absolutely. Unless you are constantly practicing, constantly nourishing. . . . Soen-roshi often said, "I am just a simple monk. I am practicing just like you. I have to do it, all the time." And I think somewhere along the line these people felt they didn't need to, that they'd arrived, or else they allowed other things to distract them.

Lenore: Do you think sexuality is inherent in the relationship between male teacher and female student?

Maurine: Well, think about the psychoanalytic relationship. That doesn't mean that it's out of control. What you *do* with it is the important thing. Sexuality and spirituality are together. This is a dynamic force in us. But how do we transmute it? Not use it for anything frivolous, but use this powerful, wonderful energy in us to further our practice, use it in some pure, unpolluted way.

Lenore: Because it's so akin to love?

Maurine: It's the warmth of it. It's powerful, and it can easily get out of control if people are not careful. If you have been sitting for seven days with somebody, you feel a wonderful tenderness, a really deep affection for that person. And if you embrace them and something goes [snaps fingers], it's very easy to say, "Oh, let's go on with this." Instead of saying, in the case of these roshis, "I love you, *but* . . . I do have a wife, I do have family, I do have other responsibilities to consider." But certainly it's there. It's a powerful force in us. And not to be repressed—you know that.

Lenore: I can see how not acting on it, but experiencing it, allowing it to course through you—how that could enhance . . .

Maurine: . . . *everything*. Yes. When you play the piano, what is coming through? Loving sexual energy. I don't have to put that label on it, but it certainly is a part of me, and a very important part of me. And to play with energy, to play with warmth and passion—*that* is transmuting this.

Sometimes Maurine talks about her "female lineage," the three powerful women who have been her teachers: her grandmother, her mother, and Elsie Mitchell. It was Elsie Mitchell whom Soen-roshi directed Maurine to find when she moved from New York to Boston. Elsie was one of the earliest converts to Buddhism in this country, traveling to Japan in the fifties, recording Buddhist chants at Eiheiji Monastery (later released as a Folkways record), and writing a very interesting book about her travels, Zen training, and teachers (*Sun Buddhas, Moon Buddhas,* Weatherhill, 1973). She has been described as the very model of a New England "lady." Yet for three decades she has been intimate with many of the most important figures in the development of Zen Buddhism in this country. And in a characteristically invisible way, she has quietly helped nurture much of its growth.

Maurine's first meeting with Elsie took place five months after her arrival in Boston in 1970. Obedient to Soen's instructions, she had tried to find her earlier, but neither Elsie nor the Cambridge Buddhist Association was listed in the phone book! Finally, Eido-roshi and a group of others from New York came to see an exhibit of Zen painting and calligraphy at the Boston Museum. Eido arranged for the whole group to visit Elsie, and Maurine was invited as well.

"So that day I finally found her. I had been prepared for an old, old lady. Everybody still thinks she must be very old because she's been involved in all of this for so long. Everybody expected her to be a doddering old woman." She was actually only forty-four at the time. Maurine, expecting a "ponderous, weighty person," was shocked when down the stairs came "a beautiful young woman looking about sixteen! She and her husband asked me to come and sit with them. And so I did. I came once a week and sat in her house. And then, when she moved to Brattle Street about a year after that, I became very involved. She saw that it would mean so much to me, so she gave me more and more to do."

Soon Maurine was handling Association correspondence and learning the ins and outs of the library. It was a collection to warm her heart, and in the months and years that followed she became familiar with its thousands of volumes. She also became familiar with the people who came for zazen, and before long they began coming to her with their questions and difficulties. Elsie began asking her to conduct meetings and give talks and instruction.

"I think you have a feeling for people," Elsie said one day.

"What are you going to do about it? How can you do more to help these people?"

Maurine had never thought of becoming a priest. She was a mother, a musician, a performer. But Elsie's words kept gently pushing her along. Then one day someone asked if she would perform their wedding ceremony. She said, "Oh, no. I can't do that. I'm not ordained."

"Well," said Elsie, "you better get ordained. It's time."

So Maurine wrote to Dai Bosatsu, asking Eido-roshi if he would consider giving her ordination, since that seemed to be her karma. He replied, "Yes, it is your karma." And they began preparing together.

During the ceremony, a snippet of hair was taken symbolically, but Maurine never had her head shaved. "That would have been an affectation for me. I'm a person in the world. It would be calling attention to myself. Anyway, the important matter is inner, not outer. If it's a question of vanity or holding on to something, then perhaps you should shave your head. For men, it's different—though there are men, too, who never shaved their heads. Nyogen Senzaki never did, and so far I think he was the greatest Zen teacher in America."

Once she was ordained, it was taken for granted that she was a teacher. And her teaching style has always been to link practice with everyday life.

"I think the biggest koan study is the study of our life," she says. "It has nothing to do with ancient stories that you supply some kind of resolution to. They require a real refinement of our practice, to get deeply into them, but always in the light of what we are doing in the twentieth century. I always tell students: This is not some old Chinese patriarch—this is you, this is me, this is our life situation. I give people koans like: How are you going to get through whatever it is you have to do tomorrow? Literally, how are you going to deal with this particular life situation?"

When I asked in what way Elsie has been her teacher, Maurine answered, "By her life. By who she is, how she behaves. Her inconspicuous attention to every detail of other people's needs, taking care of business in the most extraordinarily self-effacing yet taking-care-of-herself way. An extraordinary human being. She's unpretentious, has a wonderful sense of humor, sharp intelligence, and an absolute gift for sensing people's character. I consider her my most important teacher in the last fourteen years."

Our best and truest teacher, however, Maurine says, is our own zazen. To sit down on our cushion, to regulate our breath, to be aware of our posture, to feel our consciousness changing, to feel our heart opening, to feel our *hara* strengthening, to feel that we are making a space in ourselves with which to deal with everyday life—which then becomes the teacher too. Inside and outside are the same. Everyday life is affected profoundly by sitting on the cushion, by being mindful of all our activities.

"To open our hearts, to clarify our way of looking at things so that we see them freshly, vividly, clearly, without all of our hang-ups on them. To come to something and say, 'Ah, I've never seen that before.' After five days of sesshin, to come out and see that the needles on the pine trees are sparkling at you. They have been sparkling all the time. It's just you who haven't been awake enough to see that."

It is ten o'clock in the morning on the last full day of our California retreat. We are sitting on our cushions, facing the wall. Maurine rings the bell three times and reads from the *Mumon-kan:*

> Joshu asked Nansen, "What is the Way?"
> "Ordinary mind is the Way," Nansen replied.

At the end of the story she reads Mumon's verse:

> The spring flowers, the autumn moon
> Summer breeze, winter snow.
> If useless things do not clutter your mind
> You have the best days of your life.

"So here we are," she goes on. "Fourth-day sesshin. Wonderful, clear day. Our last few hours together. Every one of you is sincerely doing her very best. So what is the Way that we are following? What is this truth of Zen? To realize this truth in our bodies and minds, some of us made a long journey to come here to practice together. And you have been listening to my talks on the dharma. The you who is listening is the I who is speaking. When our original true face appears, speaker and listener are one. Only in this oneness are these dharma matters spoken about and listened to. Listening with your whole body, listening with your skin, hearing with your eyes, seeing with your ears. After this time together, we go back to our lives in the world, and there's the real practice. This is easy. When we go home, what happens? How does this affect our daily lives? Here we have been sitting quietly, doing nothing; summer has come and the birds sing all by themselves. Getting up from this quiet place and returning to our families, friends, impressions, what happens? If someone is rude or invades our privacy, how will we react? If any number of difficult situations arise, how will we handle them? Will we have a little more compassion and wisdom? In how we deal with other human beings? In the varying circumstances of our lives? *These* are our koans."

All day we sit and walk and sit and walk until the light fades, the lamps are lit, and we are facing each other again, chanting *Ho-o-o-o-o-o-o-o-o*, each at her own pitch and rhythm, as long as our breath holds, then starting up again. Maurine's voice is very deep, very full, sustained almost endlessly. Some of our voices tremble or quaver at first, and our breath falters. But soon all that fades, and we are immersed in a river of sound that turns into music somehow, with harmonics no one is aware of producing. Later, we chant the *Heart Sutra* and the *Kannon Sutra*. Our voices blend and are strong, filling our bodies and the room and the darkness beyond. The sound is what matters, not the meaning of the words or any feelings evoked. We listen with our bellies, with the backs of our necks. We bow to each other and feel supple, held, graced.

Maurine's particular genius seems to lie in creating a setting, a medium in which practice flourishes, hearts open, and differences among people become spices, not thorns. It is safe to be whatever one is—crazy, strong, critical, confused. There is room for everything. The forms are large enough, strict but spacious, and performed from the heart. Nothing need be rejected or feared. Sometimes one senses an endless, implicit orderliness, as vast and complex and simple as Bach. Everything exists within it, fluidly, like music.

And if, like the lion I imagine she resembles, Maurine sometimes roars, it must be a rich, redoubtable roaring, straight from the *hara,* and full of love.

Update: Winter 2000

Maurine Stuart, one of the most robustly alive people many of us have ever known, died of cancer in February 1990, three years after her original diagnosis. During those years, except for the last six months or so, she slowed down hardly at all (some have said that, if anything, her level of intensity accelerated). She conducted a last sesshin at the end of January, just weeks before she died. Problematic for some people because it did not permit the expression of vulnerability, Maurine's attitude of fierce calm and insistence on being fully alive as long as she was alive was stirringly life-affirming for others.

"Health," Maurine taught us during those last months, "is not the opposite of sickness," Roko Sherry Chayat recalls in her introduction to *Subtle Sound: The Zen Teachings of Maurine Stuart* (Shambhala Publications, 1996). "Although our habitual way of thinking is dualistic, in reality we are all living with good cells and bad cells, simultaneously, in a condition of utter impermanence."

When I spoke to her on the telephone in preparation for the new edition of this book, Sherry talked about Maurine's remarkable accessibility to her students, especially after her divorce in the mid-eighties, when she was able to devote even more of her attention to practice at the Cambridge Buddhist Association (CBA). This was her central passion, Sherry said, "her absolutely fierce dedication to the dharma. Especially when she was diagnosed with cancer, she became a remarkably clear vessel, and the dharma flowed through her, completely available and charged with energy."

Sherry remembers that during this period, while rejecting expressions of pity, Maurine actually talked a lot about death. "You felt she was walking right over the edge of the precipice, and she was not afraid."

Trudy Goodman, another longtime friend and student of Maurine's, told me this story: A day before her death, as she moved in and out of consciousness, at every sound in or outside the room—a horn blowing, a bed being moved, someone's shoes squeaking on the floor—Maurine was heard to say clearly, "Thank you. . . . Thank you. . . . Thank you." And several people have reported that around the same time, a day earlier perhaps, and seemingly out of a light coma, she opened her eyes and said: "Wonderful peace. Nobody there."

After her death, the situation at the Cambridge Buddhist Association was difficult and confusing for a while. Whether for reasons complex or simple (different sources provide different interpretations), Maurine did not name a dharma successor before she died. One piece of the truth seems to be that she did not have the power to do so (that is, there was no baton for her to pass on) because of her own highly unorthodox transmission from Soen Nakagawa, Roshi. During a private interview in 1982, with no one else present, Soen Roshi had simply said, "Tell your students to call you roshi." That was all. There was no formal ceremony, no inclusion in the official record of lineage. Still, Maurine did what she was told, while adding in characteristic fashion, "Please call me Maurine."

Another piece of the truth may be that none of the senior students at Sparks Street was perceived as solid or seasoned enough to take on Maurine's mantle. Moreover, after her death, the board of the CBA returned Sparks Street to its original concept as a center for eclectic and scholarly Buddhist events of a nonsectarian nature. Today, teachers from a variety of Buddhist traditions present workshops and retreats there, and several times a week there are Zen sittings and instruction from a guiding teacher named by the board.

Meanwhile (and more important, according to a number of people I talked with), Maurine's spirit continues to flame in many places and in "a huge number of people, two thousand or more," says Sheila La Farge, who was Maurine's close assistant for many years. People's lives were changed by Maurine, she says, people of every kind, visible and invisible, living ordinary or extraordinary lives, manifesting Maurine's spirit in whatever they do. Sheila perceived Maurine as an artist who was skilled at releasing people from rigid postures, who cultivated freedom and creativity instead. "Be autonomous!" Maurine repeated often. Thus, many of the students she left behind "don't look at all like Buddhists (in the sense of shaved heads and robes)," Sheila says, "but they carry that flame of understanding within their everyday lives."

Over many of the years since Maurine's death, and mostly with her own hands, Sheila has created a zendo in Harvard, Massachusetts, where people come to sit three times a week as well as all day once a month. "The sitting protocol is like Maurine's, more or less formal Zen," she wrote me. She is unequivocally determined to avoid "the insidious blurring of meditation and psychotherapy which reduces what Buddhism has to offer to something psychological."

Her "other main conundrum" is how to grab people's attention without being a "personality," speaking the dharma in fresh, contemporary language while remaining "a gentle, ordinary person who doesn't wear robes."

At the same time, Sherry Chayat, who received official dharma transmission in late 1998, is now abbott of the Zen Center of Syracuse, located on five acres of land at the southern edge of Syracuse, New York. Maurine's presence, she says, is "very much a part of everything we do. We include her name in our dedication recitations, just as we include Nyogen Senzaki, who never received formal transmission." Both teachers went their own way, she says, and both are extremely important for American Zen today.

So Maurine's spirit is no longer located in any particular place or person. In a recent letter, Sheila La Farge wrote me: "The real point, after all, is that Maurine touched many lives, was an example of dedication to practice, urged people to address the koans in their own everyday lives, admonished people not to become slavishly devoted to teachers but [to] work on autonomy and responsibility, reminded us that we lived in New England and not Japan, insisted that we clarify and distinguish between the time spent practicing on our cushions and the time spent (in whatever way each of us chooses) to offer the fruits of our practice to others."

An array of people, then, around the country and probably around the world, are carrying on different aspects of Maurine's teachings. "Her spirit is free," Sherry Chayat said. "It's in our own zazen that we meet the true understanding she would have taught. She wanted us to become unfettered beings. To get to Maurine is to get to the place that has no name."

3

Pema Chodron

Out of the brown earth
the sunflower sprouts
golden petals

tuned to the sun
her face (light-filled
unshielded) salutes
each new-born moment

each day
from root to crown
one bow
—Lenore Friedman

Under the huge expanse of a New Mexico sky, her body silhouetted against the brilliant light, a young woman in a dress of pale lavender stood alone on a rocky hill. It was the era of the flower children, and although she was past thirty, her long blond hair and bangs, her bare legs, and the easy abandonment of her body to the air and the elements all proclaimed her a free spirit. From below, a young man caught sight of her, stood there motionless for a moment, and then approached. What he said was shocking and disturbing to her, and antithetical to everything she felt about herself at the moment. His words were: "I just had a vision of you as a nun."

When I first saw her, some fifteen years later, in the fall of 1982, I was waiting for the start of a weekend retreat at the Dharmadhatu center in Berkeley, California. The large, high-ceilinged shrine room was full of quiet, expectant people. The polished floor was covered with bright red-and-yellow cushions, the walls hung with brilliant silk banners. The teacher we were expecting was Bhikshuni Pema Chodron. I knew virtually nothing about her at the time, did not really know why I was there. Then she appeared through the heavy wooden doors behind us, walked around the rows of upturned faces, and smiled. She was dressed in a maroon woolen robe that was draped over one shoulder, the other revealing a sleeveless yellow silk blouse. Her hair was cropped close to her head. What struck me in those first moments was something both personal and impersonal in the gaze with which she regarded us. "She is a real teacher," I told myself.

There are three things that I remember from that weekend. One was its quality of gentleness and humor. Great gentleness with our shared human idiosyncrasies. And a mischievousness and wry amusement at our tendency to take ourselves seriously. The second was something Pema said about the attribute most useful to the meditational path, or as she put it, the quality to place in the center of our mandala. This was *curiosity*. Endless curiosity. Endless interest in whatever is arising in the present moment.

The third thing I remember took place the morning after the retreat, as I walked with my dog along the ascending trail above Strawberry Canyon, a place that often nurtures my best thoughts. For some time the idea for a book about women spiritual teachers had been percolating intermittently in my mind. I had made one false start the year before, with a rather ambitious and ultimately unworkable format. Now I thought, "Here is a woman teacher, right here in Berkeley. If you're going to do this, do it now! Don't lose this opportunity to make it real."

And without giving myself time for vacillation, I ran back down the trail. I composed a short note and left it at Dharmadhatu with Pema's name on it. I had had no personal contact with her during the weekend and knew my name would mean nothing to her. But that evening, at a small gathering in someone's home where she gave an informal talk, she walked in and immediately looked over at me and smiled. "You're the one who left me the note!"

Afterward, when I asked her how she knew, she said, "I just knew." She was enthusiastic about the project and agreed to spend some time with me later when I could come to Boulder. In the meantime we would write, and she would send me her ideas.

So Pema was crucial to the launching of this book. (Thank you, Pema.) One irony, however, is that I never got to Boulder. The year after we met, there was to be a conference on the Feminine in Tibetan Buddhism at Naropa, which I planned to attend, and we scheduled interview time afterward. But at the last minute, the conference was canceled. Since everyone expected it to be rescheduled, we agreed to defer our meetings till then. In fact, the conference never took place. But in the meantime Pema came to Berkeley for another weekend retreat, and I was able to talk to her there.

Pema is a fully ordained *bhikshuni,* or Buddhist nun, one of a very small number of Western women, one of an even smaller number of women in the Tibetan tradition, and certainly the first American in the Vajrayana tradition to undergo the preparations and ceremony. The particulars of this ordination had in fact been lost for women in both Theravadin and Vajrayana Buddhism when Pema, in 1977, was instructed by His Holiness the Sixteenth Gyalwa Karmapa that it was time for her to take full bhikshuni vows. As a result, she not only ultimately accomplished the ordination herself, but with dedicated sleuthing and a few miracles along the way, unearthed the intricate rules and details of the ceremony and began the painstaking process of having it translated from Chinese into English. This may ultimately make it possible for women to be fully ordained in the West.

Pema, however, had to go to Hong Kong. It took three years before all preparations were complete, but in July 1981, she found herself at the Miu Fat Temple in Hong Kong, ready for the full bhikshuni ordination. She was the only Westerner there. No one else spoke English. It was extremely hot and humid, and the extensive preliminary stages were strenuous, sometimes grueling. The culminating ceremony involves the burning of incense cones on the bare scalp, a Chinese Mahayana tradition that has several purposes: one, to test one's capacity to bear pain, in preparation for the bodhisattva role of taking on the suffering of the world; two, as a purification, the burns being located on crucial meridians; and three, as a proof of ordination.

"I have three round scars on my head which you can see when I shave my head," Pema told me.

We were sitting in the living room of the house where she was staying during her visit to Berkeley. I commented, "You became a nun very early. You chose that path as opposed to a secular path."

"Yes. And there wasn't any precedent for it because at the time I hadn't met any other nuns except for Sister Palmo [an English-woman ordained years before in the Tibetan tradition], who had a real effect on me. I met her two years before I was originally ordained, and she was present at my novice ordination ceremony. She was the one who told me what to do, what offerings to make, what my robes should be. And it was she who told me that if I ever wanted the full ordination ceremony, I would have to go to Hong Kong. She was the first one to actually do it."

But Sister Palmo did not give Pema the information she would need later to set this ordination in motion. When the time arrived, she had to start from scratch (for example, tracking down the abbot who had performed the ceremony in Hong Kong but who had subsequently moved to the Bronx!).

Pema was born in 1936 in New York City. When she was still very young, the family moved to New Jersey, where she lived on a farm, in an old revolutionary farmhouse (built in 1774) where she spent her entire childhood and adolescence, moving out only when she was married, at the age of twenty-one. She remembers her childhood as very pleasant, very gentle. She has an older brother and sister. The beginning of her spiritual life she attributes to her boarding school experience. She attended an excellent girls' prep school, which "cultivated my intellectual curiosity. I remember it as a time of beginning to go deeper, beginning to want to know, and wanting to go further."

She was married twice—"somewhat consecutively—I had never *not* been married, you might say." She was in her mid-thirties when her second marriage ended, precipitating an explosion of anger, which surprised her. She had not, in fact, experienced much anger before, and didn't know how to deal with it.

"I felt very rejected by my husband. In retrospect, the issue was that I was very dependent on him. I felt that kind of groundlessness and fear that people in a dependent relationship feel when they suddenly don't have it anymore. The feeling was devastating to me. I didn't expect to be so devastated. But one of my major stumbling blocks was dependency. So I started looking around for answers—primarily how to deal with the intensity of my anger, which scared me a lot. A major habitual tendency that had been part of my identity was gone. And that produced terror."

She began exploring different therapies. She lived with a Hindu group for a while, and at the Lama Foundation in New Mexico. Nothing seemed to address what she was feeling.

And then she came upon an article by Chögyam Trungpa, Rinpoche. She had no ideas about Buddhism, didn't even know the article was by a Buddhist. It had to do with negativity and working with the wisdom of the energy involved in it, which can teach one something. Instead of seeing negativity as evil, something to be avoided, the article pointed to its inherent potential wisdom. One could work with these emotions rather than trying to get rid of them. These ideas were the first to really address what Pema had actually been experiencing. She didn't know this had anything to do with Buddhism. "But of course it's very much a part of Vajrayana Buddhism," she says now.

Only days after she read the article, an old friend suddenly appeared who was on his way to a Sufi camp in the French Alps. She was feeling such pain and longing that she was "jumping at things." Her two children were with their father, so she was free to follow her impulse, and off she went for a month in the French Alps. It was there she encountered Lama Chime Rinpoche, had a "strong recognition experience," and asked if she could go back with him to London to study Buddhism. This she did, and for several years she went back and forth from the United States to England to study with Lama Chime.

Her two children were in their early teens at this point and would live with their father when Pema went to England, continuing their schooling in San Francisco—"so they had a good situation." When in the United States, Pema lived at the Dhar-madhatu in San Francisco. She taught at a private school during the day, in ordinary clothes, then donned her maroon robes in the evening to teach dharma classes at the center. She became a nun while studying with Lama Chime in London, when His Ho-liness the Gyalwa Karmapa came to England and ordained her for the first time in 1974. It was Lama Chime who encouraged her to work with Chögyam Trungpa, Rinpoche, each time she re-turned to the United States, and it was with Trungpa Rinpoche that she ultimately had her most profound connection.

When His Holiness the Karmapa came to the United States for the second time in 1977, he looked at Pema during a group audi-ence and said that she should prepare to take the full ordination. "But how is that possible?" she asked. She knew the ceremony was lost for women in the Tibetan tradition. But the Karmapa announced that he would give it to her himself.

That, however, was not to be feasible—it turned out he could not perform the ceremony for a woman, since the authority to do so belonged to a different Vinaya lineage than his. So Pema's de-tective work began.

"I used to call the phone number in the Bronx, but no one spoke English, so we couldn't communicate. I would write let-ters and they would not be answered, doubtless for the same rea-son. Finally I called on a Sunday and someone spoke English, and that's how I got the address of the proper Hong Kong temple—and I set off and did it."

"Pema, as you talk about all this, it sounds so simple! As if it just flowed along effortlessly. From the time you first read that article of Trungpa Rinpoche's, you just moved ahead, a step at a time, with a kind of directness and undeviatingness. How do you explain that to yourself?" I asked her.

"I think that at some point in anyone's life it's possible to re-connect with some kind of past karmic stream, and you just step into it, and then you know because it starts going forward. Be-coming a Buddhist didn't necessarily have that feeling for me. But once I started on the ordination, it definitely did. Once the abbey started, it also had that feeling. It's like facilitating something that has strong forward movement to it, and you don't have to do that much for it to happen.

"For instance, the last time I saw the Karmapa, I asked him what I could do to help, once I got the ordination. He said, 'Bring back all the texts and get them translated.' And that was a cinch. They gave me all the texts. I came back. I wrote to the man he had suggested could translate them. He came to where I was visiting in Pennsylvania. He gave me the name of someone in Taiwan. That person immediately agreed to do it. And then the Buddhist community in Taiwan paid for it. I had already collected some money for that purpose, which I had almost to force them to take! So it was very easy. And although it takes a lot of planning and work, the same is true of the monastery."

"Was there anything in your earlier life," I asked, "that in any way anticipated an interest in the monastic life?"

"No."

"Nothing. The notion was totally new. But it didn't even seem to jar you."

"Well, at the time, I wanted to put all my energy into some kind of journey of discovery. I had been married since I was twenty-one years old, had raised my children, and had a sense of completion with my domestic life. I had explored my sexuality to the degree that I didn't feel there were any dark corners or unresolved issues. I didn't want to get married again or even particularly to get into a relationship again. My real appetite and my real passion was for wanting to go deeper. I felt that I was somehow thick, and that in order to really connect with the truth or with reality or with things as they are—however you want to say it—I needed to put all my energy into it, totally. That was why I became a nun. It was this one-pointed desire to do that. It felt to me like a big step forward into the unknown. I also remember that once I had the thought to do it, I couldn't go back on it. I had to go forward."

Since she was raised as a Catholic, Pema's early impression was that nuns were somewhat repressed. Now, on the contrary, she sees that monastic life is "about passion for life. You have an appetite for realization and you just decide you want to go for it. It also has something to do with not limiting yourself to one person or situation, but actually sharing yourself with everyone."

It was dependency, then, that drove her into searching. And then, over time, "it gradually wore out. I began to find my seat. My karma and my style began to coordinate. And finally they coincided. My sense of confidence in what was happening was strong, but it wasn't dependent on anything. The exploration was lonely. All people who seek always have that journey. You do it alone. It doesn't matter how large the community is, or how deeply you love your teachers, or any of those things. You know you're alone. In fact, this is what Rinpoche has always taught me—that you have to find out for yourself. So it's the absolute opposite of dependency. The only thing you have to watch out for is that you don't become too harsh or cold or unfeeling. You stay engaged, very engaged."

Dependency, Pema says now, is something hard to understand until you're deprived of it, perhaps. *Not* being dependent is also misunderstood. "It's often called detachment, but that's really the wrong word. Because you join in the world much more. Dependency is like protection, and not being dependent is like bravery, courage."

Whatever period of your life you are in, Pema advises that you do it well. "Because it will teach you. It's always teaching you. And later, you will actually have wisdom about that period of your life, rather than something that you just resented the whole time. As far as I'm concerned, wisdom comes from applying yourself wholeheartedly to whatever you're doing. The lessons of life are in everything."

So it's important never to feed the strong human tendency toward resentment, toward blaming others or having a grudge against one's predicament, she feels. "What should be fostered is people's courage and willingness to take responsibility for their own lives. I would never want to be part of anything that smelled of blame. I think it's the most misleading thing a person can get into. And it's so satisfying to get into! Groups like to get into it. But it's just going the wrong way, the wrong way completely."

One of the people Pema suggested I contact during the early stages of my research was a Theravadin teacher and nun, living in Australia at the time, who had established an international center for Buddhist women in Sri Lanka. Her name was Ayya Khema. We had corresponded for several years, and she had just spent a week with me for the second time during visits to this country. Pema herself had not met Ayya in person yet. But during our conversation I was reminded of an incident that took place during her recent visit. I decided to toss it in, like a pebble into a pond, and see what happened.

We had been sitting around my kitchen table talking, some friends of mine and Ayya and I. After a while the discussion became so intense, disturbing even, that one of my friends could not control her tears.

"Ayya is uncompromising, you know," I told Pema. "In her words, she's 'going for broke.' She doesn't mess around. She really pokes holes in the illusions of people who think they can keep themselves comfortable and maintain certain nice things in their lives and still attain realization. So she talks a lot about renunciation. That night she was talking about *dukkha* and how she's quite ready to get off the wheel, so to speak. Just get off. Once she says you really taste what dukkha is, and how everpresent, everywhere, it is, you don't want to stick around anymore.

"I'm pretty sure that when she talks about 'getting off,'" I added, "that it's not extinction she means, or leaving this realm behind, but just letting go of the self, the separate self. But there was something so very stark about this experience of dukkha she was describing. And it seems in sharp contrast with your own appetite for life."

"Well," Pema said, "renunciation is important. But there are different ways of understanding what it means. In the translation that we chant in the mornings, it's called 'revulsion with samsara.' The way I understand it is that you can't kid yourself any longer about how you use everything to re-create yourself all the time. So you have to really work with yourself. You have to know yourself totally, all the parts of yourself. It's like studying humanness, as far as I'm concerned. It's that tendency of mind to solidify reality that you're talking about when you talk about renunciation. Now that is very, very subtle, and I think it's good for Mahayanists and Vajrayanists to come up against a real good Theravadin person who is going to really nail you on this issue."

"As Ayya surely does."

"Yes. It's so easy to deceive yourself! So it's good to be made to feel uncomfortable. There are always things that you haven't completely understood or digested or realized. It always feels like this. What's exciting is that you're always going further. But my feeling about the wheel is that you never come to the end. This whole process is endless because mind is endless. So we're always searching in the most positive sense. That's what I call appetite or curiosity. For me, it has to do with your mind opening, rather than that you get off something."

"Your mind opening . . ."

"Your reference points are no longer solid. They're shifting. Self is not the reference point."

"And mind never ends. Of course."

"I always figure that mind and space are the same thing."

"Mind and space or time and space?"

"Mind."

"Mind and space are the same thing?"

"There's this illusion that our mind is this little limited thing. But that's not actually true. However, it's our working basis. And that's where compassion comes from. Because we live in a relative world, we want to help others, it seems to me."

As mind is endless, so is compassion. It does not apply only to some and not others. It extends even to those whose acts may horrify us. Taking the most extreme of examples—say, child abuse or mutilation of animals in laboratories—if you have no understanding of how someone could do these things, you're missing the point, says Pema. "Nothing should undermine your compassion."

"How do you deal with feelings of outrage?"

"By not solidifying them into a cause. And not blaming. Then you can work with the completely open-ended feeling that leaves you with. And then—when you're willing not to get into this mentality of 'me and them' or 'us and them'—then you're in a position where you can really speak out and try to have things that are harmful not happen. But as long as you consider the other the enemy, it's just another way of feeding your ego.

"So outrage is an interesting feeling to work with," she concluded. "It's painful and vulnerable and you want so badly to strike out against somebody or something—but if you don't, it could connect you with real insight and real wisdom."

One of the other things I questioned Pema about was the prevalence of hierarchical structure and symbolism within Vajrayana practice. Coming from a background of vipassana and Zen, I cannot help being aware of the vivid, ornate, ceremonial hierarchism that seems to permeate the atmosphere of Tibetan Buddhism.

"It's complicated," Pema said. "I can say what my experience is. If someone had presented hierarchy to me as a philosophical concept, I don't think I would have gone for it. But in fact it can be extremely powerful in terms of what it teaches you. I have a lot of respect for tradition and form. I consider them like time capsules that can reconnect you to wisdom that would be lost otherwise. And hierarchy is part of that. Devotion is very much a part of Vajrayana Buddhism. But it's based, you know, on understanding *shunyata*. It's like realizing that there's nothing to depend on. Therefore one can begin to use form to gain wisdom. The Native Americans do exactly the same thing. They have elders and they have a ritualized way of relating with the universe. It's extremely similar to Vajrayana Buddhism in many ways. It's about cultivating the intellect and the heart. And in terms of the heart, it has to do with respect and gratitude."

At a recent ecumenical meeting with spokespeople from every world religion, including Native Americans, Pema said, everyone concurred that the three requisites for spiritual evolution in human beings were gratitude and humility and humor. Essentially these have to do with discovering your place in the universe. "You could be the teeniest speck of dust and because of that you could be the universal emperor or empress, simultaneously." One needs a sense of gratitude and respect, she feels. The alternative is arrogance.

When a student of Trungpa Rinpoche gives a talk, the custom is for people to stand up when the speaker walks in. It's interesting to be in that position, she said, because you could get into thinking, "Oh, I'm not worthy of this!" But it isn't Pema they're standing up for, she knows. It's a gesture of appreciation for this world.

She recalled a conversation she had with Gerald Red Elk, a Sioux medicine man, who described the etiquette in which Sioux children are trained from the time they're small. For example, they would never address an elder by first name. They would not greet an uncle as "Joe" or "Tom." When he entered the room, they would put their hands together and say, "My uncle."

"We've rejected these things so harshly because we equate them with empty form. With a 'lid.'" Pema says. "But in Vajrayana, they talk about the difference between lids and flowers. That there is a natural hierarchy in the world. For instance, if someone says, 'Don't put a sacred text on the floor,' if you don't have any sense of respect you could argue about that. 'Isn't the floor as sacred as the book?' But when you recognize how much hard work and dedication and wisdom has gone into this book, you put it in a high place, not on the floor where someone might step on it. All hierarchy is like that. It has to do with your heart being able to soften, being able to let go of holding onto yourself and being able to open up to respect the world. So they say you can take it as a lid or you can take it as a flower. It's like a seed that's being nurtured so that it can grow. I have been trained so genuinely, and my experience of hierarchy has always led me to understand why I was doing what I was doing. As a result I was able to surrender when it rubbed me the wrong way. Once you have trust in the teacher, and respect, then there is willingness to go along with what you're told, because sometimes that's the only way to get through when your habitual resistance starts coming up."

"A teacher can also help to constellate that resistance," I said.

"Right. Teachers usually squeeze you. They put you in situations where you're just hanging in midair and you can't buy it and you can't not buy it. And you can begin to delight in that, by not taking sides. Teachers are always working against your tendency to get secure in some kind of belief system."

Pema's first meeting with Chögyam Trungpa, Rinpoche, was on a snowy day in February 1972. She was teaching a class of children in Taos, New Mexico, at the time. The class was reading Trungpa's book *Born in Tibet* at the very moment when he happened to be visiting the Lama Foundation nearby. So Pema took three carloads of young children up the hill to meet him.

"We had a meeting, and all the children asked him questions, which he answered with humor and interest, downplaying any tendency they might have to idealize him or his experience. Afterward, I felt very drawn to him, and I stayed on for three or four days. There were always all-night discussions with everybody there. What attracted me was not initially a feeling of warmth, particularly—I had had that with Lama Chime. But in Rinpoche's presence I felt very exposed and able to see my incomplete karma—the things that weren't quite finished and were still problematic in my life. When I formally requested to be his student later, it was mainly because of the fact that he put me on the spot so much, and everything about him stirred things up."

It was shortly after she was ordained as a nun and returned to San Francisco that she officially became Chögyam Trungpa's student. By this time she had completed the Tibetan *ngondro* practices with Lama Chime. These preliminary practices take years. They involve 100,000 prostrations, 100,000 mantra recitations, 100,000 mandala offerings, 100,000 *guruyoga*. Pema had already moved on to a more advanced visualization practice, but when she became Trungpa Rinpoche's student, he told her to go back to pure sitting meditation—the *samatha* vipassana practice of following the breath, in particular the outbreath, and without judgment acknowledging thoughts as they arise.

"There is a lot of wisdom in this practice," Pema said. "It trains your gentleness, your tendency to let go, your accuracy of mind. I sat like this for a long time, doing month-long programs and other things. After a year I asked if I could start Vajrayana practices again, but Rinpoche said it was still too soon. So for almost three years I just sat. And then I did the whole *ngondro* all over again—all those prostrations and all the rest—for a second time!"

Afterward, like all of Trungpa Rinpoche's students, Pema took the Vajrayogini *abhisheka* and began the Vajrayogini *sadhana* practice, which she had been doing for about eight years when I talked to her. Before the end of the year, Trungpa Rinpoche would be taking his senior students further by giving them the Chakrasamvara abhisheka, and Pema would begin the Chakrasamvara sadhana practice.

"The other practice Rinpoche has given us is a Mahayana practice called *tonglen,* which has to do with exchanging oneself with others, and with cultivating the heart, cultivating sympathy for oneself and others. So I do samatha vipassana leading to *mahamudra,* I do tonglen practice, and I do Vajrayana practice—practices of all three *yanas.* This is very typical for a student of Trungpa Rinpoche. We also study the Shambhala teachings and put a lot of emphasis on mindfulness in our everyday lives."

The other teacher who has affected Pema most deeply is His Holiness the Sixteenth Gyalwa Karmapa. Although he was the first to ordain her, she did not feel that their connection was very profound at the time. She has one vivid memory, though. It was a moment shortly after her ordination ceremony. The Karmapa was sitting in front of a window, and the light poured through, reflecting on his face.

"The curtain was sort of an apricot color, and gauzy, and he sat there and he was smiling broadly. He was talking to all of us who had just received the ordination. And he said, 'You know, if you keep this ordination for this lifetime, you will be with me again after Maitreya.' He meant that he would be the buddha after Maitreya and that we would all be with him. There was something very primordial about that moment. You could almost visualize yourself there with him under the trees. And then he said, 'If you ever feel tempted to break your vows, just think of me sitting here—a fat man with no hair—and just remember my face and that will help you.' I found that was very powerful. It was a kind of transmission that he gave us right there. And it has more power than any lecturing or moralizing he could have done. Just simply to remember him there, laughing and smiling."

During the Karmapa's last visit to this country he was very ill with cancer. Pema began to feel so close to him "it was almost unbearable." Every moment felt precious. To serve him, to simply give him something to drink, to try to make him more comfortable—though he never complained and continued to teach—felt like an honor to her.

On his return to Tibet, the cancer was found to be very serious, and ultimately he was brought back to a small cancer hospital in Zion, Illinois. With him were all the *tulkus* and many of the major Kagyu teachers, including Trungpa Rinpoche. During the extended period of his hospitalization, people often encouraged Pema to visit him. But she didn't see any purpose. He was sick, bedridden. What could she do there?

But one night she could not sleep. It was not simple insomnia. She was beside herself with restlessness, and all she could think of was that she should go to His Holiness. In the middle of the night, she finally called the house where Chögyam Trungpa was staying in Chicago. Though it was 3:00 A.M., she knew he might be awake. Someone answered the phone immediately, and she sent word to Rinpoche asking if she could come and see His Holiness. "Why do you want to do that?" she was asked. Momentarily, she lost her courage. Then she said simply, "Because I want to see him before he dies."

"Then don't waste any time," the word came back. "Come tomorrow."

She flew to Illinois in the morning, was at his bedside during the day, and that evening he died. "So I saw him once again on the last day of his life. I was with Trungpa Rinpoche when His Holiness passed away, and a group of us sat up with him all that night. We just sat hour after hour with Rinpoche saying almost nothing, and it felt spacious and loving rather than sad. It was a powerful time to have been there, and was one of the most memorable events in my life."

There was a curious occurrence at the airport later, when His Holiness's coffin was being taken to the airplane. For some reason it was lowered onto the runway, and a Chinese abbot went down to it, placed over it a special cloth which the Chinese traditionally place over the dead, and began making prostrations. Then Jamgon Kongtrul Rinpoche and T'ai Situ Rinpoche and a number of other monks, as well as Pema, joined the Chinese monk and there, with planes landing and taking off all around, together they made their obeisance.

"There was this sense of a primordial ritual—a timeless experience—occurring there on the landing field. People came down and presented flowers to the coffin, and then they lifted it into the airplane."

Gampo Abbey is situated on two hundred acres of land along the wild Cape Breton coast of Nova Scotia. When the site was originally located in 1983, Pema wrote me, "It's on cliffs above the ocean and quite isolated and magical." There was one large, comfortable house on the grounds, and in the summer of 1984 the first monastic training session was held with Ven Yuen Yi, a Chinese bhikshuni with many years of experience training novices in Taiwan. "Our schedule was disciplined but quite gentle," Pema wrote. In the future she was expected to become abbess, but for the moment she was functioning primarily as fundraiser!

The following winter they held a one-month training period for the ordained sangha with Lama Drupgyu, a Canadian monk who was in charge of Kalu Rinpoche's three-year retreat near Vancouver. This was a more intensive period in preparation for the visit of the Venerable Thrangu Rinpoche (abbott of Rumtek Monastery in Sikkim), who was to inaugurate the full summer training period in August 1985. During the spring, volunteers gathered to work on the building of a new meditation hall. The hall was finished early in the morning of the very day that Thrangu Rinpoche arrived at the abbey.

Pema arrived just before him. She had left in February and remembered the big gray barn full of hay and old trunks and boxes, smelling of cows and chickens. Now she saw it transformed into a beautiful hall with high cathedral ceiling, polished wood floor, and broad windows on all sides, providing an unobstructed view of the sky and the sea.

In the weeks that followed, Rinpoche gradually transmitted the atmosphere of the ancient Tibetan monastic lineages. He had ordained many Westerners in past years, but because there was no place for them to receive training or to follow monastic discipline, many of them had reported difficulty keeping their vows. What was needed, he felt, was a Western monastery that could gradually adapt traditional monastic discipline to Western culture and experience. That summer, therefore, he introduced only a few traditional forms that were new to the participants. And in addition to his teaching and translation work and private talks with students, he took time to become familiar with local animals and plants, to walk to the cliffs to watch the whales, to meditate in the new retreat cabin, establishing a relationship with this time, this place.

"I love the simplicity of monastic life," Pema said later in Berkeley. "But what I'm finding in my short time at the monastery in Nova Scotia is that it's not all that simple! A lot of difficulties have to be worked out. Still, the archetype of monastic life is that you simplify things so that you can put all your energy into realization. That's your career, your marriage, your everything. That really appeals to me, but for others it's different. What they need to become whole is to be married, to have a child, to develop their livelihood, their intellect. What I needed to become whole was to stand on my own feet and experience my aloneness—and somehow it funneled me right into monasticism."

"Does it seem," I asked her, "that a more appropriate time to move into monastic life is after you've lived some, after you've had the family and secular experience?"

"Yes, it does occur to me that a good time to be ordained is after you've had a lot of life experience. I like the idea of people having to prepare a lot before taking ordination. Perhaps one to three years even before novice ordination. And then more time before full ordination. I also like the idea of temporary ordination. Even though they didn't do that in Tibet, Trungpa Rinpoche has often talked about it. A person could enter and appreciate monastic life without feeling married to it. It's an appealing idea for me because I've seen people being ordained and then feeling trapped by it. To minimize that sense of struggle would be good."

"It seems as if the development of Buddhism in this country tends to be more in the secular direction," I remarked.

"Yes, it does. And I think there's a point to that. If you don't

have a financial base and a social base for Buddhism in this country, it's not going to grow, and it's certainly not going to be able
to support a monastic life."

Pema herself, however, is very interested in the development
of the Buddhist monastic tradition in the West. Not as a "cause,"
she assured me, but because she's drawn to the extraordinary
richness and wisdom found in the Tibetan monastic tradition in
particular, with which she's most familiar. There is, for example,
the use of sound and dance and musical instruments. These are
practices that take years to master. "But when you see the dancing or especially when you hear the music," she says, "it has a
way of stopping fixed mind.

"It's exciting to think of these things being brought over to
the West and the possibility of their being learned by Western
students in a proper environment. And monasticism developed
quite differently in different cultures. Now that the seed of monasticism has been sown here, I'll be fascinated to see how it
flowers in the West."

At Gampo Abbey, the intention is to start very simply, with
Tibetan Buddhist students only, until they establish themselves
and basically understand what they're doing. But the real intention is to be ecumenical, and ultimately to reach out to people
of all Buddhist traditions, in fact to contemplatives of all *other*
traditions as well. That is the vision. "But you have to have some
solid ground first," Pema says.

That is what she is working on now.

Update: Winter 2000

In the years following the first edition of *Meetings with Remarkable Women,* Pema Chodron's life both blazed into orbit and
dashed her to the ground. She published three books (*The Wisdom of No Escape,* 1991; *Start Where You Are,* 1994; and *When
Things Fall Apart,* 1997—all published by Shambhala Publications). These books, and tapes of her talks distributed by Sounds
True Audio, brought her voice and style of teaching to a wider
and wider audience—until she became a star! That is, her retreats
around the country were full to overflowing, unprecedented

numbers of new people came to Gampo Abbey, and invitations poured in from every direction for teaching, travel, talks, interviews, media events of all sorts. Her visibility "escalated shockingly," she told me recently, and her quiet anonymity became a thing of the past.

At the same time, Pema's health was deteriorating. After years of baffling, undiagnosed symptoms, she was finally determined to have chronic fatigue–immune dysfunction syndrome as well as environmental illness (a sensitivity to environmental contaminants of all kinds). As demands from the outside world increased, her physical strength began to evaporate. For several years, she attempted to ignore the situation and carry on as usual. But by 1994, her body's resources were totally depleted, and she had no choice but to pay attention.

With the help of a chronic fatigue specialist, she embarked on a long-term course of healing. Complete rest was the primary prescription, and Pema had to make fundamental changes in her life. In 1995, after having been ill for ten years, she took the year off completely.

Paradoxically, Pema now believes the years of her most severe illness were also the years of her greatest productivity. All her books came out, and Gampo Abbey was born. Today, Pema considers her illness to be a major formative event. "It requires me to simplify my life," she said, "a very sane thing to do."

But the most important thing about this particular disease, she says, is that one's habitual defensive patterns—the false or limited ego structures that cover over our true natures—become unmistakable. In Pema's case, it was her "people pleasing," her efforts to live up to her own or others' expectations, that she began to perceive acutely. When these patterns arose, her symptoms instantly escalated. It was like having her teacher hit her with a stick!

Her suffering, her discomfort, became a source of compassion, of "a heartfelt connection with all those unknown people" suffering similarly or suffering much more than she was. "It can open your heart so much—or it can close it," she said. Illness leaves one groundless and vulnerable to any possible escape route, such as seeing oneself as an "ill person"—devices one must endlessly let go of in order to stay present with the unknown. Pema equates this willingness to remain open, ungrounded, and unknowing in a situation that is "bigger than our ideals" with *maitri*, a Sanskrit term for loving-kindness toward ourselves.

We learn to stand in our own shoes, becoming intimate with our pain—and simultaneously to stand in others' shoes as well—so that gradually, over time, no matter what may be happening, a sense of well-being arises, and we are not destroyed or swept away by good or bad, up or down. This, Pema thinks, must be "the point"—not a "transcendental state" but, at a gut level, experiencing compassion and openness exactly in the midst of ordinary life.

In terms of developments in the "real" world, Gampo Abbey is firmly established and bustling with activities. A three-year retreat center has been built nearby and has been occupied by male and female retreatants (in separate wings) since 1990.

Forty people, including Pema, have now completed three-year retreats. The structure of these retreats is unusual, compared to the traditional one followed in Tibet and other countries around the world. Instead of being in complete seclusion for three years, three months, and three days, at Gampo Abbey (at the request of their abbott, Thrangu Rinpoche), people stay only for six or eight months at a time, in five segments separated by periods of ordinary life at home. The retreats are conducted entirely in English, and men and women are in retreat at the same time (all of this is highly unusual for these extended retreats, according to Pema). Men and women live separately but frequently practice together.

In the summer of 1997, the first one-month practice period for young adults (age sixteen to twenty-five) took place at the abbey. They received temporary ordination, shaved their heads, put on robes, received teachings, and did an impressive amount of meditation. In 1999, the first yearlong monastic period was held. "Young people are very interested in monasticism for a temporary period," Pema says. They stay one to two years, often have a very powerful and healing experience, and sometimes go on to take permanent vows.

Pema spent the last segment of her three-year retreat at the abbey alone in her cabin. She was becoming increasingly ill and could not maintain the schedule. But it was nevertheless a very significant experience. "I have a passion for retreat now," she says, and has been doing a two-month retreat every year since then. In 1999, she expected to be in retreat for three months.

"I am a person who enjoys solitude. I need it because of my health, but it is also my inclination." (An astrologer recently told her, "You're a very private person with a very public life. No wonder you're sick.")

With regard to her individual work with students, Pema retains some ambivalence. The main benefit of such work, she believes, is that through getting to know each other intimately, the possibility arises for both teacher and student to see through habitual patterns and begin to step more and more into groundlessness. But experience has shown that many students are not yet ready for this work. Moreover, she adds, "only to the degree that I myself continue to practice and bring everything I encounter to the path will I have anything to offer to anybody else."

Pema remembered that at the time of our first interview, I had recognized her as a real teacher. "But," she said recently, "I didn't see that myself." Now, with her reputation soaring, she is confronting the perils of fame—for example, beginning to believe other people's perceptions of her, including idolization. Meditation becomes more and more important to keep her from getting caught in the facade, not being seduced by it, not solidifying it, but "just to keep going with the essence."

In the year 2000, she plans to take another year off completely, partly in California, partly in Nova Scotia. She has recently made the commitment to teach four months a year in California, where she'll also be able to spend more time with her family.

No longer officially the director or administrator at Gampo Abbey, Pema calls herself the "resident teacher" there. She continues to teach and develop the monastic training at the abbey, but she lives separately in her own cabin, where she gives interviews and writes. She thoroughly enjoys the writing process and has come to feel "that the teachings of Buddhism benefit greatly from the feminine, intuitive voice."

4

Charlotte Joko Beck

A woman's body
a bald head—
she is just there.
A smile unsmiled
informs her spine, forehead, finger-
tips, tilts her neck—
like the touch of her stick
is remembered in one's belly.

The owl sees in ten directions
not moving a bone
misses nothing
(breeze-flickered feathers
shivering night leaves)
one plunge, taste of mouse.
In the woods a doe bleeds,
the hunter gone home.

In an upstairs room
two pillows on the floor
we bow, talk in bright air.
Stay with the body, she says.
Nothing's not seen
and nothing is special.
Tea is brought in on a lacquered tray.
Embellishment falls away
like scissored hair.
                    —Lenore Friedman

Amid a pile of photographs of Buddhist practice centers and
teachers on the West Coast, I came upon one that puzzled me.
There were pictures of serious students sitting in a line facing a
blank wall with straight backs and vulnerable faces. There were

portraits set in gardens and before altars, showing the elaborate patterns of ceremonial robes. There were scenes of wry paradox: monks doing the washing outdoors, a wooden Buddha figure smiling benignly at a bottle of Joy liquid detergent. And then this odd picture: a woman from the knees up, who might have been anyone's neighbor or aunt, in the middle of an ordinary suburban street, with cars and low houses angling away in the near distance behind her. Had this picture gotten into the pile by mistake? Wondering, looking at the woman's face, I suddenly recognized it, and understood. Joko! The last time I had seen her, she'd looked utterly different: she'd worn black robes and her head had been shaved and shining. Now I bowed to the photographer who had caught her very essence, her very ordinariness. In her absolute plainness, Joko embodies the Zen quality of "nothing special." She is simply there, in each bare moment.

On that unremarkable suburban street, in an unremarkable suburban house, the activities of the Zen Center of San Diego—sitting, walking, chanting, bowing, dharma talks, monthly sesshins—go on quietly, with no fuss at all. During a weekend sesshin that I attended there, one very early morning before the sun came up, the kinhin line wound silently out the back door, around the house, onto the dark street, and then entirely around a block of dark houses and sleeping neighbors. Instead of strangeness, there was a feeling of simplicity—our walking no different from their dreaming.

During work periods, while I stuffed zafus with kapok, Joko walked past in light blue sweat pants and shirt. (In the zendo and during *daisan* periods, she wore a long plain skirt and blouse.) She stopped using her Japanese robes in December 1984. This was "part of her ongoing examination of whether the various aspects of formal practice serve to support our being more awake or more habituated," the Zen Center newsletter explained. When I talked to her a year later, she said, "There are drawbacks to not wearing robes. It's not all one-sided. There's something very beautiful about Zen robes. There's a certain dignity in the zendo when many of the people wear them. But it's a little strange to be wandering around in these ancient gowns in the middle of a city."

About her shaved head she said: "I don't care whether it's

shaved or not. It makes no difference to me. But I'm busy here. I often have to dash over to the supermarket. I really hate to have to put on a scarf every time I stick my head out the door. It's silly. Why should I do that? But I think it's great training to go through a year, say, without your hair. But I don't think we should be *stuck* with that sort of thing."

Joko endlessly punctures students' attempts to set her apart or above them. "I'm a student, just like you," she told me. She has had her special brown sitting mat, the mark of a teacher, covered over in black. Sometimes she may not sit in the teacher's place at all. "I just go sit somewhere facing the wall." She rejects all attempts at hero worship. "People like to project their power onto someone else," she says. "But I won't accept that." Once in a while she'll think it best for students to leave if their need to project is really persistent, and they may go somewhere else for a while. Sometimes she'll just say, "Look, you're attributing all sorts of things to me, and you don't even know me. That does you no good, so please, let's abandon it."

She doesn't mean that a teacher doesn't have to have authority, but she distinguishes between authority and authoritarianism. Maintaining authority, she tries to eliminate hierarchy. "I'm trying to remove all the little special bows people make to me all the time. Courtesy is one thing, but this bowing down to another human being as though he or she were vastly superior is bad for people. I'm trying to take the teacher out of the superman role. The teacher is a guide but not some magical or heroic figure."

At ceremonies in the zendo, Joko only officiates on special occasions. Otherwise, there's no particular leader, everyone joining in together, simply, without pretension. Responsible positions in the zendo, like timekeeper and bell-ringer, are rotated. Older students are encouraged *not* to be the most conspicuous. The mark of a mature student is often work done invisibly. And if anyone were to become attached to invisibility as a sign of achievement, Joko would be sure to poke a hole in *that*.

The weekend I was in San Diego, during formal talks and later during our informal interviews, Joko said some pointed things about a number of possible distortions in Zen practice. "We think too much about breaking through to the absolute," she told me.

"I think that's a very premature consideration for most people. Even if they do it, they don't know what to do with it. And for some people, the shock is too great." Her primary consideration is the kind of mature development that makes this realization possible. When the mind loses interest in its attachments, "then very naturally, what is called *samadhi* increases. And at some point there may be an 'opening,' but this is not a goal to be sought—it's just a natural occurrence when practice matures; and after it happens, we go right back to working with the basic problem."

And the basic problem we're working with in Zen practice is attachment. Yet our whole life is nothing but attachment. That's the terrain of the ego, and practice, Joko believes, is simply a matter of constantly turning back to our everyday actions and asking, "What's really going on here? How can we look at it? How can we sit with it? Where are we attached?" The line between this kind of endeavor and psychotherapy is not sharp. But there's a major difference that comes with serious sitting, and that is a total shift in our view of who we really are. There's a subtlety and an ability to observe that makes it a "totally different ball-game." And there comes a point when the depth and intensity of the process move beyond most therapy.

But Joko rarely mentions enlightenment experiences. "If you push for samadhi as a goal, you may achieve a kind of emptiness, but it is not *true* emptiness because the *person* isn't truly empty. If in your daily life you misuse other people, or manipulate them, or are interested in your own power, then the samadhi—which can be developed quite artificially—is not, as far as I am concerned, a true samadhi."

"You can have samadhi and be attached to it, I suppose," I said.

"Oh, of course," she answered. "Almost everybody is attached to their samadhi! Samadhi is almost like an athletic ability. And people even learn to use it to avoid their own suffering."

"You leap over the suffering into samadhi?"

"Yes. Not only that, but if you have artificial samadhi power, you may maintain it during the day, and it may look really good as long as there is no particular stress. But under stress such samadhi often proves to be quite fragile. It seems more useful first to grapple with all the notions you have about your life, all your particular attachments. From that kind of practice in time will emerge a genuine samadhi and genuine understanding."

"With different people, then, the shape of their practice would be different?"

"Right. When I teach I don't say much. When someone comes in to daisan, I'll usually inquire, 'Well, what's on your mind today? What do you want to say?' And as they talk, I listen to what's going on. And then I may catch them: 'Did you hear what you just said? Can you say a little more about that?' And then we start digging in."

I asked where she had learned this way of teaching.

"Years of talking to people. Years and years. You can't really teach another person what this is—it takes experience. And I don't think, by the way, that to pass all the koans means much, though it's often considered a diploma for teaching."

"What about Mu? Some teachers consider that to be the one koan you need to pass."

"I've had new people tell me that their koan is Mu, but usually they seem to find it a puzzling abstraction bearing no relationship to their life. Mu is simply this life itself, right here, right now. If you're upset with your child, that's Mu; when you probe that, you probe Mu. It's not somewhere else. But in classic practice, when this koan is assigned, the idea is for the student just to sit with this mystery. As he wrestles and struggles with the koan, he journeys through all parts of himself in attempting to solve it. And for some people, this works. But more and more when I hear stories about the ancient monasteries, I wonder. They had a thousand monks sometimes, and you hear about the star who 'did it'—but they don't tell you much about the other nine hundred and ninety-nine. I'm sure a lot of them didn't know what on earth they were doing."

"So it might not have been appropriate even then?"

"I doubt if it was, except in a small number of cases. Many monks came and went and never did know what they were doing. But we don't hear about that. Now, my students pass Mu too, but a lot of them have never even heard the word! And still they pass it. You don't need to know the word—if practice is sincere and intense, at some point there is just a comprehension of what life is. 'Oh, it's *that!*' If the mind is empty and quiet—sure, there it is. Of course there's nothing but Mu. But I observe that many people are not ready or interested or capable of dealing with the nature of ultimate reality—which is their own nature, of course. Much work needs to precede the serious investigation of this question.

"So I think we have to teach in a way appropriate for each person. I'm just as interested in students with serious difficulties as in the so-called 'strong' students. If any life can be moved a little, become more even and steady—more 'real'—that's the most satisfying thing to me. So with every student whom I encounter, I just watch and listen and feel what's sitting there. And then I deal with that. Sometimes nicely, sometimes a little bit harshly, it depends on the student. You have to be a blank space and then you adapt to this . . . and this . . . and this."

"A complete lack of manipulation on your part."

"Oh, absolutely."

Joko was in her forties before she ever heard of Zen. Like Maurine Stuart and Roshi Kennett, she had played the piano for many years. She had received a bachelor's degree in music from the Oberlin Conservatory of Music. She had been married for thirteen years and finally divorced after her husband had two nervous breakdowns. She already had four children, ranging in age from one to twelve years old. The family had been living in the East until then, most recently in Connecticut and Michigan. Then Joko got a teaching credential and they moved to California, where she supported her family for a while as a teacher. But soon that became too draining as she coped with four children at home. So she taught herself to type and became a secretary at Convair and later an administrative assistant at the University of California at San Diego, first in the music department and later in the chemistry department, where she worked for many years.

One evening in 1965, more or less by chance, she and a friend dropped in at the San Diego Unitarian Church, where they came upon a lecture by a Buddhist monk. "We drifted in, and this monk was bowing to each person as they entered. And I was struck by something about him, really struck. There were many intellectuals in the audience, and they tried to upset him with fancy philosophical questions. He answered them all politely and very well. He was obviously having a good time. No matter how they tried to twist and turn him, he wasn't twisted or turned. He seemed to me then quite imperturbable. And I thought, 'That's interesting. I've never met anyone like that before.' At work at this time I was dealing with some of the brightest minds on the West Coast. But none of them were imperturbable!" The monk turned out to be Maezumi Roshi (Sensei at the time) from the Zen Center of Los Angeles—and that was how Joko stumbled into Zen.

There were two other people sitting zazen in San Diego then, and Joko became the third. Every other month or so, Maezumi Sensei came down from Los Angeles to help the small group with their practice. And about twice a year she would go to Los Angeles. There were also sesshins in northern California in the sixties with Yasutani Roshi, who began to come yearly from Japan. These made a deep impact on Joko. Then Soen Roshi came one year, and with him she passed the koan Mu. Her reaction to this experience was to throw something at him!

"It may seem strange now," she says, "but I was really angry at the time. As is often the case with such experiences, it takes only minutes for the conditioned mind to reemerge and distort the realization." Soon after, she began formal koan study with Maezumi Roshi in Los Angeles. For five years, Joko went back and forth between San Diego and Los Angeles to work on koans, and she attended many sesshins as well. Then in 1976, she decided to retire early and move to Los Angeles. Her youngest daughter, Brenda, was already there, attending UCLA. Brenda had begun sitting some time before, and now she and her mother lived together at ZCLA.

Almost from the first, Joko began to be increasingly sought out by the other students. They were drawn to her maturity and accessibility, her common sense and quickness of mind. More and more people requested appointments to discuss problems in their lives and practice. When I first visited Joko at ZCLA in the summer of 1983, her students talked to me about her with great feeling, sometimes with tears in their eyes.

"You feel total, open, empty space with Joko," one of them said. While never harsh, she goes right to the point, arrowlike, giving precise feedback in "a very spare way." Everyone respected her rich past experience. They were aware that Joko had suffered, felt her to be altogether human. Because she's struggled herself, she's very approachable, they told me. Yet there's not a maneuver she can't see through. "You can't snow Joko," they'd say. She knows all the tricks of human nature, all the ways we deceive ourselves. Natural intelligence and penetrating insight were called her "great, great gift."

Joko was a "reluctant dharma teacher," another student told me. It was as if she had to be pushed. Yet she was always teaching naturally. Always there were people around her, inspired to deepen their practice by her dedication and diligence. One day Roshi decided that her informal teaching should be transplanted to the formal structure of the zendo. But when he said, "Do it!" it was almost as if she had to be dragged to the altar. When she shaved her head, I was told, Joko became "ageless," and a certain fixed identity dropped away.

Again and again, words like "cut," "penetrated," "turned around" were used to describe Joko's way of seeing through and toppling belief systems. With the simplest statement, I was told, she "turns you upside down." Her unassuming style only increases the power of her "killing sword" (*prajna* wisdom). But on the other side is always compassion.

In 1978 Joko became Maezumi Roshi's third dharma heir. "But don't think of dharma transmission as some mystical thing," she told me. It simply means that at some point the teacher feels that his understanding and the student's are the same. "It's no big deal," she said. "People make a lot out of it, think the heavens open up or something. It's just that the student is now seen as prepared to assist others in clarifying the basic issues of life and death."

As time went by, however, Joko found herself questioning

more and more the traditional methods of teaching. She was curious, interested in reading about and exploring the ways of other Buddhist teachers as well as other traditions and disciplines, including psychology and psychiatry. She was beginning to see how they interpenetrated and complemented each other. At the same time, the "giant confusion" of many students disturbed her. She began to suspect that classic Zen training—pure concentrative use of the mind—was not of much benefit to many of them. For some, it even seemed harmful. It enabled them to circumvent issues in their lives that needed addressing.

What practice really is, for Joko, is being willing to be with whatever is, at every moment. Being with our bodies. Being with the physical sensations that appear and disappear. What is anger, for example? Aside from the thought or picture in our mind, she says, it is pure sensory input in our bodies. *Experience* it. Fear? Experience that.

All the emotions are our practice, Joko says. And dealing with them is absolutely basic. In themselves, emotions are fine, but when we cling to their thought content, they obscure life as it is. "That's where everybody's *stuck*. Show me anyone who isn't. Do you know anybody? Everyone's fascinated by their emotions because we think that's who we are. We're afraid that if we let our attachment to them go, we'll be nobody. Which of course we are!" The question is whether the brain runs the body or whether the body runs the brain. When the brain runs the body, we feel anxious and tight. When the body runs the brain, things go more smoothly. Practice slowly turns our machinery around.

Zazen teaches us to be with the present, constantly to be with the present. "When you wander into your ideas, your hopes, your dreams, turn back—not just once but ten thousand times if need be, a million times if need be. It's the patience to do that, and the courage, which is the life of the bodhisattva."

That patience, that willingness, is hard-won. The *last* thing we seem to want is to be as we are. So the truth of life escapes us. All of us, Joko says (including herself), make the error of rejecting our life as it is, right here, right now. And this leads to the fundamental anxiety that haunts our lives.

This very moment, she urges, "Just *be* what you are. Each of us is a precious jewel. How do we make it shine? By just being what our life is at each moment: that is the jewel. That *is* nirvana."

Nor does this preclude change, or addressing the snags in our lives. In fact, the best way to effect change is to completely be with our situation, exactly as it is. "If we're completely willing to be what is, our vision can clear and we know better what to do." Each time we do this, she says, each time we go into the suffering and let it be, our vision enlarges. Letting be *is* nonattachment, what practice is all about. It's like climbing a mountain. As we ascend, we see more and more. And the more we see—the clearer our vision—the more we know what to *do*, both personally and on the level of social action.

"In talking to many, many people, the main thing I notice is that they don't understand suffering," she says. "Of course I don't always either. I try as much as anyone to avoid it." But at a talk in 1983 during the Yasutani Roshi Memorial sesshin, she distinguished between true and false suffering. False suffering, she said, is when we feel we're being "pressed down," as though the suffering were coming from outside of ourselves. True suffering is just bearing (as in "carrying") it, not opposing it, but absorbing and *being* it.

"Of course if you're anything like me, you'll avoid it as long as possible—because it's one thing to talk about this kind of practice but extremely difficult to do it. Yet when we do it, we know in our very guts who we are and who everyone else is, and the barrier between ourselves and others is gone."

The mind that creates false suffering arises constantly in sesshin. "There isn't one of us who isn't subject to it. Last night just before sesshin began, I noticed it in myself. I could hear my mind complaining, 'What, another sesshin?! You just did a sesshin last weekend!' Our minds work that way. Then, hearing that nonsense, we remind ourselves, 'What do I really want for myself or anyone else?' Then our mind quiets down again." Patiently, we turn back to the only reality: this present moment. Then our focus and our samadhi deepen. "So in zazen, the bodhisattva's renunciation is that practice, that turning away from our personal fantasy and dream into the reality of the present. And in sesshin, each moment that we practice like this gives us what we can't get in any other way: knowledge of ourselves. Then we are facing this moment directly; we're facing the suffering. And when finally we're really willing to settle into it, just be it, then we know, and no one needs to tell us, what we are and what everything else is."

Almost two years later, in San Diego, in January 1985, Joko gave a talk on appreciating our life by having no hope. "It sounds terrible, doesn't it?" she said. But a life without hope is peaceful, joyful, compassionate. "Anyone who sits for any length of time sees that there is no past and no future except in our minds. There is nothing but Self, and Self always is here, present. It's not hidden. We're racing around like mad trying to find something called Self, this mysterious, hidden Self. Where is it hidden? We hope for something that is going to take care of our little self because we don't realize that already we *are* Self. There's nothing around us that is not Self. What are we looking for?"

The paradox is that in totally owning the pain, the joy, the responsibility for experiencing our life—if we grasp this totally— we are free. We have no hope, no need for anything else. But when we live in dreams and hopes, the wonder of the man or woman (ordinary, unglamorous) sitting next to us escapes us. Hoping for something "special," we fail to appreciate the miracle of life as it is.

Real practice has nothing to do with hope or fantasy. "We're saying, once again, that zazen *is* enlightenment. Why? Because as you sit minute after minute, that's *it*. If you really practice like this, it takes everything you have. What will you get out of it? The answer, of course, is nothing. So don't have hope. You won't get anything. You'll get your life, of course, but you've got that already. This life *is* nirvana. Where did you think it was?"

Joko keeps reminding us that experiencing our life directly means experiencing our physical sensations. The more our attention is on them rather than on our thought processes (thinking *about* our experience, analyzing it, worrying about it), the more "our expectations begin to shrivel, to dry up like withered leaves, and just blow away." Then a new kind of life is born. With nothing extra added, moment after moment, we let life be the way it is. "Not fancy, not dramatic, very plain." Our basic nature. That's it.

In the fall of 1983, Joko officially left ZCLA to take charge of the Zen Center of San Diego, a good-sized sangha that had grown from the original trio who started sitting there together in the mid-sixties. Her long-time friend and assistant, Elizabeth Hamilton, had been commuting back and forth for a year between San Diego and Los Angeles doing preparatory groundwork and organization.

At first, Joko functioned in San Diego much as she had in Los Angeles. She knew there were changes she wanted to make, but the process itself was important, and she didn't want to rush things. Even before the move, she acknowledged that Zen in the West must change. "But it mustn't be too fast," she had said in our first interview. "Some of these traditional forms are not just meaningless forms. They've developed for good reasons: the formality of the zendo, for instance—the severity of it—performs a certain function. If you are too casual, the zendo tends to lose rigor. You can't assume that all traditions are 'bad' just because they look strange. You can't be so black-and-white. If you take the traditions and say, 'Throw them all out,' you're going to have some difficulty. For instance, I am always amazed at the transformation that takes place in people in a long sesshin; they are much more open, more genuine at the end of it. And yet some of the more traditional activities have a lot to do with this transformation. Of course, some ways of traditional practice can be thrown out or altered, but we have to be careful. Even though I'm personally pretty informal, I've come to value the formal training I've had, and the way it can assist us."

In Los Angeles she had already begun teaching differently. She was using a much wider range of approaches with her students. "A person can't look at himself until he has become strong enough to do it. To increase this strength, I may use some vipassana techniques, or classic Zen techniques (including koans), or many other approaches, depending on the needs of the student. That's just the way I see teaching right now. Maybe I'll change even more."

In February 1984, Joko initiated a series of meetings at ZCSD called "What Should Zen Practice Look Like in America?" Everyone (but especially those who had been sitting for a few years) was invited to take a "broad and thoughtful look at our practice—examining and questioning everything, from what we wear to the format of sittings. Nothing is sacred." The meetings were spirited and lively, especially at first. But rather soon it became apparent that about half the people wanted to keep everything absolutely traditional, and the other half wanted to be more innovative. "And the only answer to that is that I do what I want to do!"

Joko laughed. We were sitting in her apartment in the house behind the zendo, after the end of sesshin. It was now February 1985. Joking aside, she said that neither tradition nor innovation is the point. The point is, what best serves a live, vital practice? All changes should arise from that consideration.

One change I had noticed was the elimination of full prostrations during daisan. Instead, there were three simple standing bows. Joko said they'd been making about one change a month! The next one was going to be replacement of a formal Buddha statue on the altar with an uncut stone that only vaguely suggests a Buddha figure. "A stone is life, which is what an altar represents anyway. Again, anything can change if it serves practice. If you come down to San Diego again, it might look different. It might look more traditional, but I doubt it somehow."

Later, she said, "I question everything. At the moment I don't intend to do anything about it, but I question accepting any fixed format for sesshin as sacrosanct. I'm willing to look at *everything*. What I do is think and feel and let it turn over. I don't think there's anything holy about *any* of this. I recently did a sesshin in New York City, and at first I was horrified: since they had no way to prepare food for lots of people, everyone went out to nearby restaurants and had their meals. And it worked beautifully! They really maintained silence. So I am learning that anything can be looked at.

"Our last sesshin here, we ended up doing the final kinhin along the ocean. We rode in cars to the beach and then walked in silence along the water for an hour, came back to the zendo to chant the *Heart Sutra,* and it was wonderful. You can imagine, at the end of a long sesshin, to hear the roar of the ocean for an hour! So who said you had to do it any particular way? I'm coming to think you don't have to do *anything* any particular way."

There are limits, of course, whether we are considering changes in the forms of practice or in the sitting itself. All changes must be based on a clear understanding of what practice is. "Otherwise you'll have a circus. Our sesshins may not be polished, but they're not a circus. Sitting is strong. And despite everything I'm saying, this still looks like a Zen center!"

But the point of practice is not to use hierarchy or ceremony or robes as vehicles for ego attachment. Joko feels that many zendos are, unfortunately, the very picture of the ego in action (people trying to be important, vying for position) and that many Zen teachers are heavily invested in their own power and authority and the role they play. In other words, what true practice teaches us to *look* at (i.e., the ego in action) is being blindly fostered.

"It seems to be human nature to take anything that works (ceremony, for example) and then make it solid and rigid. It's when we put ego and solidity and rigidity around it that we make a problem. But if something like ceremony becomes too rigid, we need to attack that rigidity until once again we have a more open and fluid reality. All of life is that flow between one pole and the other—nothing wrong about it. I tend to like a more open, informal structure for a center because that's my tendency as a person, and problems may result from that. But that's the nature of life: to deal with 'What problem do we have in *this* moment? What can be done *now*?'"

At ZCSD there are communication meetings, open board meetings, even open financial records. Nothing is hidden. There is almost always a question-and-answer period after any talk given at the center, and an open discussion period at the end of Wednesday evening sitting. The center is set up so that Joko can be removed as teacher in five minutes. All the board would have to do is call a meeting and vote her out. Politically, she has essentially no power. And she likes it that way. But in the realm of practice, she has the final word. "If someone were to come and say, 'I think we should have fifteen-minute sittings,' I would say, 'No, we're not going to have fifteen-minute sittings.' There's no democracy in *that* area!"

Joko believes that the primary function of a teacher is to help us perceive what we already are, what we already know without realizing it. She began a talk at the Berkeley Zen Center a few years ago with the words: "I always wonder what people expect to get out of a talk like this. What have I got that you don't? Of course I don't have anything that you don't have. There's nothing I know that you don't know. But I'll admit that maybe to be aware of this is what practice is about." Too often, students want to put her *up* somewhere. She sees herself rather as an experienced friend: "not always a sweet friend, but an experienced friend."

"I'm not saying we don't need teachers, centers, or techniques. We need them very much. But when we think that something except ourselves and our own correct effort is going to effect some sort of transformation in our life, we're deluding ourselves. Any teacher is there simply as a guide so that you can get in touch with the wisdom you already are. Anything that's done is to assist you in doing that. Be careful. Idealization, blind faith in a teacher's 'superior' wisdom, a belief that the teacher knows something the student doesn't, spells trouble for everyone. It's always up to us."

What our "own correct effort" always comes down to is attention, attention, attention (as old Zen master Ikkyu once wrote three times when a disciple asked for a word of the highest wisdom). Years ago, Joko discovered that practice with the body was the clue. She likes students to cultivate precise awareness of the body's reaction in all types of circumstances—and then to attempt to elucidate the basic ego structure that *is* this behavior. What's *really* going on here? she wants to know. How can we look at it? How can we practice with it? How can we sit with it?

"I used to teach like anyone else," she told me. She might assign the koan Mu, challenging students in the classical way: "What is Mu? Really penetrate it!" But not anymore. Students are too various, she says. Some need their egos strengthened, not torn apart. Some need simple counseling. Others are ready for the slow dismantling of the ego structure which is the work of classical Zen training. "But more and more I find that strengthening the ego (what much therapy is thought to be) and eroding the ego (what Zen is thought to be) interweave and resolve nicely when we work steadily on seeing our attachments."

Joko wants to know everything about her students. And the fact is, she usually does! She might at one time, say, be working with a man, his wife, and his mistress. With each of them she simply probes the ego attachments underlying the situation and, when these are seen more clearly, the situation tends to settle itself.

Or someone may come in and say she is obsessing about a new boyfriend. Joko will say, "Fine, just obsess, but stay awake as you do it. How do you obsess? Have you ever looked closely at how you do this? What's going on in your mind? What does it feel like in your stomach? Stay awake—don't miss anything!"

Before long, Joko says, people are teaching themselves. She may say, "You be the teacher," and she'll present a problem: Imagine you are facing three new people and one of them asks, "What is Zen practice about? Why would I want to do it?" What would you tell them? If the student says, "I don't know what I'd tell them," Joko will answer, "But you *do* know—and I want your practice to be to see that you do know, and that you can clearly express what you know. Next week come in and let me hear what you would say." And so Joko listens, listens, listens. "That way we learn a lot." And people's practice comes alive.

"I want people to see the sense of their practice. I want them to ask themselves (even for months): Why would I work so hard at this? What does it mean to me, really? Why put in this kind of effort? Why should I get up half an hour earlier to do it?

"The point is, everybody *knows*—and all you have to do is listen hard enough to find some way for them to tell you what they know. It is the skill of the teacher to give them ways of doing that. We are our own teachers, see? The external teacher is to enable you to be your own teacher."

It's not hard to see that Joko enjoys teaching, is energized by it, even. After hours of daisan during sesshin, she will have picked up energy, rather than lost it.

We were approaching the end of my stay in San Diego, and a question still nagged at the edge of my mind.

Lenore: I wonder if we could take a few minutes to clarify something you said in daisan yesterday.

Joko: Sure.

Lenore: You asked me about my "inner decision," and I said that from the time I was small, my inner decision was to be *good*. Then I filled that in a little more and said I could feel myself contracting into something very, very small, hardly being there, certainly having no needs—and you said that was more pertinent to what you were after. And I'm not sure I understand.

Joko: Being good is the ego structure we're talking about. At some point, each one of us decides we can't survive in this universe unless we have a strategy. For some, the strategy is to hit out; for some, it's to become small and invisible. Your strategy is in being good, looking a certain way, pleasing everyone. But the basic strategy for anyone is always: I'm going to preserve myself, no matter what, and it doesn't matter at whose expense either. This strategy in time becomes a basic decision which runs our life (the ego) because we are unaware of it. Our practice (attention) is to be clearly conscious of it, not in our heads but in every cell and bone of our body.

Lenore: You're saying that the bodily sensations are the clue to the ego structure.

Joko: Yes. For instance, what you describe—this shrinking into almost nothing—you wouldn't do that if it were not the manifestation of a decision. At some point you decided that the only possible way you would survive was to use this strategy. You learned (probably without being aware of what you were doing) that in a threatening situation you should shrink. And what you've learned in your life so far is to do what? To meet all threats with what?

Lenore: Disappearing.

Joko: Right. Sure. And what we must do in practice is to increase awareness of the unceasing activity of our ego. And when we sit with intelligence, we're doing that. To elucidate this ego strategy—feeling our physical sensations, hearing our obstreperous thoughts—allows us to see how it continuously dominates our life. Only then can we truly appreciate that this tiger which tyrannizes us is an *empty* tiger and that we do not have to be at the mercy of anything unreal. Our decision might not have been foolish at one time, but now it's foolish and inappropriate. We don't need it anymore.

Lenore: Well, of course to a large extent I don't—and yet I do!

Joko: And yet you do. We all do.

Lenore: I see that. And the more I look the more I see.

Joko: And then the question is how to practice with that.

Lenore: Yes. That's *exactly* my question!

Joko: Well, what we talked about in daisan was the need for research. What I see as effective koan practice—and I think it started out this way, before it became a very formalized and almost dead system—is to begin re-creating moments of your life and to do this for a teacher; and to do it in a way that assists you in seeing the ego structure as thoughts and physical sensations—make it conscious, in other words. When it's so conscious that you can't avoid seeing its emptiness, it will no longer run you. It's something you hold, and that's a vastly different state of affairs. Then you can begin to let it go, which means to see its emptiness. And this kind of practice works; I see it working here. The problem for the teacher, you see, is how to make all this clear, to be more and more skillful in conducting the whole practice. I'm constantly looking for better ways, and that's what makes teaching fun, and also very demanding.

In a tiny bedroom in the back house, next door to Joko's, a beautifully polished harpsichord takes up most of the space. This is Elizabeth Hamilton's room. I sit cross-legged on her bed, listening, while a few inches away she practices a Bach harpsichord concerto for a concert coming up in only a few weeks. A tape recorder on the bench next to her plays the orchestra part. Beginning as a child prodigy, Elizabeth has played and performed for many years. But only recently, she tells me after her dexterous fingers finish the first movement, has she begun to understand what *real* playing is about (that is, *being* the music, allowing it to come through her). She talks with the same agility, precision, and sparkle with which she plays the harpsichord.

Elizabeth: Joko teaches that we have to look at the manure that grows the roses in our life. We have to examine our personal version of suffering. She keeps pushing us back into what we have hoped to use Zen practice to avoid. We might come here to get enlightened to avoid misery. Or so that I personally can be an enlightened self and have lights radiating out of my head! She cuts through that right away, thank heavens.

You have to fully experience something before you see that it's empty. If you're evading fear, you're never going to see the fear's empty. It's going to run you from underneath. You may sit in deep samadhi and see the oneness, but it's almost a concept because when you stand up, there you are, landmines and all. And someone comes along and criticizes or even corrects you, and you fall into *rage*. And you're supposed to be enlightened now!

Lenore: The seductive thing about samadhi is—you said "concept," but it's not, it's an *experience*.

Elizabeth: Not even an experience. Samadhi is what we are when we are sitting as the present moment, open to everything. This is very different from a samadhi of one-pointed concentration which blocks out everything else. When you sit in that "blocking-out" kind of samadhi, you have no problems, you may sense the oneness. It *can* be very seductive; you can even have moments of great insight. But if you're still unaware of or trapped in your conditioning, your blind spots are down there under your samadhi, getting a good rest, like a two-year-old. But after his nap he's going to come marching out and run your life. We can even use samadhi as a narcotic, to block out thoughts and emotions, and have a false sense of our accomplishment.

If you look at what's been revealed over the last couple of years about all the people with titles, you can see just how hard practice is. I personally have no interest in making a big deal about "enlightened" people. That's a notion that implies permanence and solidity. The issue is only whether we're awake in *this* moment. And this moment. And this moment. And having been awake in 1975, perhaps so awake you were given a title, doesn't mean you're awake in 1985, or in all situations.

Lenore: Yet we get caught in the notion that there's somebody who knows, who knows better than we do, and who can tell us, or show us the way.

Elizabeth: Yes. So many of us have suspended our discernment in the interest of thinking there was someone out there who could do no wrong or might be doing the most outlandish things, but they were "just to teach us" and there was clearly a purpose behind them. I feel badly that I've actually supported people in being outlandish because I thought there was something I just didn't see. So I've colluded by putting them outside my common sense. It's sad to see how diligently we've deluded ourselves in the name of practice. When practice itself should be the work that clarifies the hurt, the anger, or the confusion—and brings understanding and growth. Maybe Americans are now nineteen years old spiritually and we're ready to leave home and be on our own.

Lenore: Would you be willing to talk personally about any of this, of the way you and Joko have worked together?

Elizabeth: Well, I had to be willing, that's the first thing, and sick of pretending. Before I sat, I never was angry. I just had ulcers and asthma and hives! I had to finally start going into my physical reality—I mean, I could be the oak tree in the garden, no problem, but I couldn't be *myself*. Without having all this self-centeredness come up, this *self-defense*. So I started looking at what was already coming up for me. She didn't have to tell me what to look for. I knew. She knows that we know. And she's patient. She's willing to wait until we're ready to look.

For example, with performing, I performed for twenty-five years, I guess, without knowing that underneath there somewhere I was a nervous wreck, frightened that somehow I wouldn't be approved of. I had it divided up into audience, performer (me), will it be okay? And I finally got down under there and saw what I was covering up *with* music. I wouldn't blame anyone for not wanting to look.

In a way, we have to hear it over and over. Like yesterday morning, when she said, "Come back, again and again, to that reality of the present moment, which is always based on the physical." The more I just *be* the shaking, *be* the tight muscles, then the more there *is* a stillness, that still point, that sanity, that nothing-at-all.

There was a marvelous moment after I'd been sitting for three months. This was September 28, 1975—I'll never forget it. It became obvious to me that the *Heart Sutra* was true. For two weeks it was quite obvious to me that this was the case. And then it slowly started to fade. But my memory of it became more and more *solid*. I spent the next two years trying to recapture that historical moment. Which is delusion. But if your view of practice attaches great significance to such a moment of insight, you now have a notion of solidity pasted on top of it. Then there's even more reason to think you have something to protect. So it's all quite counterproductive.

Lenore: Those moments of clarity don't *help* cutting through delusion?

Elizabeth: Well, I must say you can never quite put Humpty Dumpty together again, *quite*. In a way they're crucial. But chances are, even if the curtain goes up, it's going to slowly come back down, into your clouded ways of seeing things. It's like being a monk can become just a tremendous ego trip. I'm glad not to be wearing robes right now. What's a robe? *This* [touching her body] is the robes. It's so easy to become cultish or sectarian if you think these are the ornaments of the Buddha. What are you when you're in your nightgown? I prefer not to be portrayed as a Buddhist or a non-Buddhist, monk or layperson, or anything for that matter. Those categories have caused so much confusion. You can use *anything* to stir up that muddy water again, and forget.

Lenore: You can use anything; you can even use practice.

Elizabeth: Absolutely. I have. I do! I *will!* We don't want to look. We don't want to see what we're up to. It's sobering and humbling. Maybe that's the only way you get any real humility after a while.

It's interesting to me that in all the approximately 1,700 traditional koans, there are almost *none* dealing with emotions or self-centered and inaccurate thinking—the things that are running the lives of most of us (including some so-called advanced Zen practitioners, myself included). I really appreciate Joko's working with our emotional confusions as koans. She's creating such koans for students to *become*. Although it might appear to someone who hasn't studied with her that she is working on a "strictly psychological" level, it's *not* that if one infers any separation between self and world, or self and situation (me-and-my-problem). Skillful therapy can be very valuable; however, usually its intention is not to bring one to the ultimate realization that there is no separate self. The emotion-related work Joko sometimes includes in practice involves going straight into whatever arises, as one does with a koan. At first one is aware of, then experiences, and finally *becomes* the upset (or confusion or anger) in order to see its nature. This doesn't mean acting out—that just helps you become good at being angry rather than *being anger,* which in fact doesn't feel like anything at all.

In living with Joko it's inspiring to see that she doesn't *know* anything I don't know. She's just been going through the territory of her own mind, seeing her own reactive mechanisms, for a long time, and can therefore be of use to others as a guide for them to do the same. She doesn't portray herself as having "arrived." Where can you arrive, after all? We're already here!

She lives what I would call a life-centered rather than a self-centered life, although if she were to hear me say this, she'd say, "Oh, come on!" But she's a reminder that our lives can really manifest the sutras, the precepts.

We've known each other for fifteen years. She's a most ordinary, ordinary, ordinary person. It's useful to have a student-teacher relationship—I prefer to regard her as a consultant—but whatever term you use, there's no implication that she's better, or more spiritual, or anything like that. She's a great reminder of what's already so. It's like a Greek chorus. Have you ever seen a Greek play? The characters onstage are walking across the bridge, and the chorus comes on and says, "They are now walking across the bridge." It's already happening—nobody really needs to tell us unless we're totally distracted! As far as I'm concerned, the function of a teacher is to assist one in seeing the obvious, what's immanent and observable right now. Certainly nothing special.

So there we were, back to "nothing special." Sitting at my typewriter now, I remember that sesshin, the shadows shifting on the zendo wall, the sound of passing cars, children shouting in the street, a birdcall at dawn. At breakfast, the spurt of fresh orange on my tongue. In a narrow closet, a tower of fat black pillows. In a plain yellow house on a plain, plain street.

But just inside, from a table in front of a corner window, a beautiful Kwan Yin smiled with absolute grace. By now she will have been placed elsewhere, and on the table, simply a stone.

Update: Winter 2000

Since I visited it in the early 1980s, the Zen Center of San Diego has grown significantly, not so much physically (the same house still holds most of the activities, though Joko has moved next door) but in the number of people coming to practice there. During sesshins, there are often students from all parts of the world. Joko stays in touch with many of them by phone (and there's a lot that can be sensed and cut through on the phone, she says).

We, in fact, talked by phone one late autumn afternoon in 1998. Her teaching, she said, has not particularly changed since we first spoke years ago, though it's probably "less general, more specific, more sophisticated." That means seeing things from many different angles and tailoring instruction to each individual.

More and more, Joko respects how people's differences—their degree of willingness, their age, their previous preparation—affect what works or doesn't work for them in practice. But the unwillingness to practice—to be directly *in* one's life, in the present moment, without thought—seems to be universal. "We don't think we are unwilling, but we are." How best to deal with this, however, is different for each of us.

Her own teaching may seem quite psychological at first. "But we don't stay there; we move past that." She doesn't believe she's "doing psychology" because to practice well means to see through your self, in a slow process of disillusionment. And we can't leap over anything, to reach some abstract goal. "We have to really come to terms with this peculiar notion of self we have." Enlightenment is not a thing you can chase but simply "an absence of clinging to the personal self."

She perceives how people are stuck without knowing it. "What is that? What is this stuckness?" she asks. It's like a koan: "What is it?"

But most people don't really know what practice is for at least two years, she says. For some, it can take ten, twelve, fourteen years. To learn how to keep your mind in the present moment in the midst of ordinary ups and downs takes a long time. We begin to clarify our everyday lives, and then, very slowly, the "under-pinnings" come clear, too.

Always, the crucial point is to experience *this second* of life rather than to think about it. Then "something drops away, and you are just left with the absolute." But she made clear: "You are constantly practicing with the absolute, do you see what I mean?" It is a very subtle process, learning to directly experience body sensations without thought. But she said, "that *is* the enlightened state."

Joko loves the one-on-one part of teaching, experiences it as effortless, never a burden. "It's fun to see people begin to wake up." For eight hours every week, she communicates by telephone with people living far away. "An awful lot of nonsense can get wiped out over the phone." In fact, some very strong students have been developing over the years almost entirely by telephone.

Joko is now eighty-four years old, still doing five-day sesshins and working intensively with individual students. Elizabeth Hamilton and Ezra Bayda, two of her five designated dharma successors, help Joko conduct sesshins as well as leading their own. Three other successors direct affiliated centers in Oakland, California; Champaign-Urbana, Illinois; and New York City. There is also an affiliated center in Australia. The Zen Center of San Diego can provide further information.

5

Ruth Denison

Ruth would wade through the mud to get to the stars and tell
her students to do it too, but with this proviso: "Do it with
awareness, dahling."

—Student of Ruth Denison
Summer 1986

She is a changeling, a will-o'-the-wisp, a conjurer. She is by turns
a *deva*, a queen holding court, a street urchin, an old-world peas-
ant kneading dough. She can be the embodiment of compassion,
a prima donna, a bodhisattva in velvet and lace, a wizened crone,
selflessness itself.

To meet Ruth Denison, or to talk to anyone who knows her
well, is to come away with a kaleidoscope of shifting impressions.
The one element they share is a vivid intensity.

My first encounter with her was in the winter of 1983 when she
came to Berkeley to lead a weekend retreat. The evening before it
began, I was invited to join a group of her old students who
gathered together to welcome her, share a meal, and talk with her
informally. The atmosphere in the house was festive and full of
expectation when she came down the stairs with her assistant,
Julie. Both wore long dresses, Ruth in brown, Julie in black.
Ruth's long honey-colored hair was loosely pinned back and
hung to her waist. There were necklaces and strands of beads
around her neck. As the two women reached the bottom of the
stairs, everyone below formed a double row and joined hands to
create a curving archway for them to pass through, singing a song
of celebration. Faces were shining. Feelings of love and mutuality
spun a palpable web all evening.

Ruth's face is lined and lived-in and full of animation. She has a
husky, highly expressive voice with an accent from eastern Eu-

rope, which that night traversed every nuance from gruff and no-nonsense to gentle, tender crooning. Her rapport with the assembled women was almost magnetic as she told stories of her recent adventures, listened to their replies, relished the food. Later, sitting in a circle, she elicited news and personal details from many whom she plainly knew well. (Toward me, a new face to her, she manifested little interest.) She was jaunty, serious, dramatic, empathic—and she orchestrated the flow of exchanges until far into the night.

The next morning the retreat began in the elegant shrine room of the Berkeley Dharmadhatu (a center for local students of Chögyam Trungpa, Rinpoche). It glowed with primary colors: red-and-yellow sitting cushions; red, blue, green, and gold silk banners; the shrine resplendent with flowers. Though spacious, the room was crowded. ("Eighty-seven people came, and eighty are women!" I was told.) Over the two days, cushions were arranged in different patterns, often three long rows facing three long rows, with Ruth walking up and down between them. Sometimes they all faced the front, with Ruth giving a talk or directing a guided meditation. Sometimes they were pushed to the walls so that people could move freely in the center. Sometimes we snaked in and out among the rows, experimenting with different kinds of walking. If people were expecting a traditional silent vipassana retreat, they didn't get one that weekend.

The retreat *was* about mindfulness, however. About meticulous attention to the mind-body process, introduced and guided by Ruth. The goal, she says, is opening the heart to all beings, without distinction. In the stillness created by meditation, separation between self and other dissolves. Negative factors, resistance, and hindrances disappear—and our natural humanness is expressed as compassion, loving-kindness, and wisdom.

Ruth directed our attention to our breathing, perceived at the base of the nose and upper lip. We were to be aware of all other mind-body events that arose without judging them. Restlessness is okay, she said. Boredom is okay. Resistance is okay. Stubbornness is okay. Discomfort is okay. (However, if it becomes too intense, stand up or sit on the benches at the sides of the room.)

But there were no long, silent sittings. The sittings were always punctuated by guidance, encouragement, clarification.

Walking meditation was presented with care, with minute attention to lifting each foot, reaching, stepping. Four circles of people walked very slowly for periods of twenty to thirty minutes around the long rows of cushions. Then there were breaks for stretching and massaging both oneself and a partner.

On the second day Ruth led us in many different varieties of walking: fast; on toes; stiff-legged; one leg stiff, one lifted; circling; circling on toes and singing; slow; and finally reaching for the hands of the person opposite, raising arms, looking into the other's eyes, seeing them as your own, closing your eyes, lowering arms, then moving to our places for a final sitting. Also that day Ruth led us in a "sweeping" meditation taught by her teacher U Ba Khin, in which microscopic attention is directed to each part of the body in turn, from the top of the head to the toes, inside and outside (e.g., the space between the ears, the throat, the outside of the neck, the scalp)—all counterpointed with breath awareness. My own concentration and awareness became very heightened during this experience.

Throughout the two days, Ruth sustained a loving atmosphere. The final sitting was graced with flowers, and, as we faced each other (three rows facing three rows), she led an extended *metta* (loving-kindness) meditation.

Later that evening I was able to talk with Ruth for an hour or so before she left town again early next morning. (Her students describe her as endlessly coming and going, often arriving or leaving unpredictably.)

Ruth was born in 1922 in East Prussia, near the Russian border. In the 1940s she became a civilian prisoner in a Russian labor camp, but near the end of the war managed to escape, running ahead of the Russian troops while the Allied bombing was going on. When the war was over, she returned to look for her family but was caught and placed in another camp for nine months. The inmates here were mostly women—about two thousand of them, she said—and most of them died "like flies" of diseases, though she herself stayed healthy. In 1956, she moved to the United States and began working as a teacher in Los Angeles. There she married a man from an old American family who for some years had been an ordained monk in the Ramakrishna Order (Vedanta). In the early sixties they were socializing and hosting seminars for people like Alan Watts, Laura Huxley, Krishnamurti, and Gerald Heard. It was during this period as well that she and her husband traveled to Burma to study with the renowned meditation master U Ba Khin at the International Meditation Center in Rangoon.

For endless hours Ruth would sit in a little hut below the temple. At 2:30 in the morning the master would arrive and say, "You sit here and watch your breath," and there she sat till 11:00 at night. She saw her teacher only ten minutes a day. At 7:00 P.M. U Ba Khin would come back to check on her. One had to stay at least four weeks at a time. "But I took to his teaching like a duck to water, darling," she said (pronouncing it "dahling" in her striking accent). "It was so clear and convincing. I had delight in it and progressed rapidly." She received dharma transmission in 1969. Only four Westerners were acknowledged in this way, and she was the only woman. But her "depth, confidence, and clear understanding" apparently overcame any hesitation there might have been on this score.

Ruth speculated that her teacher might be shocked at the way she is teaching now. "Though probably not," she decided. "He too was a pioneer" (having given a Western woman transmission of the dharma). "When there is strong awareness, one can be creative. A new approach is no problem." *Change* and *observation* are the keys to her teaching. Sitting in the traditional way is not enough for dealing with all our neuroses, trips, and daydreams, she believes. So she uses body movement to make feelings and sensations more vivid and available. When people are having a difficult time in meditation, she can say, "Okay, let's stand up now and move." Then the mind becomes more stabilized, and interested too. And awareness develops more quickly. "After all, in a weekend I only have two days to teach the entire dharma!"

When Ruth conducts retreats she uses "spirit power," not her mind. She feels tuned in to every person in the room. "I bother with everybody," she said. "I teach like the Buddha." Whatever she does comes from the heart, from wisdom energy, in her words, and not from the thinking self.

"What I'm interested in is the transformation of society," she went on. Through true attention to the body, mind, and heart, people become more sensitive, less violent, more balanced in their thinking. "It's not so important if I have them sitting cross-legged or in a chair. The method is just a vehicle."

She was pleased with the quality of mindfulness during the past weekend. Had I noticed people's responsiveness? How they were "tuned in" even at mealtimes? "I was really touched, darling."

Ruth also underwent Zen training for two years in Japan (1964–1966), studying with Soen-roshi, Yamada-roshi, and Yasutani-roshi, and she did koan training with Maezumi-roshi in Los Angeles. Soen-roshi, she said, was particularly supportive of her vipassana background. While some of the greatest Zen masters understand the importance of the Theravada tradition as a base, it is unfortunate for many Zen practitioners, she feels, that the accurate teaching of mindfulness is often forgotten in that tradition.

Ruth is not particularly interested in talking about her private life. The teacher should be in the background, like a good friend, she says, "What we want is to reduce 'I' and 'self.' People get so hooked on the personality of the teacher that all their attention flows into that. Why is my personality so important?" She feels that her approach—with its intensity, devotion, and openness—invites people to open their hearts, to see themselves as they are, and to *let go* of personality.

When she is not teaching, Ruth lives in the Hollywood hills with her husband and is "inventive as a housewife," she says. She gardens, bakes bread, feeds wild animals and stray students. These days she particularly enjoys working with women students. "I like them. They're like myself." She appreciates their pioneering spirit, their sense of inquiry and search for new values. Many of her students, especially on the West Coast, she said, are women who have challenged traditional forms of society and who have turned away from heterosexual relationships. She emphasized, however, that "we are not women gathering as a group against men. But, to find our own strength and new responsibilities, we need this time to be by ourselves."

On the East Coast and in Europe, by contrast, most of her students are men. With all of them, she said, she gives her whole heart. It is not unusual for her to hold interviews till midnight.

"But that is my life. I feel my time is their time." It isn't even a matter of choice anymore, she said. "You just notice this dharma energy in yourself, and you cannot do otherwise." She feels her personality has subsided and that there is no longer anyone to choose. She simply does what has to be done.

As we said goodbye, her last words were, "Have a good Christmas, darling."

In order to augment my relatively brief contact with Ruth, I spoke at some length with two of her long-time students. The first had been her assistant for two years, living with her at Dhamma Dena (Ruth's retreat center in the California desert) and traveling with her to retreats in different parts of the United States. Now she has settled in northern California and is leading retreats of her own.

When she first met Ruth, she had already been involved with vipassana meditation for some time. She was on the staff at the Insight Meditation Society in Barre, Massachusetts, and for two years had been living the life of a renunciate—"the closest you could get to being a nun that I knew of: a simple, surrendered kind of existence," that included wearing the same cotton Indian dress day after day.

Then Ruth arrived. "She flowed in, in her lace and velvet, and I was so stunned! It took years before I really integrated it, but now I realize that what Ruth succeeded in communicating to me was that it was okay to be a woman in that [Theravada] tradition. It was okay to be outrageous. It was okay to be who you were." She had been so accustomed to reserve, humility, and self-effacement. And here was this outspoken woman, unabashedly polarizing people in all directions.

"She fully understands that she makes people uncomfortable. She says, 'They're sleeping out there. Wake them up!' I think she has a bit of the Zen master in her. At Dhamma Dena, you're fair game at all times. If you get into her space, she assumes she has the right to work with you. When challenged she says, 'When you come as a student, it is my duty to teach you rightly the dharma.'

"I remember one night we were getting ready for a retreat, and she had just arrived from Los Angeles with her big station wagon loaded with produce, and it all had to be unloaded and put away. Finally, about midnight, it was done, and I was so exhausted, and the retreat started next morning. In comes Ruth and says, 'Darling, why don't we bake bread tonight? It will be so hot in the morning, don't you want to bake *now* while it's cool?' But I'd been working all day, making granola and all the other things you do before retreats, and I was exhausted. I couldn't believe she was suggesting it. I don't know what I said, but she took one look at me and said, 'It's okay, you go to bed and I'll make the bread.' And my mind just stopped. What became clear was that what I was calling exhaustion was primarily resistance to what was happening in the moment. I realized it was no different than somebody saying, 'Why don't you meditate all night?' Ruth has a way of showing up when you're right at your edge and suggesting that you go beyond it.

"It's almost as if she plays the part of the roshi and also all the other officers in the zendo who come around and prop you up and poke you and wake you up. She's playing all the roles, and that can be exhausting! It took me a few years before I could say, 'Thank you for your teaching, and I will go to bed tonight.'"

"Does Ruth have inexhaustible energy?" I asked.

"She has very, very long-running energy, yes. A lot more than most of us, and she feels she is just doing what has to be done. Dhamma Dena is a very busy place. Something is always being built or renovated. There's never an end to what's going to be done there. It took me a long time to realize that, that there wasn't going to be an end to it. She sees work as part of the practice. And she sees her function as the awakening one, the one who stirs things up."

I recalled that there was not a lot of silence at the retreat I'd attended, and I asked if that was characteristic.

"She does more talking and guiding than most teachers. It's difficult for me at times. You have to know what your limit is *and* you have to take the whole package. My role is not to judge her but to love her. Also to let her know how things affect me, which I didn't do in the beginning, except indirectly, which isn't very skillful. This is a new part of my relationship with her, and a new part of my own development in relationship to authority and power. There's such a division between that person over there who's 'the teacher'—even if it's a woman—and the people out here who are 'learning.' It creates a separation (produced by our egos) that we ultimately need to go beyond.

"But particularly with Ruth, what I see is that the more I trust my own perceptions with objectivity and nondefensiveness, the more she trusts me and we can see each other as equals. And that's when we begin to have fun together!

"Ruth has done an incredibly pioneering thing, you know," she went on. "Her teacher U Ba Khin didn't teach people to move around the room and feel their hand touching the air or moving through space. She has a gift for very carefully guiding a group experience that evokes a vivid physical presence in the body, an experience of awareness that reaches a cellular level." (My own experience at the weekend retreat confirmed this.)

She had brought along some pictures to show me, of Ruth conducting vipassana meditation by means of movement experiences during a retreat in Germany. "She guides movement in a very spontaneous, intuitive way that brings you back again and again to where you are."

"What I see in the pictures is great simplicity and naturalness of movement," I said.

"Yes. It's natural and it's aware. Not frivolous at all."

She went on to describe the way Ruth has combined the clear, focused "linear" approach of the traditional teaching (where one may sit alone in a cell all day minutely observing one's physical sensations, feelings, and thoughts) with her own spontaneous kind of movement/awareness. "Given my own conditioning, I think it was perhaps helpful to me that I had experienced more traditional, structured retreats before I met Ruth. However, I see that many people, particularly women, connect right away to her intuitive approach."

She feels that Ruth's body-centered integration of the two approaches—her cultivation of awareness through psychophysical movement—is a pioneering feminist contribution. I asked if this might explain why Ruth has attracted so many women, and especially lesbian women, to her center in the desert.

"Yes—aside from the fact that she was the first to hold retreats for women at all—I think it is her intuitive use of movement which brings women together and adds joy to the training. It's also the way she improvises with the daily structure." When I asked for details, she said that one can't count on anything, things are very spontaneous, and the day just evolves and unfolds.

"You mean no schedule?"

"There is a schedule, but within that Ruth is very flexible. For instance, sometimes we'll end up sitting again after everyone thought they were ready for sleep. Because she gets you up and moving, you start experiencing yourself again, you're present, and then—oh! There's the energy again! She's also a master of ritual. She incorporates ritual for its true purpose of evoking awareness. She brings it all back to the dharma."

She became reflective and then added, "I remember one night at a women's retreat, she had turned on some music, and we were moving, dancing. Then she noticed that some of the women had begun moving carelessly. She turned off the music and said, 'You must stay conscious. You must move sensitively. I go into the fire with you! We're not doing this to entertain ourselves. We're learning to be aware and to know what we're doing.' She gets under your skin. She doesn't let you drift. It can be very uncomfortable. And you have to take responsibility for yourself. You can't just 'hang out in the sitting posture.' She'll say, 'You old students— you petrified ones! You've been sitting like that for years. What are you doing?' She has a way of using language that brings us back to ourselves, that wakes us up."

R. is a thirty-nine-year-old political activist, lesbian, and performance artist who has been a student of Ruth's for eight years. Once she started attending retreats and practicing on her own, she was an assiduous student and was acknowledged by Ruth for her "right effort." Nevertheless, she "hated every minute" of it for a very long time.

From the beginning, it was important to R. that Ruth was a woman. She wanted to be free of male judgments, male values, and male standards of linear thinking and intellectuality. One of the most striking aspects of Ruth's teaching for her is that "she allows herself to be everything she is." She dares to make mistakes, be angry, be wrong. "Sometimes she's outrageous. But her outrageousness serves the purpose of getting our attention. She's always looking for new ways. And she's so loving. Amazingly loving." For many women like R., who have had negative relationships with their mothers, this can be transformative.

But for two and a half years, she hated it. "I hated the meditation. I had so much restlessness. It was the dharma talks that got me. I saw there was another way to live. There was more to this existence than was apparent on a superficial level. I'd had glimpses of it, but didn't know how to go deeper, because that takes discipline, it takes form, it takes a teacher. And it takes a long time. I never would have been able to sit in the traditional way—sit, walk, sit, walk, sit, walk. I still have a hard time with that.

"But when I sit with women, it's different. One of the things about Ruth is her flexibility. And she's completely impromptu. She creates rituals on the spot—any celebration that comes along: Halloween, full moon, Mother's Day, dedication of the zendo. Once her ninety-year-old mother was there, and we dressed up in all these bits and pieces of things Ruth's collected over the years. She's a scavenger, collects everything. She's built up Dhamma Dena—aside from student's contributions—through scavenging a lot."

R. said she'd been on mixed retreats (with men) as well and had noticed that Ruth allows more of her spontaneity to come through with women—her "Ruthness" rather than her "teacherness." In Europe, on the other hand, she's reported to be much more formal, "Mrs. Denison," with a wholly different persona. With each group of people, or each individual, R. says, Ruth senses and responds to them where they are, in their own language.

In addition to the way Ruth works with body awareness, breathing, and movement, R. described her presentation of "seeing" as a path to awareness. Perhaps at sunset she would take them all outside and ask them to close their eyes. Then they would be asked to open them slowly, to look down, and simply see what was right in front of them, all the tiny things close to their eyes. Then, very slowly, they'd look up and see the sand and the bushes and the mountains in the background and, still farther up, see the clouds, and way up, all the way up, see far into the distance, seeing the haziness or the brightness or the colors in the sky. And then come slowly down again, lingering on a detail here and there, perhaps closing and reopening their eyes, feeling the sensations inside their eyes, feeling the walls that hold the eyeballs there, the "envelope" and all the tissues.

R. said that she felt happy there for the first time in her life. She always slept outside in the desert, watching the incredible night sky. Ruth would say, "Take it all out into the desert. The desert can hold it all." And there was a lot to hold. People often had a hard time. There would be tears and sobbing. "You meet yourself, you meet all those places that have been covered over and you don't want to meet. I was in resistance for almost three years. I used to count the minutes till break. How long till lunch? How long till sleep?"

The desert in the springtime is extraordinary. One year it had rained more than usual, and everything was greener than it had been in fifty years. The entire desert floor was green and covered with flowers. And there were rabbits and coyotes and rattle-snakes. In the fall there are tarantulas. The tarantulas aren't poi-sonous, R. said, they just move along in the desert with you. When you're doing walking meditation, you find a path and walk back and forth, and you can walk along with the tarantulas. They go very slowly, she said, and are actually quite beautiful.

One day, after working with Ruth for about three and a half years, R. had an experience in the zendo of deeply letting go, sinking into herself, and "feeling the movement of the breath and beingness." Her restlessness had ceased. When she saw Ruth she felt very quiet and just told her she was happy. And Ruth began to cry. She had seen this student coming to retreats three or four times a year, hating every minute. Now her tears came, and for R. it was another precious experience of Ruth's ability to be there with her in the present moment, whatever it happened to be.

Another time, R. was struggling with feelings of jealousy that had surfaced for the first time in relation to Ruth. She wanted her all to herself! Ruth helped her see that the jealousy—attaching her suffering to the suffering of another—was where she was stuck. And one evening, in a flash of insight, she actually per-ceived her envy leap out of her body and attach itself to another woman. It was unmistakable that she was the source, she was doing it, it had nothing to do with anyone else. "All of our stuff is like that. It's us. It's me. We project it."

This is not a psychological realization, according to R. "It's on a different level. One thing therapy never gave me was compassion for myself." For her, Ruth's particular strength is teaching compassion—for oneself, for the world, for human suffering. She manifests compassion in a very nonattached way. And before R. ever "got the awareness stuff—the meat of meditation—I got the compassion." She says she had all the hindrances to right-mindedness: sloth and torpor, restlessness, doubt, aversion, and desire. "I was sunk in all of those, especially restlessness. And doubt. And self-hatred."

But Ruth began to teach her to be happy even when she was miserable. "This is your livingness," she would say. "This is a living being, and this is your beingness at this moment."

"When you grow up depressed, as I did," R. reflected, "how can you open to life and not judge it? How do you accept the experiences that come to you? It's not easy. It's not something you're taught in Western civilization at all. It's that tiny difference that's made by the witnessing mind that separates you just a tad from what you're going through."

R.'s early conditioning was to be highly intellectual and judgmental, of herself and everything else. Ruth has given her a tool that cuts right through her judgments, and that tool is compassion, which Ruth manifests all the time, she said, in everything she does. She also feels Ruth has helped her plumb the darkness in herself, "the power of the deep feminine which is the pathway to the self."

Ruth manifests a woman's consciousness and a woman's sensibility, says R. "And we want it from her. That's the fine-tuning you pick up. Because of her complete immersion in the dharma, she stretches herself in a unique fashion, giving us the gift that allows each of us to stretch ourselves the way only we can stretch."

Some teachers teach vipassana. Ruth *is* vipassana, R. concluded. From the very beginning she taught that the Buddha did not have to be a man, that the enlightened mind has no sex, and that it is present—right now—in each one of us.

RUTH DENISON

Update: Winter 2000

Ruth Denison is seventy-six years old now, and she has begun to notice how formidable the summertime desert heat can be in Joshua Tree, California, where her center, Dhamma Dena, is located. "Sometimes I chant when I walk through the heat," she told me, in her quite noticeable Prussian accent. "It gives me strength to endure that enormous impact. I am close to fainting sometimes. People can die here from the heat, but I do not fear that. I chant my vows. I know I'm in the service of the dharma, and I move through (while everyone else is quivering with fear, thinking I should stay inside)." Nevertheless, all summer long, she "commutes" from her office to her house (it takes 375 steps and three to five minutes to cover the distance).

Her husband, from whom she has been separated for many years, has Alzheimer's disease now. She honors her commitment to care for him and has brought him to the center. "He is eighty-eight, just living in pajamas, and not walking except with the aid of a walker. He comes out and says, 'What are we up to?' I say, 'Darling, maybe we have some breakfast.' 'I'm not hungry!' Then, after a while, he asks, 'Well, what's for breakfast?' A minute later, he does not know what he has said, so I sometimes cook three times for one meal."

Close by, there are six small, fully equipped cabins that belong to the center. Ruth rents them out inexpensively to students who wish to live a simple life near a dharma center. At any one time, there might be an ex-professor, a pizza company executive, a sculptor, and a burned-out musician living separately in each cabin. "I can hardly cover expenses," Ruth says, "but I am feeling good. They are in a good place."

Until recently, a recovering alcoholic with advanced cancer was living in one of the cabins. But during the annual monthlong winter holiday retreat (attended by thirty full-time people and about seventy who came for shorter stays), this man moved close to death. Ruth had never sat with a dying person before. Still, "Three nights without sleep I was with him. He trusted me, and I would say, 'Tom, I came to breathe with you. Would you like it?' 'Groannnnn.' So then I soothed his blistered mouth with water, and I would talk. This man was not a meditator and had no sense of mindfulness or of his body, so I guided him through the steps of paying attention to breathing and the body in very elementary ways. He then got calm and could breathe better and in a more relaxed way. He got into more rhythmic, quiet breathing and was more accepting of what he was doing. He knew he was dying. 'Tom,' I would tell him, 'do not be afraid of where you are going now. Breathe out into the desert, where there is love and a wide, beautiful space, and where you will be comforted. You will be received in it. There is nothing to fear. And when you breathe out, breathe out to the coyotes and to the rabbits and to the tortoises. Go forward. Come and tell us, we are behind you, we want to know. Be the leader and go!' After the third time of such encouragement, he breathed out, and it was finished. Interesting, this phenomenon of life and death. I had not studied the process or assistance of dying, but after Tom had died, I went to the *Tibetan Book of the Dead*. I found that I had naturally or intuitively been in accordance with its teaching."

(Ruth encouraged me to relate these aspects of her daily life because she believes that some teachers these days are getting lost in techniques while losing the breadth and connectedness of the dharma. Her own strength is bringing the spiritual realm "into this plane" and not expecting anything in return. "No more karma for me," she said.

I do want to convey something of the poignance and particularity of this unique teacher and hope some taste of it comes through.)

Dhamma Dena now comprises 17.5 acres, with four substantial buildings and many smaller outbuildings. Over time, flushing toilets have been added, but some people still prefer the more water-conserving outhouses. Last year, the zendo was enlarged, and a whole new addition was built, which houses a tea kitchen, a small library, and a bathroom. Today, Dhamma Dena can comfortably accommodate at least thirty-five guests.

At this writing, twelve to fifteen of Ruth's senior students have become teachers themselves. Guiding and inspiring students to take the Buddha dharma out into the world is one of her passions. Everything she does on the physical plane (managing and sustaining her land and center as well as this intensive work with students) is dedicated to nurturing and spreading the dharma in the West, keeping the roots safe, so that it becomes part of the culture here and not just "an enthusiastic temporary thing."

Looking out at the world, seeing the extent of individual and environmental suffering, Ruth says: "I feel the pain of dukkha, yah! Deep, deep, like the Buddha, when you read his discourses on the First Noble Truth. He says there is no subject more important to contemplate than suffering. I begin to comprehend the pervasiveness of it. I see the grief and the pain from the prisons to the hospitals to the dentists [she laughs], to the farmers, to the low-income people here in the desert where I live. It flows out, my compassion, to the forest and the whales, to all beings, including animals and plants."

When one deeply understands what the Buddha is saying, Ruth believes that qualities like compassion are "no problem; it is there!" She feels there is no limit to who we are: we are a field of energy endowed with consciousness that can flow out to everything there is. "I am not a separate entity; I am rather without boundaries, yah? Because in all phenomena, the same energies function. The physicists tell us we are not a solid mass of something; we are just energy in flux, like everything else, animated and unanimated. Wherever you look, you are in contact and see the context, and the situation presents itself clearly as it really is in true nature. Life."

The desert, she feels, is especially conducive to this kind of perception. One lives in a field of "open space, vast, a mesa surrounded at the horizon by mountains, with snow peaks until June. So barren, so naked, so truthful. Nothing is hidden; everything is presenting itself as it is."

6

Bobby Rhodes

If you need good words to feel good about yourself, then it's devastating when someone gives you bad words. Neither one needs to touch you. Your mind doesn't have to move with either. You're right there the next moment. I think that's the goods you get from sitting and practicing. That is Zen—being able to answer the next moment with no trace of the last.

—Bobby Rhodes

A beautifully crafted temple gate, bearing Oriental characters on both tall wooden stanchions, is silhouetted against a clear New England sky. Beyond it, above a small rise, a graceful two-story building is topped with a dramatically curving and ornamented roof. Chinese? Japanese? a passer-by might wonder. Actually, it is of traditional Korean design, executed by the American students of Korean Zen Master Seung Sahn, or Soen Sa Nim, as his students call him. A wooden plaque at the top of the gate announces that this is the Providence Zen Center (though technically it is in Cumberland, Rhode Island). It comprises a large community of about fifty residents, with a new monastery for male and female monks, and a strong traditional daily practice.

As I was to learn firsthand, every day here begins at 5:00 A.M. with 108 full prostrations in the dharma hall—a strenuous, exhilarating way to greet the morning. After fifteen minutes for rest and tea, the first sitting of the day starts at 5:30. Bowing and chanting are very important aspects of Korean practice and precede most periods of zazen. The morning and evening bell chants, performed by senior students, are hauntingly beautiful.

In the fall of 1983 I spent several days at PZC, following the daily schedule, talking to students, and interviewing Barbara Rhodes (known to everyone as Bobby). She was one of the first two students to be named Master Dharma Teacher by Soen Sa Nim in 1978. Today she is one of six, but still the only woman. In addition to her teaching duties at the center and elsewhere, she is a part-time registered nurse, a wife, and the mother of a young daughter, Annie. Bobby's manner is direct, totally unpretentious, totally human.

At the time of my visit, she and her family lived across the street from the center in a smallish downstairs apartment in a house shared with other students of Soen Sa Nim. Bobby sorted and folded laundry at the kitchen table as we talked. (This was her own family's laundry, but someone told me later that she does all the center's laundry as well.) From time to time she also had to check the basement where a broken cistern had caused some flooding. There is nothing esoteric about Bobby's life. And that is entirely consonant with the style of practice presented by her teacher. "Doing your job one hundred percent" is what it's all about. "If you just pay attention moment to moment, then you'll become a Zen master," she said. And at that instant it was not clear who was talking, Bobby or Soen Sa Nim.

Bobby began her life in Providence, Rhode Island, in 1948. She was the second of four children in a Navy family that moved at least every two years during her childhood. (She spent first grade in California; second grade in Newport, Rhode Island; third and fourth grades in Wisconsin; and fifth grade through half of ninth grade in California.) I commented that she learned early about impermanence.

"I did," she replied. "And that was really important for me. Because it's hard. In fifth grade I went to three different schools. I was eleven years old and just starting puberty. My breasts were starting to appear and all those hormones were starting to work. My parents were not getting along, my mother had severe asthma, and it was horrible. Yet, when I look back on it, I see that it was a really good situation. Soen Sa Nim always says a bad situation is a good situation. It was so bad it was good. I began to really question, 'What is happening?'"

Bobby was the one her mother turned to when she was very ill. "I've always had nursing-type karma," she said. Still, it was "heavy duty" to be called home from school to take care of a mother unable to breathe.

Afterward, in nursing school, she perceived an entirely new realm of suffering. Her inner questioning became more intense. She wasn't like the other women around her, who were mostly "into giggling and all-night parties." What she calls her "Buddhist karma" had already taught her to rise early, without effort. She would be up at 4:30 or 5:00 to study every morning.

When she completed nursing school her life looked quite rosy. On the physical plane, she could have had anything she wanted—money, car, boyfriend, apartment. "But it was empty. I was very straight in a way, and if I didn't get married and have a house in the suburbs, it was unclear to me where I was going." She applied to the Peace Corps, but there was a long waiting list for nurses, so instead she went to California to work at a free clinic for Mexican farm laborers. This was the psychedelic era of the mid-sixties, and in due course she was introduced to psychotropic drugs. Suddenly she realized that human consciousness was vaster by far than anything she'd experienced before. "I got in touch with the trees and the earth, the moon, people, and myself. Before that I'd always had a 'big question,' but I didn't have any elevation of consciousness."

The Episcopal Church, in which she had been raised, had felt "dead" to her. But now she began to have experiences of God that were alive. She used drugs to "get clear," as a kind of meditation, often out in the woods with a friend. But after two years the experiences started to repeat themselves. She realized she was no longer learning anything new.

And then someone gave her a book about Zen. It was D. T. Suzuki's first book, *Manual of Zen Buddhism,* and it was "perfect," she says. Although it did not refer to meditation at all, it was the philosophy that struck her: that truth is to be found right here, in the present moment. She was galvanized by Suzuki's statement that enlightenment is equivalent to paying attention, moment after moment after moment. She began looking for a Zen master. And, almost immediately, she met Soen Sa Nim.

Her parents had retired to Rhode Island, and Bobby was visiting them there. She was unclear about almost everything, except that she was looking for a teacher, but decided to look for an apartment. At the very first one she looked at, she discovered a Korean monk living downstairs who repaired washing machines. "It could have been anybody, but it was Soen Sa Nim." Though he knew very little English, he was soon teaching her about Buddhism. And gradually they set up a schedule, sitting at regular times of the day, getting up at a certain time in the morning, and other people began to join them. Bobby had a nursing job, working nights from 11:00 P.M. to 7:00 A.M. After dinner with her parents she would drive to the center to chant and sit from 7:00 till 8:30 P.M. Then she'd sleep for two hours. Soen Sa Nim would wake her and say, "Time to go to work." And she'd dash off to work and come back to sit and chant again the next evening.

On the weekends there would be a dharma talk, with Soen Sa Nim speaking in Japanese and someone translating into English. Gradually it began to sink into Bobby's consciousness what it was she should be doing when she meditated. Soen Sa Nim did not stress breathing techniques or holding koans. "He always just said, 'Go straight, don't know.' As soon as he learned to say that, that's all he ever said! So that was it. And it's been great because through the years I've realized that's one of the best things you can tell someone, and just let them flounder, let them try it. Specific techniques are helpful to some people, but I think that ultimately you have to let go of those things and just ask: *What is this?*"

In recent years Bobby has visited other centers and experienced other teachings. When she comes back and talks to Soen Sa Nim about them, he'll say, "Yes, that's good, that's okay, but most important is 'don't know.'" His emphasis is on the clarity of your mind, moment to moment in everyday life, not just on the cushion. Ninety percent of our life is spent outside the zendo, Bobby says, "bouncing off our situation." Soen Sa Nim's strongest teaching has always been just "What is this?" No technique, no koan, no particular kind of breathing. And there's a very subtle difference, she feels, between this approach and even letting go of Mu.

"For me right now, for instance, it's just to look at your face and to experience your face. Mu is you," Bobby said. "Soen Sa

Nim says, 'Don't let Mu get in between you.' Between you and your child or between you and your car when you're driving." At Providence Zen Center, she said, people are more interested in bodhisattva action, in trying to make their communities clear, than in having a very strong sitting practice. This reflects their teacher too. For Soen Sa Nim, sitting itself is not the priority.

Once Bobby did a retreat with Robert Aitken-roshi in Hawaii. She was impressed by the focus on breathing as a kind of anchor and as a means of deepening the meditation. When she returned to PZC she thought she'd experiment a bit with this technique in her own retreats. She suggested that people breathe out "Don't know" rather than "Mu." Soen Na Nim was away at the time, but when he returned and heard what she had done, he "just gave me hell. He really screamed at me for a minute, which is his Korean way of dealing with things. He didn't have to scream, but it was okay. He really impressed me with it."

"It was okay?" I asked.

"It wasn't okay at the time. I felt very upset, but that was his way. And I really accept him as my teacher. He didn't have to scream. I would have heard him if he had sat down with me and looked me in the face and said, 'Now, Bobby . . .' But that's not his style. If he's upset he just flares out. It was all right. I started to cry. But that was okay. We stayed with it for quite a while. He saw I was upset and hugged me and said, 'Bobby you're wonderful, but I just want you to listen to me.'"

"You're not supposed to deviate at all?"

"Yes, somewhat. But he wants us to all talk about it before we do it."

Interestingly enough, Soen Sa Nim gives his students authority to teach earlier, Bobby thinks, than any other teacher. She had been practicing only five years when, along with one other student, he gave her *inka* (dharma transmission). When someone is clear, he recognizes it, Bobby said, man or woman. "If someone is shining, *everyone* wants it, loves it, recognizes it."

If there is a lot of male energy at Providence Zen Center, Bobby was well prepared for it by her early family experience. "We lived on Navy bases quite often, with a male structure, and I figured that was the way it was. In the dining room my father had the only chair with arms on it, and he always sat at the head of the table. The message was very clear. And he still has an important place in my life. He is very strong and in some ways wise and honest. I took it from my father and I take it from Soen Sa Nim. And I don't feel that I *shouldn't* take it from them. My father can still intimidate me. I don't like the intimidation part, but I can appreciate some of the authority he has over me. It's okay.

"What's great about Soen Sa Nim is that he teaches you to believe in yourself. The more you understand yourself, the more you see that it's neither male nor female nor both. It's just you. It's your energy. It's what you've got right now, your collected karma that makes you you. A lot of masculine energy sometimes comes out of me, too. The clearer we get, the more we use reserves from both those sides, and they don't feel like two sides. It's just you.

"There's a part of me that is more accepting of some of the limitations that have been put on women, that some women get angry about. I don't feel like going out and pounding nails on the temple all day long, building buildings, or dealing with administrative or legal matters the way my husband does. I don't have that kind of energy. It's not that I value these things differently. Someone needs to be doing the things I'm doing at home. And I'm good at it, and it feels right. I'm doing what I'm doing and that's me, and that's neat. I think that's what we all need to get to. Plus," she added, characteristically, "try to do a little more."

More disquieting, perhaps, were incidents that have taken place during trips to Korea with her teacher and her husband, Linc; during a large international assembly that took place at PZC when she found herself "in the shadows, completely"; and during visits to Korean families in this country. Bobby was one of Soen Sa Nim's first students and became a dharma teacher before Linc did. But he has a doctoral degree from MIT and was abbot of PZC, credentials which Bobby told me are impressive to Koreans. So invariably, upon meeting people from that country, Bobby suddenly becomes "Linc's wife" and is introduced only after he is. She understands the cultural dynamics, but her "small mind" still sometimes cares, and her ego wants to shout, "Recognize me, too! I'm just as important as he is!" It's not easy when Soen Sa Nim starts acting "very Korean" and treats her more like an attendant than a student ("Get me my shoes, get me my coat, you sit here and I sit there"). But she also feels that it has helped her practice, that it is good teaching, although it may seem severe. It's a matter of seeing what's necessary in each moment, she feels, not getting hung up on form, but following the flow of the immediate situation.

Bobby agrees with Soen Sa Nim that women have a different job than men, not better or higher class, just different. "And men have different hangups than we do," she adds. "I think they're a little more attached to power than women are. If we were as attached to power as they are, we'd be up there being army generals too. We need to learn from each other. I need to learn from Linc how he puts so much energy out into the world. And he needs to learn from me how to be more intimate."

On the second night of my visit, there was a high-spirited Halloween party at the center. People loaned me scarves and feathers and other oddments so I could put together a costume, and everyone dressed up in fanciful disguises. There were skits and contests and food and general hilarity, and we all got to bed very late. Nevertheless, most people were up before dawn the next morning and bowing together in the meditation hall at 5:00 A.M. This is an example of what Soen Sa Nim calls "together action." If you follow his teaching, there is no vacation. Every day of the week there is practice, without exception. He says, "If you have vacation mind, then you can't finish your work, your great work of life and death. If you have vacation mind, you never grow strong."

But after breakfast that day my eyes were smarting and it was hard to keep them open. Bobby and I continued our conversation, and she admitted that it had been hard for her also to get up that morning. But she knew that if she went to practice, it would help everybody else. "To me, practicing is perseverance," she said. No matter how tired she is, when she is working full-time and doing all the household things as well, she will almost always be in the dharma room on time. (If she needs a fifteen-minute nap, an inner alarm will wake her in time to get there.) Just getting there, day after day, year after year, has helped her more than her actual concentration power on the cushion, she believes. "If you keep going, then you start to burn your karma." The whole point at PZC is long-term "together action," letting go of one's opinions, conditioning, and personal situations, and acting with others over and over again. Eating with others—taking just an orange, perhaps—even if you're not hungry. Attending work periods and practice even when you need a break—if not 100 percent of the time, then 95 percent of the time.

As she talked, I had the uncomfortable feeling that if I were to follow such a schedule for an extended period of time, I would probably begin to feel like running away somewhere, just for an hour by myself. "What would you say to me?" I asked.

"You should run away if you need to and find your own balance," she said. It's her conviction that a Zen center should have a reasonable schedule, but also a *difficult* schedule. Otherwise, growth will be slower. There is something to self-denial, she feels, and to working hard, to getting a little less food, a little less sleep. It may seem like hard training, but her observation is that this generation in America is ready for it. In Asia right now, there are no lay communities like this one. But because in the last couple of decades many Americans (often young and middle-class) were ripe for this kind of discipline, teachers like Soen Sa Nim, Maezumi Roshi, and Suzuki Roshi came to the United States when they did.

"Soen Sa Nim brought his monastic system to us, and we bit. We wanted it. It's still wonderful to me. Getting up with everybody and bowing and chanting this morning—I loved it."

Bobby believes it's a lot harder to keep one's practice strong if one lives outside a Zen center. It's a rare person who can keep strong practice going without the support of formal structure. Regularity is crucial. Soen Sa Nim uses the analogy of water dripping on a stone. If it hits the same spot month after month, year after year, it will make a deep groove. So he says we need to hit our practice in the same place day after day, month after month, year after year. If you're not consistent and play games with yourself, there is a host of demons who will sabotage you.

For Bobby, living in the Zen center keeps her practice "hot." For example, she had been asked to cook lunch that day because no one else had signed up. And that was great, she said. Not that she felt like cooking lunch. She was tired too. But she agreed to cook lunch nonetheless, and she believes that made her stronger. She finds her tolerance a hundred times greater today than it was twelve years ago. Many people get anxious or annoyed when they feel they're being pushed. "Me, I'm so used to getting pushed or pulled that I hardly notice it—and it's helped me grow. It's not everybody's correct situation, but it's a great way to practice if you can do it. Dogen said that one moment of clear mind is one moment of enlightenment. Whatever your job, if you do it one hundred percent, that's enlightenment."

The dining area at PZC is a long, narrow, sunny room at the bottom of a short flight of stairs just outside the kitchen. People sit silently in two rows, facing each other, arranging their bowls and utensils meticulously in front of them, repeating the mealtime chants, bowing to the servers. Everyone follows the ritualized procedure for accepting or refusing food with the proper gestures, using the proper sequence of bowls, eating quickly and without pauses, correctly receiving hot tea for washing up at the end of the meal, washing each bowl and utensil in proper order, drinking down the used tea, receiving clean rinse water from a server (in the most economical amount possible), and drying and rewrapping bowls and utensils in prescribed fashion, silently, with no extra movements. The whole process can be a graceful collective expression of gratitude and appreciation for the food received, a means of maintaining practice-mind during these regular interludes of replenishing our bodies, and a most efficient way to accomplish community mealtimes with great dispatch.

For me, however (a slow eater by constitution or conditioning), this part of the daily schedule soon took on a tone of high stress and strategy. Since one has to finish every morsel of food in one's bowls before washing them, and since each phase of the complicated dance has to be completed by everyone before the next one begins, I found myself desperately resorting to shameful tactics. Once I stuffed almonds up my sleeve. And once I pressed cherry tomatoes under the elastic ankle bands of my sweat pants. Once I actually dropped a bowl of rinse water. In the ensuing silence my face flamed and my heart must have been audible to all my neighbors.

How much of this predicament, I wondered, was created by my own mind? How much of it was what Soen Sa Nim calls "checking"? When I asked Bobby, she said she thought it was, in fact, a good example of "checking."

"You're feeling as though you have to perform exactly like everybody else. But if you were completely clear about what you're capable of, then you would just take a tiny amount of food and tell someone you had to eat afterward as well. 'I'll do this ritual with you, but at this point in my practice I know I can't do it and get enough food at mealtimes.' The 'checking' part is feeling that you 'should' be able to do it perfectly."

"You're right," I said. "It didn't occur to me I could get something to eat later."

"The kitchen master or the guest master would be clear enough to see that that is your correct situation at this point. That you're being genuine and that you could be graciously given some more food afterward. That's something that this community needs to learn more about, actually. We've had a few people come here who were either older—two women in their sixties recently—or physically handicapped. And they couldn't get into the routine. They needed a slower pace and fewer demands put upon them. But we didn't really see clearly enough at the time, weren't quite sensitive enough. And they ended up leaving.

"Maybe the first time we saw you having difficulty eating, we could have come to you and said, 'You know, let's work something out here.' Sometimes Soen Sa Nim will drop the structure completely for some people and just act like a grandfather."

I was surprised. I had never seen Soen Sa Nim act like a grandfather. But admittedly I had not spent much time with him. Bobby said it happened often. It's a way of encouraging people, of giving them "juice." And he's a master at that. But it's not manipulative, she said, "just kind."

Bobby, though, is clearly someone who thrives on the Zen center schedule. It's her best medium, her natural habitat. Laziness and self-indulgence are not her demons. But I was glad I had seen her cavorting in the hot tub one night with her little girl, Annie, so I knew she had another side, a playful, funny side. And a year later, at a large conference, I heard her give a whimsical and pointed dharma talk based entirely on a picture book she had just read to her daughter. She had brought the book with her and held it up frequently so everyone could see the illustrations.

It's a matter of balance, she understands. We need to be honest with ourselves about where our practice is going and what it needs to be. Within that framework there's lots of room for hot tubs and picnics and movies and walks with one's friends. PZC is a high-powered place, Bobby admits. Mostly she relishes it, but she also enjoys her time away—time alone and with other people.

"I think everybody is practicing in some way," she said. "We're all working things out, you know. But some people haven't quite reached the stage of really taking their practice seriously." They have more negative karma and cater more to the five desires (food, sex, sleep, fame, wealth). Other have more of a vow, or a big question, and seek to help others first. She hasn't reached that place yet, Bobby allows, but she thinks it *is* possible to disconnect the five desires from one's ego. Then, she says, you wouldn't eat or have sex or be famous or have money for yourself, but always for other people. It would just flow in and out. "The longer I practice, the more those things feel that way. It gets there. Not from just thinking about it. It gets there from self-denial, I think."

She doesn't mean this in a moralistic way, but in a practical, everyday way. She'll stop herself before doing some habitual thing—buying a doughnut, for example. There it is: you can either buy the doughnut or you can turn around and *not* buy it. It's a matter of seeing the larger picture, or the largest picture, all the time. "It's not shoulds and shouldn'ts and guilt, you know—all that crap we get into with our practice. But if you're right there with it, then your practice has really arrived."

Bobby remembers her mother telling her: "Everything in moderation, including moderation." There's a nice analogy there with Soen Sa Nim's repeated teaching about nonattachment to our opinions, even those that feel most sacred. Vegetarianism, for example. Bobby became a vegetarian not for health reasons, but because she became sensitized to the suffering of animals. As a result she began to feel quite judgmental about meat-eaters. "How can they continue when they know what animals go through?" she would think. But she's learned a lot from practice and from Soen Sa Nim's philosophy of acting with others. "Before you can save people from hell, you have to go to hell," he says. Bobby still can't eat hamburger, but the past Thanksgiving was the first time in eleven or twelve years that she'd eaten turkey with her parents. It meant a lot to them. After that they came to visit the Zen center for the first time—and had a meal there. Then Bobby went to church with them for the first time in many, many years. "I had communion, took the wafer and the wine, the whole bit. And then a whole bunch of other walls broke down." They asked questions about the center, the newsletter, her life. "But first I had to go over to their team. I had to act with them."

The word most frequently used to describe Bobby by people who know her is "honest." She has a great willingness to share her own experience, to talk *with* people and not talk down to them. She manifests a sense of unshakability to some people. One described her as unsqueamish and completely accepting of the physical side of the human condition. (She cleans toilet bowls by hand, not with a brush, I was told!) She doesn't particularly enjoy "hanging out" with people, would much rather hang out the laundry with them instead. She likes to work—likes to shovel manure, drive a tractor. "Her style is so simple and so pure that you have to allow yourself to be more simple to understand and appreciate her," one person said. Another told me how funny she can be, how she can tell a good joke and laugh at herself. He also quoted something she said in a dharma talk three years before, something he said he would never forget. It was: "Remember, whatever happens, no matter how far out your mind gets, *just believe what's right in front of you.* That's your direction. No matter where your mind goes, return to that. *Just believe what's right in front of you.*"

Bobby can say without false humility that her practice is growing. What tells her this is that she feels herself loving people more. She has more energy, can take on a bit more all the time. "What I would like for myself and the whole world is just increased communication and love. I want to reach out to lots of people." Since she was a little girl, her only wish was that people would love each other. In recent years she has developed a vision of a broadening network of clear-minded people in this country working together for positive change. There is so little time, and things are beginning to feel urgent. "We need to talk about how we can help this world," she said. "The answers aren't clear, but if you're honest with yourself, people will trust you and listen to you."

Then she smiled and added, "I do have to leave soon to make lunch."

Update: Winter 2000

Seven or eight years after our interview at the Providence Zen Center (PZC) for the first edition of this book, Bobby Rhodes's life changed dramatically. In a two-year period, her father died; she was divorced; she moved out of the Zen center with her daughter, Annie; and she started a relationship with her partner, Mary S. Bobby is still affiliated with PZC but teaches only one seven-day retreat there every year. Her house in Providence has a little dharma room in the basement. Once a week, people come to sit and chant with them. Annie is now nineteen and a sophomore at Oberlin. Her father lives only a few blocks away, so he and Bobby have been able to raise their daughter together.

Bobby continues to work full-time as a nurse, but her current job, which she loves immoderately, is at Hospice Care of Rhode Island.

But less than three months before our recent talk, I was startled to learn, Bobby had had open heart surgery. This followed a stroke last summer, which had paralyzed her briefly. Tests done at the time revealed a large hole in her heart, present since birth, which required her heart to pump twice as much blood per minute than normal. Her hands turned blue sometimes, but "I never noticed it. And I didn't think I was any more tired than anybody else."

Before the heart surgery, "I used to be really driven," she admits. But after that two-year crisis period, she began a course of Hakomi therapy, an intuitive mind-body work that she found immensely helpful. For the first time, she was able to allow herself to receive attention and care. "I needed to have someone ask how I was and not feel I was selfish." Her instinctive "helper" role had been out of balance. Now she needed to help herself, to listen to herself closely. As a result, she believes she's become a more sensitive listener to others. In her work with patients and students, she notices body language, has more empathy. "In the past, if someone came in angry or frightened, I would ignore it and deal with the content of the koan instead." Now, she'll say, "You look angry [or scared]. Is that true?"

Her retreat talks have become more and more relaxed: she never thinks ahead of time about what she's going to say. "Most of the time when I arrive at a retreat, I've been working all day in hospice, and I'll often use an example of something that's happened with a patient. I can do a whole dharma talk around what someone said to me that day—because people in this situation are so open, so real."

The love Bobby has for her work is transparent. She is responsible for fourteen to fifteen patients at a time and deals with a death about every two weeks. "The light will be in someone's eyes one second, and then you see them take their last breath, and the light goes out of their eyes. It's someone I've gotten to know quite well, and I see them die. What a gift! To know I haven't really lost them, nobody's lost them, just breathe in, breathe out, in body, out of body—same thing, you know."

Bobby says she always feels like a "total phony" being called a teacher. Though it's important for people to take that position and do it well, "there has to be a lot of humility and honesty. Just try to be yourself and not hide anything and not be pretentious. People fall off the platform all the time. And there but for the grace of God go I. The grace of God means each moment being honest, trying to see yourself, and if you're confused, put that into your teaching. Then it becomes *your* teacher."

What's "good" about her, Bobby says, is her enthusiasm for the practice, for the realization that what the mind really needs is to rest. The Kwan Um School teaches: Put it all down, put it to rest, and *just be here*. "I have tremendous enthusiasm for that simple, simple practice.

"The nature of me is nothing. There is no Bobby Rhodes. I'm just trying to point toward something I really respect, and that's being awake."

Bobby currently conducts weekend retreats twice a month, circling from New Haven to Chicago, Denver, and Tallahassee. She does biannual retreats in Washington, D.C., as well as her weeklong yearly retreat at Providence Zen Center. In Providence, she also sits weekly with a Zen group and gives interviews as well. (All of these activities are under the aegis of the Kwan Um School of Zen in Cumberland, Rhode Island.)

7

Jiyu Kennett

If you're afraid of being grabbed by God, don't look at a wall.
Definitely don't sit still.

—Roshi Jiyu Kennett

We arrived at the gate to Shasta Abbey toward the end of an afternoon in late October. There was a smell of early winter in the air.
A friend and I had made the six-hour trip together from the San
Francisco Bay area, and we had driven right beneath Mount
Shasta without seeing it. The cloud cover was dense, reaching
most of the way to the bottom. But we caught a glimpse of sun
on a sloping plain and the beginning of snow. There was a sense
of mystery and hidden immensity.

Inside the main abbey gate we were met by the assistant guest
master, the Reverend Kinrei, a tall, smiling young man with a
fresh face and large dark eyes, wearing a heavy black robe with a
short cape and a woolen Siberian-style cap. He phoned the main
house to announce our arrival, and soon thereafter the guest-
master himself, the Reverend Kinsei, appeared, even taller (six
foot five, we learned later), in brown robe and cape and brown
fur cap. I began to feel I was in a Russian novel. Later, when I
commented on the handsome cut of the robes and capes, Reverend Kinsei told us they'd been designed by Roshi Kennett herself
and were sewn there at the abbey.

The wind was rising, but there was an hour before dark and
dinner, so we left our bags in the guest room and followed Reverend Kinsei on a walk around the grounds. The large circular
cloister had only recently been completed but now connected
most of the buildings. There was a sharp smell of freshly cut fire-
wood, which was neatly stacked around the inner wall. The sky

was dramatic. Layers of gray-black clouds alternated with strips of dark blue sky.

We visited the library, full of Buddhist texts and scriptures, including the entire Pali canon and *Tripitaka* and many taped talks and lectures. Novice monks spend part of their evenings here, we were told. We passed the ceremony and meditation halls, which we would visit later, and looked briefly into a large, bustling kitchen. Then we passed through a fence and around a hill to the goat barns. Nestling among the grasses and stones on a steep slope below were a large number of beautiful female goats of many colors. They provide all the milk used at the abbey, which also makes its own yogurt and cheese. The male goats are kept in a separate pen, some distance away, Reverend Kinsei told us—otherwise their bad smell would spoil the flavor of the milk.

By now it was becoming chilly, but we elected to climb the steep path to the cemetery. Established only a few years before, it holds only a handful of graves, but many other sites have been purchased by members of the extended congregation. The unspoiled, rocky hillside is covered with low trees and shrubs, with an inconspicuous shrine here and there containing flowers and candles. I could imagine, on a clear day, the awesome presence of Mount Shasta close by.

After dinner that night, we were assigned places in the *gaitan*—a long, narrow annex off the meditation hall, where visitors, lay members, or postulant monks sit for meditation and chanting before they take vows. In the dark next to me I was dimly aware of a small person who, when the lights came up, turned out to be a boy with dark red hair. Next to him was a little girl with hair of the same color. They walked out silently with a small, quiet young woman who had to be their mother: she wore a long brown cape, and the color of her hair echoed theirs.

Again and again at the abbey, one is aware of color, of an aesthetic sense, of verve, even *style*. Monks stride by in contrasting shades of black, red, brown, and white. Long capes and short capes swirl as they walk, as they briskly turn corners. Winter caps of pleasing design appear on every side. One thinks of the brightly colored covers of Roshi Kennett's books, published at the abbey. And I remembered the rose-colored summer robe in which I first saw her, and the lavender rakusu that she wore over it. Whatever the rigors of training at Shasta, visually it has vigor, drama, and spice.

Inside the ceremony hall, above the main altar with its massive golden Buddha, there are two graceful garudas (peacocklike mythical birds) beautifully inlaid in gold. They were made by a gifted artist who was then a monk at Shasta. The Buddha, too, was constructed by artist-monks. And circling three sides of the ceremony hall, high windows are painted—in a process reminiscent of stained glass—with scenes of Roshi Kennett's third *kensho*. This remarkable experience (described as a "kensho-in-slow-motion" by her disciple Daizui McPhillamy in the preface to her book *How to Grow a Lotus Blossom*) took place in 1975–76 after a series of traumatic events that occurred in rapid succession. First, during a period of increasingly debilitating illness, Roshi Kennett was told by her physician that her heart would probably fail within three months. A week later she was shocked by the sudden defection of her chief disciple and heir. Finally, a highly regarded Oriental healer informed her that her entire way of life and teaching were false and were responsible for her illness.

Challenged to her core, she embarked on a period of intense inner questioning and meditation practice that lasted a year. Renouncing all other commitments (and medical treatment as well), she used all her strength for uninterrupted meditation. Determined to examine every corner of her life and belief, she hardly left her room for four months. It was during this time that she began to experience intense visions not usually associated with Zen Buddhism in the West. Her faith and health were both gradually restored. The following year, risking the repudiation she knew could be provoked by this sort of material, she published a full account of her experiences in *How to Grow a Lotus Blossom*, with plates illustrating each phase that were later used as sketches for the painted windows at the abbey.

"Love is not an emotion! It is the basic stuff that makes us tick."
My friend and I were listening to a tape of Roshi Kennett's before we went to sleep. It was from a talk given during a conference at a Catholic seminary some years before. Someone asked,

"What's the difference between Christianity and Buddhism? You sound like a Christian."

"There is no savior in Buddhism," Roshi Kennett answered. "You have to do it for yourself. No one else will meditate for you. At the time of death you will judge yourself. The Lord of the House will never judge you. That Which Is, simply is. The ability to die in peace means the ability to live in peace. The Cosmic Buddha has no hell to hold over us. We make our own hell. The only judging that is done is done by ourselves—and thus we hide ourselves from the Cosmic Buddha. Everyone possesses Buddha nature (or, as the Christians call it, the soul). It is only hidden from our view because of our opinions of ourselves.

"The art of meditation," she went on, "removes that separation, so that we can return to our basic nature and truly know it. Meditation has nothing whatever to do with self-improvement. It is an extraordinarily deep, prayerful experience, and its purpose is to become one with the Cosmic Buddha—or, if you like, have an experience of God."

On the tape, Roshi Kennett's voice is by turns commanding, funny, sardonic, rousing, hortatory. She sometimes seems to be scolding or shaking her listeners, as a nanny might scold her beloved, naughty charges. My friend affectionately dubbed her "the cosmic nanny."

Roshi Kennett was not well at the time of our visit to Shasta Abbey, so I did not see her that weekend. I felt her spirit, though, behind the friendly reception we received, and behind all the arrangements made for us to explore the abbey and to meet and talk with members of the community. I felt concerned about her health, however. I had met with her twice in Berkeley the previous summer, and she had told me how her body had never been the same after her years in Japan. She had experienced an extraordinary weight gain, a hundred pounds in one month, probably due to the onset of diabetes as well as to the complications of an operation she had received in Tokyo for a large growth that had, incredibly, been missed for a long time because it was too large! The Japanese doctors had simply not seen it on their x-rays because it did not conform to their ordinary expectations. Today, despite excellent medical care and a strict diet for her diabetes and heart condition, her health is precarious. "The physical condition of my body weighs incredibly on me," she told me. "It's very difficult for me to be up and about."

Yet here was the abbey, vigorous and thriving, blooming up from the remains of an abandoned motel. The number of practical decisions, the organization of effort, not to mention the physical labor involved, seemed staggering. Originally there was no electricity, no gas, no phone. For a couple of weeks after the community moved in, they slept on the floor of one house. Opening the door one morning, they found seven feet of snow in all directions. All they had was a sack of carrots and a sack of onions. So until they were rescued two weeks later by the one person in town who knew they were there, they subsisted on carrot and onion soup.

Now the monastery has an excellently provided kitchen and is well known locally for the quality of its bakery products, which are periodically sold to raise needed cash. The monks make all the abbey's bread (about thirty-five loaves at a time) and its cheese (about 120 nine-pound wheels each year).

Because of the intense heat of the summer months in Mount Shasta, Roshi Kennett generally spends part of each summer in Berkeley, where the climate is more temperate. I spent two mornings talking to her there, at the Berkeley Buddhist Priory, an affiliate of the Order of Buddhist Contemplatives, which she established in 1973. The priory is located at the lower end of a long, winding street that drops, sometimes precipitously, from the top of the Berkeley hills to the bay. Toward the bottom, it widens out into a broad, curving residential street, and it would be hard to distinguish the priory from neighboring homes on either side except for a small bronze identifying plaque.

Two alarming-looking but evidently mild-mannered English bulldogs greeted me as I arrived. "That's Winnie and Gawain," was the first thing I learned from Roshi Kennett. She was waiting for me in a small sitting room just inside the back door, along with an attendant monk, Reverend Koten, who remained with us for the interview.

Roshi Kennett is a large woman, forthright in style, her voice at once hearty, robust, and cultivated—and in her eye and manner an immediate twinkle. She retains the aristocratic accent and rolled *r*'s of her early years in England, which, together with her emphatic speaking style, should be remembered in reading the dialogue to follow. I had asked Roshi Kennett for her views on lay practice versus monastic life.

"It all depends on how far you want to go. If you want to go the whole way, you must become a monk. You must be willing not to be married, you've literally got to give up everything. You cannot go the whole way unless you completely control, and no longer need or want, sex and anger. Those are the two things you really have to give up completely. To go the whole way.

"It's very clear if you read the Theravada books on the subject. There are the four kenshos, the four stages of understanding. A married person can very easily reach the first, and probably can't reach the second, definitely not the third or fourth. This does not mean that marriage is wrong, it merely means you have to decide how far you want to go. And anyone can get a first kensho. It would seem to take between seven and ten years of celibacy before you can really go further."

"I know of one teacher who is married but has been celibate for years."

"If you get a first kensho and you then decide to get married, you won't go further. If you're married already, and then decide to give yourself to the Eternal . . ."

"Then sex is the important thing, and not the relationship?"

"Well, that's what I said, but the relationship does enter into it, because once you've had a kensho you can't even marry for the sake of the relationship—because then you've taken something away from the Eternal, as it were, and given it to someone else. You have to give up everything. The scriptures specifically say: give up everything. And 'everything' means what it says. Immediately people ask: does that mean I have to give up . . . I just said *everything?*"

"But lay practice can include a first kensho?"

"Oh, yes. But one of the interesting things about our particular church is that it would never confirm one for a layman. For the simple reason that a layman is not under the sort of discipline that the church members are under, and you'd have people going off and saying, 'I've had a kensho,' and perhaps doing harm."

"Like people going to a seminar and having an 'experience' and calling themselves teacher."

"That's why the church would never give a certificate saying they've had one. They'd simply say, this person studied well. Which would actually mean he had a first kensho. I see their point."

"When you say the church, you're talking about . . . ?"

"I'm talking about the whole Soto church, either in Japan or here. Soto Zen pickles should taste like Soto Zen pickles!"

We took a short break and somehow got onto the subject of evil ("Evil is the result of ignorance") and sin. When we started up again, I said:

"A little while ago, off tape, you said, 'If you sin, sin vigorously.'"

"Yes. It was Martin Luther who said that. And I agree with him. Don't piddle about. If you're going to do it, do it. You're still going to carry the consequences, you might at least enjoy it. And do it up right."

"In *How to Grow a Lotus Blossom,* there was a strong sense that what you cared about most in your lifetime was—"

"—knowing the Eternal."

"Yes. Being a monk. Knowing the Eternal and teaching those who want to know. And there was a very strong emphasis on not making a mistake, on 'growing a perfect stem.' What exactly did you have in mind there? Does it have to do with the precepts, with morality?"

"It has to do with looking at everything that one does from the point of view of asking yourself three questions: One, am I doing this out of ignorance? If so, it will be evil. If I can answer no to that question, I can go onto the next one. Am I going to be doing good? If I can say yes to that question, I can go on to the third one. Is it going to be good for me, or is it going to be good for others? In other words, am I going to be doing something that will cause others to do wrong? And if I can say no to that question, then I can go ahead and do what I'm doing."

"That's the purity you're talking about?"

"Things *have* to be done from that angle. There's nobody outside you telling you what you shall or shall not do. You yourself must look at what it is you're doing. Where can I do the very least harm? And still be willing to take the consequences. The fact is that you have to do *something*. People come to me and say, 'What's the Buddhist teaching on pacifism?' And my answer is: If you go into the army, you will be required to kill. And there will be consequences. If you are a pacifist, the law of the land says you will go to jail. If the war is such as in World War II, where millions are being harmed, what does your conscience tell you you must do? There is no savior that can say, 'Thou shalt not.' The only person who can do this is yourself. And whichever way you go, you're going to take the consequences. And that's why I tell people Buddhism is not pacifistic. 'Oh, you're belligerent!' No. I'm not belligerent either."

"Buddhism is often not this, not that."

"There is a third position, which means you've got to be a full adult. This is a religion for spiritual adults, not for spiritual children, with a big daddy and a big stick."

"You said in another place that Buddhism is often mistakenly thought of as a way of life and not a religion."

"That again can be disproved by one of the oldest scriptures in the Pali canon, the *Udana* scripture, wherein the Buddha says (about the third position, as I call it, between good and evil), 'O monks, there is an unborn, undying, unchanging, uncreated. If it were not so, there would be no point to life, or to training.' Buddhism states what the Eternal is not. (I use the term *Eternal* rather than *God*. *God* has the implication of a deity with a beard and a long stick.) It does not state what it *is* because if it did, then we would be stuck with a concept. Buddhism states specifically what we know for certain. It will not state that which is taken on faith. We can find this for ourselves—that it is unborn and so forth—but we cannot state what it is. Therefore we call it Mu or 'nothing' or 'emptiness' or, as my master called it, 'the immaculacy of emptiness,' which is the fullest description I've ever bumped into. So it's definitely *not* irreligious. It's very definitely a religion."

She told me she was working on a new translation of the *Denko Roku* with one of the priests at the monastery. We talked for a while about problems in translating scriptures from the Japanese, and Roshi Kennett gave the example of older translations using the word *predestination* for what she currently translates as "past life experiences." She said there was "one *heck* of a difference" and I asked her to amplify.

"Because of a tiny bit of ignorance centuries ago, a mistake was made. And that mistake was continued down the past lives. I was not *predestined* to make that mistake. All I had to do was train at any time to clean it up. But I was not predestined to it. There was no God that predestined me to make the mistake. The mistake had been made once, and I was free at any time to end it, and that's the big difference between predestination and past life experiences."

"Okay. I think I get that. Would you say a bit more, though, about understanding past lives without a sense of continuing *ego* or *self*?"

"Well, if you once think that *you* are in it, then you cause the thing to entitize. And then what you've got is a bunch of ghosts and you're into witchcraft and spiritualism."

"It isn't entirely clear to me how you get rid of that."

"You just know that when they come up, this is not *you*. In you is all that is left of this person or this animal. But it isn't *you*. It's just like a shadow that you've been carrying around with you. And once you saw the mistake, you could put it right. And the thing disappears and no longer affects you. Something was done wrong, a grave mistake was made, and it left vibrations around. Imagine you have a bag in which you've brought home some fish. You eat the fish, but you carry the bag around and it still smells of fish. That's an impregnation. We all carry the impregnations of past lives. But they've got nothing to do with *us*."

"But there's a continuity down the line?"

"We tend to pick up stuff that made the same mistake. And that's how you can make the mistake of predestination."

"So we do each have our own particular series of impregnations."

"But they're not our personal ones."

"In the sense that we're not personal either?"

"No. You see, we're part, if you like, of a great central ego. We all have a spark of the Eternal. Each one of us is therefore here as a bag of karma. Our duty throughout our lives is to cleanse that karma so that part of the Eternal has got rid of that much. We're probably a very, very religious holy being, in other words. And we have a definite purpose, which is cleaning this stuff up."

During our conversation Roshi Kennett referred elliptically several times to incidents involving other Buddhist groups in this country that were apparently demeaning to her as a woman roshi.

"The treatment of women can be anything from abominable to ambivalent to really first rate," she said. "It all depends on the master, not the sect. It's not consistent. The only reason the Buddha made the comments he did about women was because of the culture at the time. We know that."

"Well, he refused to ordain women for a long time."

"Yes. In the end he got annoyed and said, 'All right, it'll probably bring the thing down, given the culture, but go ahead.'"

"He thought it would result in Buddhism's lasting only half as long."

"Yes. But that was given the culture he was in. And in those days he was probably right. That was then and this is now."

We talked about her first ordination in Malaysia, for which three monks who knew the full traditional ordination scriptures were smuggled out of Communist China.

For the elaborate ceremony they brought with them "a whole bunch of the most incredible real lotuses from the garden of the big temple where all the ordinations were formerly done. And this is while the Communists are going strong! I said I wasn't worried about the Chinese Communists. Every forty years the Chinese change their government. Like clockwork. And precisely forty years later, look what they're doing now! You've got to remember that in the tenth century Buddhism was wiped out by the Chinese, and look how it came back again. And it'll come back again now too—I'm not worried in the least. I have never seen any people so competent in making their lives comfortable, whatever the government. They don't change at all, basically, whatever the government. It is a Buddhist tradition to quietly do what you have to do, work for the good of all people, and quietly change things from within."

"Skillful means!"

"Yes. They do that, and suddenly it's not a violent land, it's a green land. You don't start quarrels. It may not look spectacular—you just do what needs to be done."

Women had only just won the right to vote in England when five-year-old Peg Kennett started school. It was a "very snooty, very expensive private boarding school" for children of the wealthy upper class. But its teachers were largely militant suffragists, not above chaining themselves to railings to dramatize their demands for equality. Now, flushed with victory, they wasted no time impressing their small female charges with the absolute conviction that they could do or become whatever they dreamed. "You should know what we've done!" they said. "We fought for you. This is your right. Now you keep those rights." All through school the message was clear: You are not inferior! You are anything *but* second class.

The little girl who today is Roshi Kennett, abbess of Shasta Abbey, learned that lesson well. What *she* wanted to become was a monk.

This had been clear to her from the age of four when she saw a monk for the first time on the streets of London. She had announced her intention immediately to her startled mother, a conventional woman who continued to be startled as her unconventional daughter grew up. When I asked for more information about her mother, Roshi Kennett said, "There's really nothing more to say. How do you say anything about someone you've never met? I've put that in the *Goose* [her book *The Wild White Goose*]. How do you say goodbye to somebody you've never met yet? Oh, we lived in the same house. But we never met each other. We were a couple of ships that passed in the night and said hi."

In her boarding school, alongside their advanced notions of feminism, her teachers taught a distinctly blood-and-guts variety of Christianity. Yet it was there that, quite by accident, it seemed,

Peg Kennett was introduced to Buddhism. It happened that the father of one of her schoolmates sent his daughter a beautiful marble Buddha from Burma, for the school museum. The headmistress decided it was too big for the museum but was just right for the mantle in the lecture hall.

"Now, the lecture hall is where you have prayers every morning. And here was this very narrow-minded Scottish Calvinist talking dire things about hellfire, brimstone, and everything else that happened if you dared so much as to think you looked attractive or didn't do your hair in pigtails. And here was this lovely cool statue of a Buddha sitting in meditation. When we were singing hymns like 'where every prospect pleases, and only man is vile,' and 'the heathen in his blindness bows down to wood and stone'—I'm thinking, I *prefer* it! If you're listening to blood and guts every morning, and there's something else sitting on the mantle looking good—that's where I got converted to Buddhism!" (Today there's an exact replica of that Buddha in the library at Shasta Abbey.)

Yet, for years after she finished her university education in music, Peg Kennett worked as a church organist. It seemed the most likely route at the time toward her goal of spiritual training. She was, if anything, overqualified. But she was also a woman, and the Church of England was not then of the same mind as her schoolteachers. Often, in order to get in the door for a job interview, she used the ruse of putting her initials, rather than her full name, on applications. "It was very obvious that they didn't want women. I kept thinking that maybe I'm wrong, and I would apply for jobs and I'd get them, and as soon as they found out I was a woman, I was out. One parson informed me that the only women he wanted in his church were the ones who cleaned it." Another, after hiring her, insisted on sexual favors. She resigned. He came to her house and tried to force his way in. She threatened to tell the bishop. He said, "He won't believe you. You're just a woman."

Finally she found a very poor church that couldn't afford a man and, after working there ten years and doing brilliantly ("I am not swollen-headed when I make that statement"), she was informed that a man had been found who was willing to work for the "miserable pittance they were paying me. I was fired, after ten years, for being a woman."

Decades later, in a pamphlet on women and Buddhism published by Shasta Abbey, she wrote: "This is the situation women have been in for centuries. This is the situation that needs to change. The damage done to me I cannot tell you. However, out of it came *something* good. It sent me back to studying my own original religion, Buddhism. It sent me to the Far East, making possible the discovery that I *was* adequate. . . . In the beginning I was looking in the wrong direction. I was looking for equality in work instead of knowing that true equality came from within. I was looking outside myself for recognition instead of knowing that I must first recognize myself as whole.

"Once one knows of one's own adequacy, once one knows one's own Buddha-nature, once one knows one's own soul, there can be no problem whatsoever with adequacy or inadequacy; *and* it no longer matters whether one rocks the cradle or digs the coal in the mine—or works as a lawyer or a doctor, all work being equal in the Buddha-mind, all work being that of a Buddha."

The only reason she turned away from Christianity, Roshi Kennett told me, was her incredibly deep calling to become a priest. And, as a woman, "there was no way I could become a priest in Christianity." It was the sexism of the Church of England that compelled her to cut loose from Christianity and finally become a monk in a foreign country, in a foreign religion, in a foreign language.

It was no easy task. The story is told in detail in the two volumes of her autobiographical work, *The Wild White Goose*. It chronicles extraordinary hardships to body and mind—including beatings, malnutrition, ostracism, illness—as well as the attaining of that heart of religious experience which transcends words, labels, denominations. Peg Kennett found what she had left England and Christianity for. Despite much to the contrary in her experience in Japan, she was inspired and supported by words in the Buddhist scriptures like these: "A little girl of seven, even, may be the teacher of the four classes of buddhas, and the mother of true compassion to all living things. One of the greatest teachings of Buddhism is its insistence upon complete equality of the sexes." This passage from the *Shobogenzo* by Dogen-zenji, a thir-teenth-century Zen master, was shown to Roshi Kennett by her Japanese mentor, chief abbott of one of Japan's major training temples, while she was a junior trainee. "That was why I was able to put up with all that idiocy in Japan," she told me. "It's all right, I don't care, people being fools is fine, so long as the great have said this is true, I believe 'em. That was what I based my faith on. I kept my consciousness on those who mattered and not the idi-ots. There are always idiots. And always will be. But the more churches say women have equality, the less vulnerable we're going to be. Once the churches say we're equal, the rest of the world isn't going to matter. And as soon as the rest of the world doesn't matter, it will come. As soon as we *know* we have full rights, they're going to give them to us anyway."

The Equal Rights Amendment, she says, is not about who does what job "but who has a soul and who has not." It is the spirituality of women that lies at the heart of it. No woman will be certain, absolutely, that she is equal "until she knows with the certainty that I know, that her own Buddha-nature, or her own soul, exists."

She believes that women will probably lose much, in the worldly sense, in this generation. But "at least our daughters will reap the benefits of that spiritual adequacy if we fight for it now, for then the work that was denied to us will be open to them. When men know that spiritually we are the same as they are, they will have to judge us on our merits and our ability and not on what someone said thousands of years ago. We need to leave behind these nar-row-minded doctrines. We need the wide-mindedness of those who *know* that spirituality exists evenly in the entire universe. The Buddha himself did not keep women down. It was some of his stick-in-the-mud disciples that did that."

Now she feels it absolutely essential for women to know un-equivocally that they are spiritually whole. Initially she was afraid to throw away her music for fear of discovering she had no soul, no spirit. "But I was so desperate that nothing mattered any longer, not even life itself. I went ahead, threw away everything, and gained adequacy."

Roshi Kennett: Nobody wants to be treated special, but they do want to be treated like everybody else. I'm not asking for a reserved seat in heaven. I'm asking to be able to get in through the door.

Lenore: That's often the other side of the coin. Women are either treated as enormously special, being up on some terrific pedestal—

Roshi Kennett: That was one of the problems I had in Japan. I was either lionized on one side or hated on the other. And you know, when you're batted about like a shuttlecock, you tend to sit back and say, Enough of all that! As long as you're kept down to things you don't have—a soul, or Buddha-nature—eventually you tend to believe that. And that is why women have not made it in the past, because there's always been that little voice inside saying, Well, just supposing the bishops are right, or just supposing the Catholic Church is right? There's always been this little doubt. I even had an American man who came to stay with us once and got extremely angry when he found out it was an *abbess* who was in charge of the monastery. He'd heard that this was an abbey, Shasta Abbey, and obviously there would be a man in charge. I said, I'm awfully sorry, but I happen to be a female.

Lenore: There's a lot of ambivalence in Buddhist scriptures and teachings about women as well. In some places you find you have to be born into a male body to be enlightened.

Roshi Kennett: Well, there's an interesting thing about that. It says you have to be reborn as a man *once*. What they don't mention is that you have to be reborn as a *woman,* if you're a man, too—because you have to be beyond both. When you have a really deep religious understanding—kensho, as it's called in Soto Zen—you literally become male for a time, in mind, if you're a female, and female for a time, in

	mind, if you're a male. And you can't have a kensho unless you can knit the two together and get beyond them. They leave that bit out of the scripture!
Lenore:	Reading about your kensho in *How to Grow a Lotus* was startling in some ways.
Roshi Kennett:	That was very interesting. A lot of people think you can't have visions. The teaching is, if you have visions, don't get involved with them. But once you've had a first kensho, visions will come, and you don't get involved with them, you learn from them. There's a big difference.
Lenore:	A part I really wondered about was your disciple's becoming part of the experience, seeing the same things you saw.
Roshi Kennett:	When I was very ill in 1975 and came down to Oakland, Daizui pulled himself into a first kensho within the first few days of my being there. He was seeing some of the things I was seeing. The reason he was pulled into it was that he was so anxious that I should get better, he sat down in meditation one day and literally yelled *Help!* He yelled it in the right way, and the Eternal heard him.
Lenore:	What's the right way to yell 'Help'?
Roshi Kennett:	That's the secret of a koan. What's the sound of one hand clapping? "I give up, I don't understand it, help me!" When you do that the right way . . . That's how koans work on you. You can't find an answer. You have to find the third position: The Eternal. He was yelling "*Help,* I want her to get better. I don't know what to do. *Help!*" (He experienced kensho.) And he's a psychologist, with lots of ideas and theories about things!

Our second morning at the abbey dawned cold and crystal-clear. Hurrying through the cloister for 7:00 A.M. meditation, we caught brief glimpses of the magic mountain. Its twin cones were blanketed in luminescent snow against the early-morning sky—a dream tapestry in blue, gold, and white. We had only time to gasp and run on. But later, after meditation and before breakfast, we took time to stand in a spot of sunlight and let the glowing mountain shine down on us.

The setting of the abbey is so beautiful, portentous even—but Roshi Kennett declares it was purely an accident.

"I came to the United States to give some lectures but had no intention of staying here at all. I had been in Japan, at a little temple I'd been made priest of, and had been very ill and they'd operated on me, but the doctors couldn't find out what was wrong. When I was offered this job to come over here and do some lectures, I thought, well, why not get myself checked out by a Western doctor at the same time? At the time I wasn't at all sure what I was going to do. I presumed I would probably go back to Japan. Or maybe go on to England if I was found too ill to return to Japan. This was the spring of 1969. They'd operated on me in the autumn of '67 and I'd gradually found that my legs were losing their power to move. I was getting to the state where I couldn't walk. I came over here and in less than a month I collapsed, and they took me along to UC hospital. They discovered I had diabetes. I had got it somehow or other from malnutrition in the temple and possibly something done wrong in the operations. It looked like all the electrolytes had been messed up. And I was now incapable of walking at all. But I started getting better, thanks to the help I was getting at UC.

"In the meantime, a bunch of people had gathered around me—a lot of them were people who had been with me in Japan. They'd been with the armed forces there, Americans. They were saying, Why don't you stay in America and run a temple here? I'd no intention of doing this when I came over. I said, Well, I want to go home to England first, and I may possibly go back to Japan, I just don't know.

"I'd been in Japan eight, going on nine years. And I'd made no arrangements. I didn't want to resign from my temple. I owned it, I was the legal priest of it, and at that stage I really thought I was going to get better and go back and live the life at my temple again."

"Did you say you *owned* it?"

"Well, I was the official priest of it. By law in Japan the priest of a temple owns it—I mean he owns it and he doesn't really own it—you know what I mean? Anyway, I went on to England the following April when I was able to move again reasonably. I could never really walk properly again. When I got to England it was very obvious that they were not interested in Soto Zen. They want only Rinzai there, thanks to the influence of Toby Humphreys. And I kept receiving letters from people over here saying how much they'd like me to return. So I came back over and started a small temple in San Francisco.

"Within a very short time we discovered that the building wasn't big enough. So we found a place in Oakland, a very nice large house up in the hills overlooking Lake Merritt. But then *that* became too small. I think within two weeks we had fifteen people who wanted to live there. They were the actual people who had been with me in Japan, or their relatives or friends. Very serious. But we'd got absolutely no cash. And here we are, developing a training monastery! And the temple is getting bigger and bigger, bulging at the seams.

"It occurred to me that we might be able to find something bigger in the country districts that was reasonably close to a freeway so people could come and stay *and* visit. One thing I hadn't reckoned on was the *size* of America. A temple in San Francisco isn't much use to someone living in Newark, New Jersey. That being so, it really didn't matter very much where we put it because the majority of them were not in San Francisco, they were all over the place. And since they would be coming in for weekends or weeks at a time, any place that was reasonably easy to get to was going to work. That opened up a big possibility.

"We started looking on the freeway for a suitable building and land that would do the job. And by accident, completely by accident, we stopped off in Mount Shasta on one occasion to get some gas for the car. Anytime we stopped off, we'd ask, 'Are there any big houses for sale here? What land is for sale?' And this time they said, 'Oh, there's a lovely old motel down the road. But the only thing it's fit for is a monastery!' Nobody else would buy it. It was almost fifteen acres, right beside the freeway, and it was just the perfect place to be developed."

"What year was it that you actually established the abbey?"

"Nineteen seventy. November 1970."

"So San Francisco Zen Center was already established at that time?"

"Oh, yes, they were going strong."

"The need was huge, wasn't it?"

"Yes, the need was huge, but there's always a tide in such things. The tide of interest in something which had been going on since the late fifties, early sixties, was beginning to wane somewhat. And in a way that was a godsend. Because you no longer got the people who thought, 'Let's see what it's like, we're curious.' You got the real people who wanted to stay and be established with it. When you just have the curious, when something first starts, it's not nearly as permanent and as good as when that high goes down."

Then I asked, "What is it like at Shasta? What happens every day? What's the schedule like?"

Roshi Kennett turned to the monk at her side, her close assistant, who obliged me with a detailed account of the day's events. Later I talked to other abbey residents and obtained personal stories by mail as well.

You are a junior monk. Together with thirty others, you live in the meditation hall. Only monks can enter this space. One side is for women, the other for men. All your belongings are stored in a small cupboard during the day. At night your sleeping mat is rolled out at your sitting place.

Forty-five minutes before dawn, the bell rings to wake you up. Following the sun, you rise earlier in summer than in winter. Whatever the hour, you must be quick. Fifteen minutes is all you have to dress, stow away your things, use the toilet, wash and be in place, facing the wall, for the first meditation period of the day. After thirty minutes of deep silence, a bell rings, and you turn around in your place and face the center to chant.

From west to east, unseen, flowed out the
Mind of India's greatest sage, and to the source
Kept true as an unsullied stream is clear.

> If, from your
> Experience of the senses, basic truth
> You do not know, how can you ever find
> The path that certain is, no matter how
> Far distant you may walk? As you walk on,
> Distinctions between near and far are lost,
> And should you lost become, there will arise
> Obstructing mountains and great rivers. This
> I offer to the seeker of great Truth:
> Do not waste time.

Then, in silent procession, you move to the ceremony hall where, together with the rest of the community, you chant the remaining morning scriptures.

> When one with deepest wisdom of the heart
> That is beyond discriminative thought,
> The Holy Lord, great Kanzeon Bosatsu,
> Knew that the skandhas five were, as they are,
> In their self-nature, void, unstained and clean.
> O Sariputra, form is only void,
> Void is all form;
> O Buddha, going, going, going on
> Beyond, and always going on beyond,
> Always *becoming* Buddha. Hail! Hail! Hail!

In the early light, Oriental drums and bells punctuate the service, while the organ accompanies your singing.

Singing?

"Yes," Roshi Kennett said. "I was once a professional musician, you know. And one of my specialties was medieval music and composition. When the Vatican threw out all the ancient chants, deciding to become modern, I looked at them all—and they were so beautiful! If someone believes in throwing the baby out with the bathwater, I believe in picking up the baby!"

"Are you talking about Gregorian chants?"

"Yes. I picked up all the ones they threw out and set some of them to our scriptures. First I turned our scriptures into poetry: you keep the same words but you move the order a little. Or you make the lines a slightly different length, but it comes to the same thing. If you use what they call blank verse, you don't actually rewrite anything. Blank verse is what the psalms are written in, and interestingly enough, all Buddhist scriptures are written very much like the psalms. In the psalms, you have a verse in which one half asks the question and the other half gives the answer. Each verse is a sentence, one half complementing the other. And that's exactly what happens in Buddhist scriptures. So it was very simple. All I had to do was fit them to the music. It was very, very simple—we just fitted the whole lot together. And the Japanese are so pleased with them, they've made them the official versions in English."

"Are people shocked or surprised that you've done this?"

"No, they don't even notice! As I knew they wouldn't. You see, Gregorian chant is fundamental to Western people. It's the fundamental music that's been with us for century upon century. And it was that which made it so easy for people to change over from what they had before to what they've got now. From the Christian words to the Buddhist ones. Because here was a vehicle that they knew. Oddly enough—well, not oddly enough, it's quite reasonable psychologically—what they found was they'd got a medium that made the transfer extremely simple. They'd got an old friend so it didn't sound strange to them."

"There's a particular quality, a devotional quality—"

"It depends which one you use. There can be a terribly clingy, emotional quality. There can be. But not if you choose the right ones. You see, there are about twenty-four different types of scale. Our ordinary music has only two types."

"The major and the minor?"

"Yes. But there are twenty-four in Gregorian—and there are peregrinating ones as well. Which means if you choose the right ones, you can avoid the emotionalism. Interestingly enough, regarding our major and minor scales, the major is one of the twenty-four, which is the war scale. All our major music is written in the scale that encourages anger and violence. And all our minor music (which is the aeolian) is the death scale, in which people made all their funeral music. So what we've effectively got is war and death! But if you go into the others—for example there's the fire scale, one that can create heat in the body. And these things do, they really do create these effects, if you know what you're doing. I do most of mine in the phrygian, which is very cool and starry and still. And it gives the perfect effect. I also use the peregrinus mode because that's extraordinarily good for very long lines. It doesn't stick to any one mode. It's the equivalent of going into a lot of chromatics, although it never *moves* to a chromatic. It's a psychological chromatic. I felt that the phrygian and the lydian were the best for Buddhist chants. And it works."

For about an hour and a quarter you have been singing. Now it is time for morning chores—sweeping, cleaning inside or out, milking the goats. You bow to other monks as you disperse or as your paths cross in the cloister. In late fall and winter the air is cold in your nostrils, your shaved head covered with a warm hat.

The first few years here are the hardest. You are prepared to give up everything. At first this seems appealing, a relief, a cleansing to the core. There is a freshness of energy, a freshness of commitment. But, inevitably, the novelty fades, the romance pales. You wake one morning to bare bones. For the first time you grasp the absolute starkness: giving up everything means *everything*. Most especially it means your ideas about things. Old concepts and images begin to crumple, disintegrate like ashes underfoot. Everything seems alien, forbidding. How do others find it so easy, so natural?

You talk to one of the senior monks. And you discover you are not alone. You feel understood, acknowledged. Your crisis is only one stage on the path of training. Like any other it can be experienced fully. No judging, no turning back. Defiance, doubt, disenchantment will arise. You feel them and let them go. Boredom, anxiety, fear, resentment—these too you embrace and move on. Gradually you strip away all the layers of conditioning that you thought were "you." Sometimes the loneliness is acute. Sometimes the questions seem too huge. But the structure of your days, the example of the older monks, the support of the scriptures and meditation, and the compassion that is the bedrock of Roshi Kennett's teaching, all feed your growing faith and help get you through.

The bell rings for breakfast. Most times of year this is a formal meal, Japanese style, in the meditation hall. It is followed by a half hour of scripture reading, and then comes the longest work period of the day. For two hours you do your assigned job—one of the many needed to keep the temple running smoothly. Then come lunch, a rest period, and an afternoon work period.

You try to do each thing you are assigned to do with a willing heart. You try to maintain awareness, try not to yield to boredom or irritability, try to learn from your mistakes. If resistances arise, if you fall into automatic behavior, reminders are everywhere, built into the structure of your day. Then for a moment you sit in zazen in the midst of activity. Meaning returns. And gratitude fills your body in great waves. Going on, going on: this is the life of a monk.

At 3:30 the big bell rings and you have midday service, a recitation of the rules of meditation (the *Fukanzazengi* by Zen Master Dogen) back in the meditation hall. It's also the "closing of the gate." At 11:00 A.M. the big bell rings for the opening of the temple to the outside world. And at 3:30 it rings again, for the closing.

Through the simplicity of this life, the bare bones of it, a subtle, cell-by-cell cleansing process takes place. You allow it, give yourself over to it. Everyone, everything, becomes your teacher. Humility arises like a gentle fountain.

Training here means you give all you have. It is a letting go, over and over again, of all the tendencies that once governed your life, causing all your disasters and ecstasies. Now there is no turning back. There is no other life. Taking one step at a time, in gratitude, you go on, you go on.

Before dinner you have another work period and another scripture reading; after dinner, a rest period and a cleanup period. At 7:00 P.M. there is time for recollection, meditation at 8:00, then more singing of scriptures, tea, and bed.

A rigorous schedule, I thought.

"It's identical to the one they had in Japan," Roshi Kennett said. "The only difference is that we have used familiar terminology for some things. For example, it was outlandish to use the term *Fukanzazengi* for the scriptures just before going to bed. But if you use the term *vespers*—which meant the same thing, the last music of the day, or the last scriptures of the day—you could tie it to what people have been and what they are now. It's not contrary in any way to the Japanese tradition. But we have to use our own language. We're stuck with it. And you have to use a language that has meaning. You can't keep adding in new words. It's very frightening to people if you keep adding in new words. Words like *vespers* and *recollection* people can look up in the dictionary. I could have done so much better in Japan if I'd had it in English."

"Some people say that the meaning isn't that important in chanting, that the sound is what matters."

"I hate to say this and I don't want to tread on any corns, but as far as I'm concerned, and as far as Soji-ji was concerned, that is called atmospheric training. The purpose of training, as Dogen has put it very clearly, is to understand birth and death completely, so that they both vanish, and you find the third position, as it were, which is nirvana, a place where there is neither birth nor death. Where you are beyond those opposites. Because there *is* a third position. And you can find that place. That's what you do meditation *for*. The scriptures say it very clearly. The first scripture tells you to have faith—that's the *Kanzeon* scripture. The second one tells you what sort of signs you're going to have (this is the *Sandokai*) when you're getting close. The third one says: Don't come too close, don't go too far away. It's like this, it's like that. And these are all done in this order in Japan. And they're done in Japanese. The Japanese therefore can understand them; they're not done in some ancient language.

"So the third one's telling you how to do it, and all the pitfalls, and the fourth one—the *Scripture of Great Wisdom*—tells you what it's going to be like when you're there. So what you're doing each morning is a rehearsal, you're rehearsing what's going to happen, and when the moment comes for you to have genuine understanding, something in your brain says: Don't get too close, don't get too far away. Do this, don't do that. You've got it all programmed in.

"I can remember Koho Zenji having a quarrel with a couple of people in Japan over this. They said, 'She doesn't need to know anything in English.' And he said, 'Until she knows the scriptures in her own language and they become part of her blood and bones, she's not going to be able to study Zen properly.' He had me and another person translate them together. Then we had to explain their meaning to him, from the translation.

"He made it very clear that if the teachings are not in the language you understand well, you will not be able to get to this place of kensho—understanding—nearly as quickly. And people have sometimes said to me, 'How is it you seem to have got so many people who've made it to roshi?' And the answer is very simple: They've got the thing in their own language, and they know what the pitfalls are, know what they're doing."

"What does *roshi* mean, actually?"

"It means: gone beyond the fear that the opposites generate. They've gone beyond—if you like, they're people who know the Eternal. Even if it was only for a few minutes. They know the truth. And you can never be as if you'd not known it."

"Well, you're not saying that if you've had a kensho, that makes you a roshi . . . ?"

"If you've had a kensho and have been trained to teach, you become a roshi. Kensho by itself can't do it. You have to be trained to teach and keep your training up. That's the main thing, to keep your training up."

"It never ends, does it?"

"Never. And you can lose the title if you start letting your training down. That's the difference between Rinzai and Soto. In Rinzai, once you've got the title of roshi, you're fixed in your everlasting seat, which I find very dangerous. Soto is not. If you stop behaving like a roshi, then people will stop using the title to you. And that seems to me fair."

"You use the term *Lord of the House*. Do I understand that that comes from Keizan Zenji?"

"Yes. In the *Denko Roku*. It's a term that implies the unborn, the unchanging, the uncreated, the undying. It is what Shakyamuni discovered. Now what people normally talk about Shakyamuni discovering is the Eightfold Path and the Four Noble Truths. That was what he taught about how to *get* to this. But in the *Udana* scripture he says what there *is,* though using the *via negativa*. You are not saying there is a God. Keizan called it the Lord of the House. It's the *essence* of God. It's knowing the fullness of Emptiness, which is immaculate."

"And the term *Lord of the House* is an attempt to make that accessible?"

"It's trying to explain the inexplicable in words, none of which are ever going to work, are ever going to be adequate. Because however much you use words, they're going to imply something to somebody. They're going to imply God or atheism or something where there's nothing, or nothing where there's something. They're going to imply negativity or positivity. All you have to do is go with your gut feeling. And when somebody says the Eternal or Lord of the House or X, Y, Z, if that's what turns them on to it, that's *it!* In some cases it may be what someone means by the term *God*. You can't turn away from the term *God* simply because mankind has given it a bad connotation. You've got to go on beyond it without pushing it away."

"The term *Lord of the House* may be problematical for some people because it has patriarchal connotations."

"Fine. Say 'Lady of the House'! I don't care what you call it. Just know it in your guts, and go with whatever word is best for you. For me the term *Eternal* makes it. A lot of people, even in Japan, have trouble with Keizan calling it the Lord of the House. For a lot of people I find that to say, 'I take refuge in the Eternal'—rather than 'in the Buddha, Dharma, and Sangha'—is a lot easier. Because the word *Buddha* has got its own connotations. What you're looking for is the essence, and something that, for you, expresses it."

"We talked last time about some of your experiences as a woman, both within Christianity and Buddhism, and the kinds of difficulties you encountered. Would you say that you turned to Buddhism out of that conflict?"

"The only reason I turned away from Christianity was because I felt incredibly deeply called to be a priest. And there was no way I could be a priest in Christianity."

"As a woman."

"Yes."

"How did you discover this potential within Buddhism?"

"Oddly enough, I didn't. It was obvious that Christianity did not really want women, and while most of my life I'd been exposed to books on all the religions, I began reading more books on Buddhism. And somehow I felt that this seemed to offer the most to women. I do not believe in predestination, but something seemed to guide me to the right place."

What happened, in fact, was that the very week she resigned from her last job as church organist (because of sexual advances from the parson), Koho Zenji, abbot of Soji-ji Temple in Tokyo, invited her to Japan. For some time she had been working for the London Buddhist Society and had been making arrangements for Koho Zenji to come to England.

Toward the end of our second talk, I returned to something Roshi Kennett had mentioned in our first interview. I asked if she would say more about what she meant by a psychology beyond psychology.

"A Zen Master does things psychologically that the average psychologist would not do, simply because the psychologist is a doctor and presumes people are sick. The Zen master is a priest and is going to take psychology to a much higher place, presuming people are *not* sick. I can give you an example, We have found that on the whole, people who are very feminine or very masculine really don't make it very successfully in a monastery, because the instant they get there, they begin looking for a member of the opposite sex to get involved with. Now, a Zen master has to grow people out of that, so that what they're looking for is the Eternal rather than a mate. A psychologist tries to help people to become more mature, able to stand on their own feet. We take it from there. So normally you would not let into a monastery someone who is extremely feminine or extremely masculine— until maybe they've done some work with a psychologist and gotten more independent."

"By feminine or masculine you mean sexually charged?"

"No. You know the very clingy type that feels she must have a man to do everything for her?"

"That's not too common nowadays, is it? Maybe you mean that all of us have both sides in us, but some people have only one side developed."

"Or much *more* developed, and need to balance it more. That's one typical example. It doesn't mean that somebody like that can never train. It may mean that he's got to wait a year or two, to get the other side up a bit. Because you presume, when a person comes into a monastery for training, you *presume* that he's completely sane. Completely normal."

"So you must have a rigorous screening program. Does it extend over time?"

"It can do. The point I want to make is that the average psychologist mainly wants people to function in society without causing danger to themselves or society. He'd *like* them to be able to function at a higher level, but he usually settles for less. Now, a Zen master cannot tolerate that. We've got to push it to a much higher level."

Our second afternoon at the abbey, at my request, we met with a group of senior women monks, two of whom were roshis. (There are currently four women and nine male roshis at Shasta Abbey. As explained above, Roshi Kennett attributes this unusual number to the fact that her training has been carefully Westernized, making it much more readily comprehensible to Americans, thereby speeding their progress. The higher number of male roshis reflects not sexism but the fact that for many years far more men than women were attracted to Shasta Abbey. That has now changed dramatically—there are slightly more women today than men—and it is expected that in the next few years the number of women roshis will increase accordingly.)

As the four women arrived and took off their hats, there was the initial shock of adjusting to their shaved heads. What a striking symbol of renunciation, especially for a woman! The first to arrive was Reverend Teacher Meiten McGuire. At fifty-eight, she was the oldest monk except for the abbess at Shasta, and she admitted that this sometimes felt isolating to her. She has a Ph.D in clinical psychology, worked at the Langley Porter Neuropsychiatric Institute in San Francisco, and taught at the University of Manitoba. But the intellect is a big stumbling block to religious training, she said. For the first five years she found it very difficult. She had been at Shasta six years when we met, and while she still found the physical demands excessive, things had lightened up in the past year or so since she'd been a senior.

"But the stubbornness that arose in my fists when I was first required to do gassho!" she said. "You learn how much resistance there is. You learn what you have to look at. At some point the inner and outer gassho come together. But until then it's a form of internal medicine." She has had the impulse to leave any number of times. But each time, she realized leaving was not the answer. And each time she stuck it out to face the self she had run away from all her life.

"When one is ordained, one gives up everything," she said. "It is quite painful and difficult. Though I wouldn't be anywhere else, I still go through periods of questioning and doubt." But everything at the abbey is carefully designed to help you, she said—help you stay in touch with your heart, and to grow faith and willingness. And Roshi Kennett is a genuine master. At critical times something has always happened to make things possible. "Daily life is the teacher," she said. "What is handed to me right now is what I need to grow on."

Reverend Roshi Ando Mueller was in her thirties, rosy-cheeked, crackling with energy. She was the assistant treasurer as well as pastry cook extraordinaire and had been at Shasta for ten years. She came after what she called a series of "what looked like coincidences," to try three months of training. After one week she realized this was the life she wanted, and after two weeks she decided to become a monk. She remembered feeling, "I've come home."

What she particularly appreciated was the emphasis on meditation practice and on making every aspect of daily life an expression of meditation. People here were interested in practicing the fundamentals of Buddhism, experiencing it for themselves. When she first arrived, she felt this in the senior monks. (Roshi Kennett was not here at the time. But the quality of her training was alive in her disciples. "Her spirit was here.") She immediately felt the path was right for her.

The daily discipline she finds helpful—she had expectations of far more austerity. "It was much softer, more real. People were normal, friendly. They weren't manipulative. There was the sense that 'this is what we're doing—you can join us if you're so inclined.'"

She felt immediately accepted. Which was difficult, she said, "since one is always facing oneself, one's selfish self. In a monastery there's no escape from that." She, too, had known times of difficulty and doubt, the wish "to flee from the pain of it! But of course the only way is to embrace the pain. Something inside you knows this is right, even when the surface is saying, 'How can I?' You soon learn to trust your deeper feelings, and the others fall away."

The fact that there were women at Shasta was important to her, and that there was no difference in attitude toward their training. There is true equality, she said. It was encouraging to her that Roshi Kennett is a woman, but it was the teaching that goes beyond male and female that drew her.

When she chose to become a monk and receive ordination, Ando understood that she was becoming Roshi Kennett's disciple. Although this meant the opportunity for personal interviews (*sanzen*), much of the teaching at the abbey is done through lectures or, even more, through daily life. There are responsibilities to the community, service to the community through assigned jobs, the willingness to follow what one is asked to do, to follow the master's instructions and advice. As a result, loyalty, willingness, and friendship grow. And one becomes willing to follow the master in oneself.

Sometimes people come who want to stay "forever," she said. They may have a glamorous or romantic view of what it means to be a monk. It's actually mostly plain daily life, hard work, and at times a lot of pain in facing oneself. It requires a considerable amount of faith and trust. Otherwise, when the novelty wears off, it will be too hard. The intensity may be too much to handle— not in austerity or asceticism, but in responsibility, in doing the very best one can do.

Monastic training requires 100 percent of a person's heart and energy, Ando said. She could have chosen lay training, but did not. She chose the contemplative over the social life.

"The development of faith is a very important aspect of training," she said. "It grows into certainty, that the Lord of the House is *there*. But first you have to accept doubt completely—not indulge it, but go on with it. This is essentially an experience of faith. It is not a feeling, it's a willingness."

Roshi Kennett was all her life propelled by that faith, that willingness. For women today, doors are open (or opening) all over the world for monastic training. But when Peg Kennett—a Westerner and a woman—went to Japan to become a monk, it was without precedent. Every step of the way was new. But with this indomitable willingness, she marched ahead. And today we have a beautiful monastery for Western Buddhists under a beautiful California mountain, where women roshis are being empowered to teach along with men.

I recall an incident in *The Wild White Goose,* volume 2, that comically captures these elements and ironies. Returning one day to the Tokyo temple where she was then serving as priest, Roshi Kennett was met by the chief guest master. Urgently, he told her to go immediately to the guest department. "It is very important." He did not explain further except to say, "You really must meet this lady," and he repeated, "It is very important." Upstairs she found a throng of priests and women, and she later recorded in her diary, "In the center [was] one middle-aged one who looked rather kind and who was obviously the person concerned. She smiled at me as I came up to her and, since no one seemed willing to introduce us, I held out my hand. She took it with great glee, obviously enjoying herself and thoroughly pleased with the fact that I had offered to shake hands with her. I noticed that everyone seemed to be startled but, since nobody explained who she was, I felt that I had done the right thing. To my delight, she began speaking in English, telling me how glad she was that I was there and hoping to see me again on her next visit."

Afterward, back in her room, the director paid her a visit. "I want you to shake hands with me," he said.

"May I ask why, Reverend Director?"

"You shook the hand of the Empress of Japan. No living person has touched that hand except the Emperor. You do not realize what a great thing you have done."

And then the entire staff appeared outside her door, followed by a crowd of junior trainees. They formed a queue behind the director, and each solemnly waited in turn to shake her hand as well.

Update: Winter 2000

On November 6, 1996, at the age of seventy-two, Reverend Master Jiyu Kennett, founder and abbess of Shasta Abbey in Mount Shasta, California, died of complications of diabetes, from which she'd suffered for many years. Traditional Soto Zen funeral ceremonies were held during the seven-day sesshin at the abbey immediately following her death. Afterward, according to her wishes, elections were held for the new head of the Order of Buddhist Contemplatives, which she had created in 1983, and for the new abbott or abbess of Shasta Abbey. Reverend Master Daizui MacPhillamy was elected head of the order, and Reverend Master Eko Little was elected abbot. (At present, the order includes two monasteries—Shasta Abbey and Throssel Hole Buddhist Abbey in England, each housing about thirty-five full-time monastics—and nine priories and numerous meditation groups in the United States, the United Kingdom, Canada, Germany, and Holland.)

Roshi Kennett had struggled for years with a variety of health crises, including cancer, high blood pressure, and a heart condition that nearly caused her death in 1976, as well as diabetic neuropathy and loss of vision. But the "clarity of her purpose allowed her to survive the illness of 1976 and to live for an additional twenty years," according to Reverend Jisho Perry of the Santa Barbara Buddhist Priory, writing in the special memorial issue of the *Journal of the Order of Buddhist Contemplatives.* "She had joked about the religious experience being the 'dummy run' for death."

When Roshi Kennett died, Reverend Perry drove the ten hours from Santa Barbara to Mount Shasta and found his master's body lovingly washed and dressed in white robes for the funeral. "I bowed three times and sat in meditation," he writes. "Although I have had the opportunity of being with a number of people during and after death, never have I felt the depth of stillness that pervaded that room."

Remembering the earliest days at Shasta Abbey, Reverend Perry writes that "Rev. Master drove each week to San Francisco to teach a class at the College of Oriental Studies, sleeping on people's floors at night, and bringing home a little money and twenty loaves of free bread from the Parisian bakery every week. The day-old bread and tea, sometimes oranges, were our first breakfasts at the Abbey in those first few months. . . . When I think about this now, I am amazed at how much faith she had in starting the Abbey with no money and so little support, in poor health, and being unfamiliar with the country or the culture."

In the weeks following her death, he says, the "most amazing aspect . . . was the quality of harmony in the Sangha of monks she had ordained and trained." The traditional funeral ceremonies had to be learned and prepared, and a coffin had to be purchased. Roshi Kennett had "always loved a bargain, being both single-minded and practical," he recalls, so they "all shared in the delight of getting a bargain price on a good oak coffin."

At the end of his article, Reverend Perry quotes the sixteenth-century priest-poet Ryokan: "If we attain something, it was there from the beginning of time. If we lose something, it is hiding somewhere close by."

A personal commentary on what the relationship with a true master is like, as well as a probing look at how "all is one *and* all is different," are offered in another article in the memorial issue by Reverend Daishin Morgan, abbott of Throssel Hole Abbey in London. "In the heart of a disciple," he writes, "there is the recognition that the Buddha Nature and the master are one. . . . For me this resulted in some profoundly challenging difficulties that nevertheless helped transform some of the deepest fears that underlay my sense of isolation as a separate human being. To recognize [Buddha nature] in another being opens the way for recognizing it in oneself. But . . . if one manages to avoid setting that person on a pedestal, one also sees that he or she is a human being who sometimes makes mistakes, and one's idealism is profoundly challenged. . . . One wants to get away, but one finds that to reject the master is to reject the Buddha nature. When embroiled in the feelings of love, resentment, and fear that surround this process, it will not feel as cool and rational as setting it down on paper might imply. During the time I was able to spend living closely with Rev. Master, I oscillated between an ever-deepening love and affection for her and some quite powerful projections of anger and doubt."

Citing the Buddha's words at the time of his enlightenment ("I was, am, and will be enlightened instaneously *with* the universe"), he notes that "Rev. Master taught us that the 'with' includes all the projections, ideas, and opinions within one's own mind. . . . The coming and going of emotions, thoughts, and sensations are all the 'with'; the 'I' is therefore not the egocentric self, but that which does not move, that which remains while all else comes and goes. In the end we all have to bring together the 'I' and the 'with,' regardless of the way the 'with' manifests. . . .

"It is through allowing the barriers erected by the defensive self to come down and to plunge into the confusion that results, that one discovers that nothing was ever separated, is separate, or could become separate."

Although, for a while, it did not seem possible for me to speak personally with anyone from the abbey, in the end, I had an excellent talk by phone with Reverend Koten Benson at the Lions Gate Priory in Vancouver, British Columbia. The reverend master's death was for him "like the death of a parent or spouse." He entered the abbey at the age of twenty-one, became a monk at twenty-three, and asked to become her disciple. She was the person he cared about most in the world, and his deep grief at her loss continues. "The master-disciple relationship doesn't stop," he told me. All of the disciples are still coming to terms with her death and legacy. And a whole new dimension of her achievement is becoming visible. "Suddenly, we're our own order," he said. "Before, we were standing over an abyss with our teacher in front of us. Now, there is no one ahead. Now, it's *our* ball game!" He recently admitted a new postulant to the priory whom, in time, he will ordain. "*We* are now at the edge. The mandala is changing, like a kaleidoscope. Horizontals and verticals have shifted. The abbots and head of the order are our brothers and sisters now." Others will come and bow to *him*. "You have to get out of the way to receive a bow," he said, "but you also have to be there, to be responsible, even if you don't feel worthy."

But "it's not a matter of worthiness," he corrected himself. "It's just continuing one's training."

After the death of their master, people at the abbey seem to be moving around more, both geographically and in relation to each other. The mandala no longer has a single orientation. So trust becomes primary. Not judging. Not setting perfectionistic goals. "All of it brings up the ego, which you have to be still and look at," he said.

Reverend Koten misses his teacher's humanness. Toward the end, when she couldn't sleep, he and a few others would stay up most of the night with her. Those are the times he remembers most vividly. These days, at the edge of his own particular precipice, he sits up late with his own new postulant, mustering all the trust and transparency that he can.

8

Karuna Dharma

On a Los Angeles sidewalk
ten bare brown feet in sandals
five yellow robes.
Above an inner courtyard
a muted drone of chanting
bright altar-lights, bright flowers
a Buddha's golden smile.
Among close-packed Asian faces
an old, old woman
holds a deeply breathing child.
Now a slender man bows
holds incense to his brow
presents it to Buddha
then rejoins the crowd.

Outside, a flock of children
all tender bare elbows
their pale knees exposed
a hundred washed faces
white blouses, clean shoes—
a flock of small shorebirds
all silent, on sand.

Then round the corner strides Karuna
bluff midwestern Karuna
dressed in Vietnamese robes
and to indomitable Karuna
they wave all their bare arms.
Too polite to scream or shout
still their arms yell "Karuna!"
and their breasts pound so fiercely
their wings beat so wildly
one onlooker cries.
        —Lenore Friedman

On a broad Los Angeles boulevard lined with tall palm trees, there are several handsome old two-story houses with brightly painted porticoes, well-kept lawns, and overlapping gardens in the rear forming a sort of private park where small children, cats, and dogs mingle with shaven-headed monks in yellow robes. This is the International Buddhist Meditation Center. It was founded in 1970 by the Vietnamese Buddhist scholar and Zen master Dr. Thich Thien-an. Since his death in 1980, it has been under the direction of his closest disciple and dharma heir, Venerable Karuna Dharma. In one of the buildings, a living room has been converted into a colorful zendo with a golden Buddha figure on the altar. Although there are regularly scheduled periods of zazen each morning and evening, people can often be seen sitting there at other times of the day as well. Across the street, up a broad flight of steps ascending just beyond the front door, Karuna Dharma has her apartment and office. During my visit to IBMC, I slept on the floor of a tiny student's room opposite the zendo, but my waking hours were mostly spent across the street, up that broad flight of stairs.

Karuna's responsibilities and schedule verge on the awesome, but she put aside a good part of one day to talk with me. She had informed a number of crucial people that she was not to be interrupted, but the phone kept ringing nevertheless. "I'm in the middle of an interview—can we talk later?" she repeated many times. But then, willy-nilly, she'd get drawn into brief exchanges that gave me a hint of the wide range of issues with which she's involved (from plumbing to word processors, from problems with the city to construction crises in one of their buildings). One moment she was a savvy politician ("Uh-huh. Hm, you know, he might be right. It might be advantageous for us to have his foot in the door"); the next, a commonsensical surrogate mother to someone who was ill and vomiting ("Now go to bed, okay? Stay away from fruit juice. Try a little clear water, not too cold. After that, maybe some tea, like chamomile. No, milk at a time like this is not good").

Her laugh rings out frequently. It is large, strong, and generous—like Karuna herself.

We were sitting on cushions at a low table in a spacious room filled with rugs and couches, lamps, pictures, and oddments from all parts of the world. Between phone calls, I was beginning to get a picture of Karuna's early life. She was born in a small Wisconsin town to religious parents. Her mother was a gentle, compassionate woman who had died twelve years earlier and with whom she had had a warm, open relationship. With her father, things were more complex. There was conflict between them over the years—"I think most of it in myself." He was the founder of a small church where the family attended services and where Karuna later taught Sunday school. But at eighteen, she decided that this religious tradition didn't answer any of life's real questions, and for the next ten years she considered herself an agnostic.

When she was in her late twenties, however, the idea came to her that she was a Buddhist. Curiously enough, this idea was not based to the slightest degree on real knowledge. She had purchased a number of D. T. Suzuki's books but had never read them. This was purely an intuition, but it was a strong one—so strong that when she was later briefly hospitalized for ear surgery and had to enter her religious preference on the hospital forms, she put down "Buddhist." It was partly the hunch that this was where she belonged, partly a disinclination to be visited by a Christian clergyman. But when she left the hospital a few days later, she determined to begin some reading.

By this time she was living in Los Angeles and going through a difficult time in her life, including a divorce. She had a young daughter and was teaching at a high school full-time. She felt that her life needed restructuring. "I was very tired of certain things, tired of personal relationships, particularly with men. All I wanted was to be quiet and peaceful."

It was just before her summer vacation in the late sixties, and she decided to take a course at UCLA. (If she did, she knew she would get a raise in salary.) But in the catalogue she found nothing of interest under Literature (she taught English at the time) or Psychology. Philosophy was something she usually avoided ("I did not care for Western philosophy"), but this time she noticed a course in that department on "Buddhism and Zen." She thought, "That's fantastic. I'll take this course and get a thousand dollars more a year!"

"It was summertime, and it was the evening, so one went to class twice a week, three hours at a time. I walked in, and there was this Asian gentleman teaching the course. I sat down and looked at him, and by the end of the evening I realized that this was a religion which taught what life had taught me. He started off with very beginning stuff, with the Four Noble Truths and the Eightfold Path. And I certainly knew about suffering! I thought, 'This is really real.'"

Here was a religion that might answer a need in her life that had not been answered in a long time. She was comfortable enough on the material level, but had not been touched on the spiritual level for years—had perhaps never really been touched there at all. She came out of this first class in Buddhism knowing that she would have to really study now. And she had found her teacher: the little Asian man in front of the class, who happened to be Thich Thien-an.

"I'm not usually impressed by teachers. I've never had a guru fixation. But as I looked at this man up there who was very gentle and who had this very charming smile, who laughed and giggled and didn't take himself seriously in the least, who obviously *was* what he taught—in looking at him it seemed to me that there was an aura emanating for about twelve inches around his body. I didn't really see him as real. I don't know how to explain that. I knew that he was real, that he was human. But later, when I had known him for several years and was a close disciple of his, I told him that when I first met him I felt he was not really real, not really human. And he laughed for about fifteen minutes, nonstop. He said, 'That's a really extraordinary thing to say. How could you possibly think such a thing?'

"But in the twelve years that I spent with him every day, I never lost that feeling, that he was not really real. He walked in the human world and behaved in human ways, but he was totally untouched by the world in which he walked."

Karuna described another incident that occurred during that early period of the UCLA class. Dr. Thien-an had told nobody that he was a monk, but she knew it intuitively. She wondered how one got to be his student. During a break one evening, she went outside to sit on a ledge and smoke a cigarette. When she saw Dr. Thien-an come out and sit down directly opposite her, she was embarrassed. But he looked up at her and, smiling, pulled out a pouch of tobacco and a pipe. "You see, I smoke also." She had never spoken to him before. But he was able to perceive her discomfort. She was very touched. (Later, she told me, they both stopped smoking.)

When she finally asked to talk to him after class, he suggested they have coffee together. And across the table of a coffee shop, it became clear that "he knew all about me. He knew what I'd been going through, could name all the important events in my life. That first time we really spoke, he told me that he had known me for many, many lifetimes. With great accuracy he told me things he couldn't have known about me. And conversely, though I can't explain it, I knew many things about him."

"A remarkable meeting," I said. "You're very lucky."

"I don't know how to express the feeling of gratitude I have for having met him in this lifetime and for his showing me the path. It is something I can never repay. My whole way of looking at life changed. Those things which used to interest me don't interest me anymore. And now I just feel this overwhelming gratitude toward him."

By the time that first UCLA course had ended, Karuna had formally become Thien-an's student. First she joined a small Buddhist study group that he conducted, but when he later turned it over to a young American Buddhist monk, she asked to study with him privately and, along with one or two others, was able to have frequent access to him. She was already doing daily meditation practice (it had been assigned as "homework" during the introductory course).

Meanwhile, a number of Thien-an's advanced students suggested he remain in this country and start a meditation center. When his permanent residence status was granted, he decided to experiment with this possibility. A house was rented in Hollywood, and the group agreed to give the project a year. In fact, it took off immediately. In six months they had to move because they'd outgrown the Hollywood house, and by that time were able to purchase the larger property they now inhabit in Los Angeles.

Karuna was still teaching full-time at this point (she continued to do so until 1981), and her daughter, Christine, was eleven years old. Karuna would come to the meditation center most weekends and three or four times a week from the town where they were living nearby. There were daily sittings, weekend sesshins, and lots of work that needed doing. In 1973 she took her novice precepts.

The ordination process in the Vietnamese tradition is stricter than in the Japanese, Karuna told me, adhering more closely to ancient Theravadin rules. Full ordination, for example, requires 250 precepts for men and 348 for women, and monks are required to be single and celibate. Dr. Thien-an proved to be an innovator, however. He had studied at a Japanese university for seven years and was comfortable with Japan's more liberal approach, in which monks may marry. He felt it would be more appropriate to American culture if people were free to take either kind of final ordination—that is, the vows of a Japanese Zen monk or the vows of a traditional bhikshu or bhikshuni. All those who were to be ordained, however, were required to study all the vows for three months before final ordination, partly so that they could clearly determine which course was more appropriate for them. In the end they took either 25 vows and were called dharma teachers or 250 vows and were called bhikshus or bhikshunis. Both received the same ceremony and robes and were considered to have exactly the same status.

Because of his very strong interest in bringing different Buddhist traditions together, Dr. Thien-an invited "witness masters" to the ceremony from as many different schools of Buddhism as possible.

"That seems to have set the tone one senses at the center today," I suggested: "very eclectic, very ecumenical. That was his influence from the beginning?"

"Yes, definitely," Karuna said. "From the very beginning that was his interest. We had Theravadin monks and Tibetan lamas at the center."

"I wonder if that spirit has anything to do with his being Vietnamese? One feels it also with Thich Nhat Hanh."

"Many of the Vietnamese masters *are* ecumenically inclined. It's also true of Thich Man Giac, abbott of the Vietnamese temple here. And it's true of the abbott in San Diego as well. I'm not really sure why."

"So what sort of ordination did you have? Which set of vows did *you* choose?"

"I asked to take all the bhikshuni precepts when it came time for the final ordination. Until that time I was not sure. It wasn't because I thought I could always fulfill all the precepts—I *wasn't* sure. But I wanted as traditional and as committed an ordination as I could have. Part of my life was still an 'ordinary' life—I was teaching school and my daughter was growing up. Still, I knew that in the future my whole life was going to be committed and that as soon as I practically could, I would be totally immersed in Buddhist work."

"Did you have any feelings about women having so many more precepts than men?"

"Yes, I have some feelings about that. Some of them don't bother me in the least. Some are liturgical in nature. It's hard to discuss without talking specifically, and that's something we're not supposed to do. (And I really believe in not letting people know what the precepts are.) But yes, I think that some of them are perhaps unfairly administered. But with Dr. Thien-an, we discussed what lay behind these precepts, what each one was aimed at. And they all come down to just a couple of things: the main one is to remove ego and self-indulgence. They're not extreme precepts at all, though. In Mahayana Buddhism, they stressed the spirit rather than the letter of the law."

"But that doesn't explain why there should be so many more for women."

"No, it doesn't really. I have some theories about it, but I don't know if they're accurate or not. First of all, there's some question about whether or not all of those precepts were really enforced in the Buddha's time or whether they were added on later. The second thing is that I look at the *vinaya* [monastic discipline] as rules that were laid down 2,500 or 2,600 years ago in a particular culture, and we have no way of knowing, if the Buddha appeared in twentieth-century America, if we would have the same precepts or not."

"I think you could make a guess."

"We probably would not have as many of them. It could be an entirely different ball game. The third thing is that, of all things, the Buddha was a master psychologist. Here he was in India, where women had a role of less importance almost than the cattle, and suddenly here are women being treated as total equals in the monastic order. And I wonder if some of the precepts were not put in because of the real problems men were having in relating to women? Here you have a group of Indian men, where women have no value, and suddenly they are elevated to equals."

"So a precept like nuns having to walk behind monks appeased them?"

"I wonder if it did. I wouldn't be the least bit surprised. But that's only surmise. Some of them seem to be that sort of thing. For instance, you're not supposed to talk back to monks, and you're not to reprimand them."

"And you have to bow down to them, even if they're just newly ordained and you've been around for a long time. That's one of the first ones."

"Right."

"Has anyone considered modernizing these things?"

"I had an interesting conversation about this some years ago with Walpola Rahula, who wrote *What the Buddha Taught*. He's Sri Lankan and very well known in Theravadin circles. His books are excellent for beginners. He was in town about four years ago, and I mentioned something to him about changes that would be needed for adapting Buddhism to American society. I said there are real problems regarding the role of nuns versus monks. Not only American women but American men as well really don't like this distinction. And I told him I didn't know what to do about it.

"He looked at me and said, 'You know, monks can do nothing about it because those are not their rules. It's you nuns who can make the changes, and you're the ones who should make them!' That was very interesting, I thought."

"What would it take?"

"Well, there may be a modernization to get rid of precepts that no longer apply. And even if not, they should be given to men and women alike. Zen precepts make no distinction. And my teacher made no distinction."

"Okay. So you got fully ordained. When was that?"

"My final ordination was in 1976, with 250 precepts."

"At what point did you shave your head?"

"I shaved my head in 1974."

"Was that a big thing?"

"Yes, it was a big thing. My teacher had ordained one woman before that time who kept her hair several inches long. So when I became ready for ordination, we had a conversation about it. I asked him for permission to shave my head. But he felt that in American society it would be too difficult for a woman, especially since I was teaching. I told him it didn't bother me, I could wear a scarf when I was out in public or in school. But he said no. He refused. This was six months before the actual ordination date, and we discussed it periodically from then on. When it was really close to ordination time, I said, 'Please allow me to shave my head. Even if you don't require it of the others, please allow me to do it.'"

"May I ask you what was going through your mind?" I said.

"I felt that if one could not shave one's head, then there was not absolute commitment. I felt it was necessary, emotionally and symbolically, to be completely detached from everything. So I asked again to be allowed to shave my head, even if the other women were not required to. And he said, 'No, there can be no distinctions.' I replied that he was making a distinction in requiring the men to shave their heads but not the women. That's how I finally won the argument. At least for the ceremony, he required everybody to shave their heads.

"The day before the ordination there was a little hair-cutting ceremony. We were out in the back garden and everyone was standing around, monks as well as lay people. The head monk was Reverend Suhita. We were pretty close friends, and he'd been rubbing his hands, just waiting for this curly hair to come off. Every time he'd see me, he'd go, 'Clip, clip, clip!' He could hardly wait to take those clippers to my head. There we were in the garden in the early evening, chanting the hair-cutting chant in Vietnamese, while all our heads were shaved. Then suddenly Thich Thien-an ran into the house. One of the monks went in to see what was wrong, came back, and said, 'Don't anybody go in right now.' When I asked why, he said, 'Because Suto [Master] is in there weeping and he doesn't want anyone to see him.' He was so moved by seeing an American woman shave her head. After that he decided that anyone going to be a monk must shave the head, man or woman. It was a rule from then on. And I think it's a good rule.

"If one is out in society or out teaching Westerners where a shaved head is a detriment, then one should grow hair again. But I do feel that heads should be shaved at least for periods of time, for example during the whole intense training period right after ordination. Because it's difficult to let go of hair. It really is. If a person cannot shave the head, then he can't perform the role that a monk has, because it's not a romantic life. Shaving the head is nothing compared to the things that one has to do, just being a monk."

"In that thoroughgoing, complete way."

"Right."

"I want to ask you a little more about what it means to be a monk."

"For me, becoming a monk only meant one thing, and that was I felt the need to commit myself totally to Buddhist work. Becoming a monk to me meant a promise to myself that for the rest of my life Buddhist work would be the number-one priority."

"You said that shaving your head was easy compared to other things. Could you say more specifically what you mean?"

"I think some Americans have a very romanticized idea of what being a monk is. They think it means being able to spend long periods of time in sitting, that a monk's life is idyllic, quiet, calm, and free of outside hassles. This is utterly untrue. There are more hassles. There are more problems. There are many more demands on your time. As one's training progresses, one's role increases. The teacher and the situation demand more and more of you. It's very common for really committed monks to sleep very little and to sit a lot less, because there's so much work to do. Problems are always arising, especially in communities like this one. I'd love to spend my time working on things that could be termed spiritual, but instead my time is involved frequently with administrative things, with the city bureaucracy, with conflicts between residents. When you have thirty-five or forty people living in a communal situation, conflicts arise. People here are generally very helpful, tolerant, and supportive of each other. But even in the most open, warm, and loving community, conflicts always arise."

In 1975, a dramatic change occurred in the lives of everyone at IBMC. The United States had been at war in Vietnam for thirteen years. But in early January, Dr. Thien-an told Karuna that Saigon would fall before May 1. "How do you know?" she asked. "I just know," he replied, adding, "And there is a lot of work to do." He was soon involved in arranging for the emigration of young Vietnamese monks to this country, working through the American Friends Service Committee and the State Department, and taking responsibility for the monks' welfare and continued training once they reached Los Angeles. On April 30, Saigon fell. It was two weeks after the start of IBMC's three-month training period. The phone began ringing immediately, and it virtually never stopped. Since Dr. Thien-an was then the one ranking Vietnamese Buddhist monk in the United States, he became overnight the authority on handling the sudden flood of Vietnamese refugees to the country. For Karuna, who had already been working very hard, it meant stretching her limits further. For seven months she spent every weekend at Camp Pendleton, where the refugees were initially housed, giving religious services, talks, and general support. Later, as the Vietnamese community in Los Angeles burgeoned (and at times sleeping bodies covered every inch of the floor space at the center), she had to deal with all the exigencies of a major transplantation of human beings to a totally new environment.

"It was hectic every single moment," Karuna recalls. She had to learn how to work under pressure, to stay calm in crisis. It was no longer a matter of whether or not one could do something. "*Do it.* You had no choice. And that was good, I think." She never slept more than four or five hours a night during this period, but she knew her teacher was sleeping even less. Each moment required her total attention to what was needed, without reaction or extraneous thinking.

"I learned not to resist it, to totally not resist anything. One didn't have the chance. When you don't have that choice, you know, it never enters your mind—to resist or to say no. One doesn't have that luxury."

Overnight the atmosphere at the center was transformed. Before, they were a community of thirty-five adult residents. Now they were suddenly accommodating 150 refugees, including lots of children. "They were everywhere," Karuna said. "You could not step in or out of the lecture hall without stepping on a body because we had no place to put them." Aside from the inevitable tensions created among the American community, there were the nitty-gritty problems of getting children enrolled in school, arranging for health examinations, for financial aid, for Medi-Cal cards—all the logistics of feeding and housing this huge influx of new people.

For Karuna, this experience and the resulting close ties she's had with the Vietnamese community ever since have crucially affected the direction her life has taken. She is regularly involved in any Vietnamese Buddhist activities within driving distance of Los Angeles and has a standing invitation to every Vietnamese temple in the country. She is also very interested in Buddhist ecumenicalism and in dialogue between Buddhism and other religious groups. She is an active member of the Buddhist Sangha Council of Southern California, a group that includes all traditions and ethnic groups. Already, a "tremendous camaraderie" has developed among the various groups represented, Karuna reports.

In September 1976 a second event occurred that profoundly affected her life. The sense of crisis that had marked the Vietnamese refugee period was gradually abating. Most of the refugees were adjusting well and organizing their own programs. A Vietnamese temple had been established and was thriving. Her daughter was now sixteen years old, needing her mother's attention much less of the time. Karuna began to look forward to concentrating on her own practice, ending her public school teaching stint in two years, and being free to put all her energy into what she'd long considered her true work. In August 1976 she completed her final ordination. Her life, she felt, was on course. Then, one month later, an accident killed a woman she knew, and suddenly she was faced with the prospect of raising this woman's twenty-one-month-old daughter.

At first she thought, "I can't do it. Not *now*." She was working on her doctoral degree. She had resumed her Sanskrit and Japanese language studies. She had plans to collaborate with a Korean friend who was translating from the Chinese, while Karuna would translate from the Sanskrit. But here was this baby asleep in her crib. Karuna had been visiting the family only a few days before. And there was really no other place for the child. Carefully she sifted through all the other options, and she saw that none of them was good. She could not turn away. And on what had seemed the brink of her emancipation, she started all over again a new stint of motherhood.

In the beginning there had been real problems: the child was withdrawn, spoke no English, had no patience with herself. But Karuna felt tremendous love for her from the first moment and never regretted her decision. By the time of my visit, this adopted daughter was ten years old and full of laughter.

There was a third event that radically altered her life, and it was undoubtedly the greatest, Karuna said, because "there was no choice at all." In 1980 her beloved teacher died. He had cancer of the liver, which ultimately metastasized to the brain, and he was ill for about a year.

"But it was not until about three months before his death that we saw him as being ill or that he saw himself as being ill. His surgeon told me that he must have been in great pain. But all he ever admitted to was a little discomfort."

Karuna was with him regularly, was the one who drove him to the hospital on the final day. "It was difficult spending all that time with him when he was so ill, watching that life go away, knowing there was nothing to be done, clinging to it, not wanting him to leave."

"It was good you were there," I said.

"I was glad I was there."

"You loved him a lot."

"Oh, yes. I've never had a closer friend in all my life."

His effect on her was so profound, Karuna says, that she will never be able to repay him. "The only way a student can ever repay that debt is to become as great as the master. I don't know if that's possible." She paused, and then added, "No, I think it's possible. It's not only possible, I think it's likely. Not right away. But if I work at it."

After his death there was a tremendous void and a need to restructure her boundaries. "He was so much a part of me, and I had become so much a part of him, that without the other physical being there, it was really difficult to know where my own personality boundaries lay. And that took a long time to resolve." She wasn't ready to be on her own, would have preferred to wait ten years. But it was like being shoved off a cliff. There's no time to think, "Am I ready?" or "I want to wait ten years."

Gradually, however, as the boundary lines were redrawn, Karuna realized that she would never be separated from Thien-an. "He is totally within me so strongly that he's always with me."

Karuna naturally assumed all the responsibilities of the center after Thien-an's death, and was named director of IBMC in 1980. In addition to her administrative duties, she teaches regular classes at the Thien-an Institute of Buddhist Studies. (Some recent subjects have been Lotus Sutra Study; History and Development of the Early Mahayana; Zen Philosophy, Zen Practice; Dharma Teacher's Class; Vimalakirti Nirdesa Sutra; Buddhist Philosophy; Sutra of Queen Srimala Devi; and Asian Philosophy and Religion.)

When I remarked that she didn't seem to even think about having a life for herself, she replied, "No. You don't have a life for yourself as a monk. It's totally gone. It's been gone for a long time, but particularly now it doesn't exist."

Inevitably, we talked about Karuna's experience as a female monk and teacher within a largely male environment. It was crucial at first, she remembers, to develop her sense of confidence and independence—"not something that is cherished for women in probably any culture"—and it took a while to stand on her own completely, not to rely at any time on anyone else. Women are taught from birth to turn to others when problems daunt them, she said. Men are taught they must have solutions. But today this is shifting. Men are acknowledging that they don't always have solutions. And women are seeing dependency as a crutch they need to get rid of, she said. "They have to face that directly and become totally independent. And I think I do that now. We'll see whether that's true or not! But I think I came to that point completely only after the death of my teacher, when there was nobody to whom I could turn."

"Have you had any problems with men who aren't accustomed to women having that kind of independence?" I asked.

"Oh, yes, definitely. And I can be very obnoxious at times. I try to be nice about it, but I do confront men very directly. On the other hand, there are problems with women—those who attribute all our problems to male dominance in the society. While that's true to a certain extent, it's also a way of evading one's own responsibility. So what if that was true in the past? We have to deal with it right now. I've also had women try to convince me that experiences in meditation are different in women than they are in men. I think that's malarky. Each individual experience is different, and certainly gender is involved for part of it, but only part of it. And I'm not sure it's the most important part."

Karuna does feel that it's important that we have women teachers—not just for women, but for men as well. They provide an alternative approach and perspective. But the common perception of them as gentler, softer, and quieter is an illusion, Karuna believes. However soft the exterior, "it ain't much different inside." Perhaps, even, women can be a bit more flinty than men.

"Are you speaking of yourself?" I asked.

"I can speak of myself. For a woman to get to this position, there has to be real strength and real steel underneath all that. I can be as uncompromising as any man anytime, and perhaps worse."

"I'd like to see you in action!"

"Well, mostly I'm a very reasonable person. But I'm very stripped of myself. I expect a lot from other people. One of my weaknesses is that I do not tolerate lazy people or incompetent people. I let them go. The students who can get close to me are committed in a steady, long-term way. The ones with whom I'm willing to spend time are the ones who are very hard-working and who don't say, 'I can't.'"

Although she has had no particular female role models along the way, Karuna never experienced this as a problem. "It never occurred to me that women could not accomplish *whatever.*"

In a slightly different mood later on, however, Karuna showed another part of herself. We can talk all we want to, she said, about there being no division between men and women, about enlightenment having nothing to do with sexual differences ("If there's no body, how can there possibly be sex differences?"). On a more mundane, daily level, however, we have to acknowledge perceived distinctions. And more and more, Karuna has noticed a widespread shift toward what are considered feminine values. As Buddhism moves into this new culture, she believes, it will be truly successful only if there is a great deal of feminine energy and responsibility involved.

Women in Buddhism in America, she says, are on what David Spangler calls the "cutting edge." They have to be very aware, therefore, and even "better" than their male counterparts. ("Frankly, I think that maybe we are better in some ways.") Although she anticipated raised eyebrows, she went ahead and said that in general not only are women more nurturing, intuitive, and sensitive to change, but that they are *stronger.* They're the ones on whom entire families have always depended. And at rock bottom, she said, women are less emotional than men.

I asked her to repeat that, please, and she did. "I think women are less emotional than men, much more realistic, and less romantic than men when it comes to practical, nitty-gritty, daily things. Women are much more realistic in their relationships and in their attitudes toward relationship."

"Men have always romanticized women," I said. "To our detriment, unfortunately."

"And I think women have not done that toward men anywhere near as much. Perhaps we're better grounded to begin with."

She went on to describe an incident years before when someone had asked her teacher about women becoming enlightened. They had noticed that all or most of the examples in the literature pertained to men. Thien-an had replied that in his opinion it was easier for women to attain enlightenment because many of them have already very strongly developed compassion and intuitive insight. So they are innately much closer than men to realization. Emotionally they have fewer walls erected around them.

Women, however, have not traditionally become teachers and leaders, Karuna feels, because they are less interested in power in the broader sense. And women's conditioned role has always been subordinate to men's—"This is not Buddhism, it's a cultural imposition," she said. But now women need to take their place as equals, not wait for it to be given to them. If they don't, they won't get equal treatment.

"Within the structure of Buddhism today, it is possible to just take it?" I asked.

"If one is willing to work on it, yes, it will be. And now is the time to do it. Whatever we do in these formative stages is going to have a profound influence on what comes up in the future."

There is an epilogue to the story of Karuna and her teacher. It concerns her father, with whom she'd had a difficult, thorny relationship most of her life. His ancestors had come to America 350 years ago, and he was "very English," very reserved. She felt unable to talk to him about anything important to her. Although he wanted his children to grow up to be independent thinkers, his disapproval and incomprehension of his daughter's most important life choices were clear to her. In 1975, a year after her mother died, her father decided to remarry, and when he called to tell her about it, she heard unmistakably that he was as afraid of her disapproval as she had ever been of his. At that moment, all her own fears dropped away completely.

Later, he met her teacher and spent some time with him. And, Karuna says, "that was very, very good." He started to read and study and talk to knowledgeable people about Buddhism so that he could understand what his daughter was doing. When Thien-an died, her father had just undergone knee surgery, but he said immediately he would come out to be with her. "But you're still in the hospital," she said. "You can't move around." But he only repeated that he would come.

"It was exactly what I needed," Karuna says. He began doing exercises in his hospital bed, and despite his doctor's warning that he shouldn't move for several weeks, in three days was ready to board the plane.

His very presence was immensely helpful to Karuna. All day she would be at the center in Los Angeles, surrounded by the enormous burden of everyone's grief and anxiety. There was little time for her own. At night she would drive back home to Downey, where her father would be waiting, even if it was 1:00 or 2:00 A.M. There would not be much time, and they would talk mostly of inconsequential things, but simply to have him there meant a lot. "And when he saw the thousands and thousands of people who came out for that funeral, and when he read the article in the *Los Angeles Times,* and the messages that were coming in from around the world, and heard about the ceremonies that went on here endlessly for a week, he realized where I was and the position I was in. Today he talks about me as 'my daughter, the Buddhist monk,' and I think he's very proud of me now."

So Karuna lost a teacher but found the father she had not realized was there. According to a recent issue of the IBMC *Monthly Guide,* it appears she has also found a disciple—a woman with many years' nursing experience who is now in monk's training with her and who is already leading a weekend retreat on meditation and healing. (In a recent letter Karuna writes about a new male disciple in training as well.) This was something she had talked about wanting sometime in the future when I saw her last. At that point she was thinking mostly about carrying on the work of her teacher. She had promised him that, and would keep her promise. But eventually, she said, she wanted to be able to have disciples training under her as monks and nuns, and to develop a core of dedicated people, one of whom would ultimately be able to take over the center and leave Karuna free.

Free for what? For writing, for editing several manuscripts left by Thien-an, possibly for doing a biography about him, to return intensively to her scholarship, to her Sanskrit, to read the sutras in the original, to travel occasionally to Asia, to do more ecumenical work. This would all take time, however. There was still a long stretch of motherhood ahead for her. And training a disciple to take over the center, she felt, would take at least ten years. But things are clearly moving ahead. I can see Karuna striding emphatically onward. And I can hear her laughing.

Update: Winter 2000

From our first visit all those years ago, I vividly remember Karuna's physical presence: robust and radiating abundant energy. Now, she walks with a cane, her left leg in a brace, her left arm nonfunctional. Six years ago, she had a major stroke, which left her unable to roll over in bed. Now, after rehabilitation and with a modified vehicle, she is able to drive every day. She walks with difficulty and with great concentration.

Although Karuna never doubted she would recover, helplessness was at first a huge challenge. "Becoming totally dependent upon people was a big lesson I needed to learn," she told me. Intimate details of her experience were seen in a new light. "I began to appreciate the way our bodies work, without our thinking about it." Now, she had to concentrate on everything. "How do I move this foot? What do I have to do to get down the stairs? Can I put on this shirt? Can I make my left leg move?" Simple, but so difficult. In order to lift her leg, she had to stop and think, "Lift the leg."

Most difficult of all, though, was dealing with her emotions, which were suddenly out of control. She had never cried in public before, "not even when my teacher and best friend died." Now she found herself crying at the most ordinary things. It embarrassed her at first, but soon she learned to explain matter-of-factly that it was the result of her stroke. Over time, she regained control, although she still finds herself crying easily at movies!

The whole experience was "a great teacher" for her. She saw that "whether we weep at sad things or become angry easily is not necessarily an indication of our progress along the Buddha path." At first, incontinence also challenged and embarrassed her. But she learned that after a stroke, the bladder often shrinks, and it became easier to see her incontinence as just another way that she was not in control. "What people think" keeps shrinking in importance.

To some degree, Karuna's teaching responsibilities have been taken over by senior students. For the first three years after her stroke, for example, her chief monastic student conducted the monks' training program. Tragically, this student herself died in 1996, forcing Karuna back into some of the roles she'd given up.

One area that's become particularly compelling to her is a prison outreach project inaugurated five years ago. Each week, the International Buddhist Meditation Center (IBMC) receives five to ten letters from prisoners seeking information about meditation. If Karuna senses they are appropriate candidates, she places them in a correspondence program that puts them directly in touch with experienced students who send materials and answer questions. One student corresponds monthly with more than sixty prisoners, overseeing a course of instruction for each. Now, one of the prisoners himself has taken over responsibility for orienting several new students. The goal is to train long-term prisoners to begin and sustain meditation/study groups in prisons where interest is high. One of these prison students was ordained by telephone as a brother in Karuna's order, and he, too, has been entrusted to correspond with beginners. Another monk at the center works with young people at Juvenile Hall and Camp Kilpatrick in Malibu. He teaches them blues harmonica along with meditation instruction!

In recent years, the center has hosted Halloween parties for homeless or abused children as well as a large outdoor concert for the entire neighborhood with several Los Angeles rock bands. Six weeks after the Los Angeles riots of 1992, the IBMC in conjunction with the Inter-Religious Council of Southern California organized an event called Hands across Los Angeles. Twenty thousand people stood side by side along ten miles of Western Avenue, holding hands and demonstrating the interracial, interreligious harmony that has been a central concern at IBMC for many years. (IBMC was basic to the planning and execution of the event, which had largely been arranged by Karuna's eldest daughter.)

Karuna has also noticed an increase in the number of gay people flocking to the center, probably the result of outreach by
two senior students: one has been working with lesbians on the
Internet, and the other has been leading a gay men's group at
the center. "Their gayness is not an issue with us," she says. One
gay man has been fully ordained as a Zen teacher, and two men
and one woman have been ordained as teachers in training. All
expect eventually to become fully ordained Zen teachers.

But the "biggest change," according to Karuna, has been in
the center's traditional ordination procedures. In 1994, it held
the first Grand Ordination, inviting master teachers from all traditions to participate. Thirty master teachers arrived for the ceremony, representing the Theravada, Mahayana, and Vajrayana
traditions, and Pure Land priests could be seen as well as Zen
masters. Furthermore, men and women were granted equal ordination responsibilities. For the first time in history, a female master (Karuna) offered final vows to both male and female
monastics.

The ceremony was "truly international": it was conducted in
English, used traditional forms of Vietnamese ordination, and
took three hours to perform. Each monk put on the robes of his
or her tradition and received a name from his or her master.
Twenty-seven men and women were ordained that day. Three
years later, in November 1997, a second Grand Ordination took
place. As a result, three Theravada women from Vietnam, Sri
Lanka, and Nepal have received full ordination, "which could
never have happened in their homelands," and eight Western
women have been ordained in the Tibetan tradition. Karuna
hopes that other temples will follow suit, ordaining people not
into separate traditions but into a unified Buddhist order.

She does feel some urgency about cultivating new, young students. Most of her monastic students, she feels, are "too old to
carry on with the center after I'm gone: they're in their later
forties, fifties, or even seventy. I'm going to be sixty next year,
and it takes ten years to train a student to take over. It's difficult
to find someone who can administer as well as teach. Therein lies
my problem."

But being a good teacher, she now believes more than ever, is a matter of how we live our lives "rather than giving brilliant talks." Her prison work, I think, a central part of her teaching now (and mostly accomplished by computer), is a good example. "Prisoners are desperate for contact with the outside world," she says. "Their approach is direct, urgent, often quite touching, especially those with many years left in prison. Some of them have very good insight. At first, they will write something like, 'I am just a beginner in meditation. I have come to learn that I caused most of my problems. I am not truly a bad person, although I have made mistakes. Now, I want to learn to control my life, to find peace in this place that has no peace. Can you help me by sending me some books or a newsletter about Buddhism? I thank you for taking time to read my letter, and I wait anxiously for your reply."

Sometimes, Karuna feels grateful for waking up in the morning. Sometimes, "I'm tired and want to laze around. But I don't have the time."

9

Sharon Salzberg

You might think she's too young
to speak the word compassion
and taste it on the tongue
to explain renunciation
from knowledge in the bone
to pronounce *dukkha*
and say it from the spine,
with the hairs of the skin.
But look at the eyes
at the arc of the chin.
A Giotto madonna?
A Chinese Kwan Yin?
　　　　—Lenore Friedman

The time is the early seventies and the place is Calcutta. Two young Americans are walking through crowded, filthy streets to the dwelling of an extraordinary saint and teacher named Dipa Ma. They turn down a narrow slum alley and make their way through puddles of sewage to the house they're looking for. Up four flights of steps they find a tiny room where Dipa Ma lives with her daughter. It contains almost nothing but a wooden bed and a curtain behind which a few clothes are hung. There are many such rooms, containing many families, around a courtyard below, where there is a communal water pump. At one end there is a kitchen and a bathroom that all the families share. In these surroundings, Dipa Ma sits quietly, radiating a kind of light. Sometimes she will feed her guests, sometimes answer questions if there is a translator. Often, she will just sit, totally at peace. After an hour or two, the Americans leave her presence filled with a strange happiness. They descend the narrow stairs and walk through the abysmal streets as if in a heaven world. They traverse the puddles of sewage and see the beggars and the lepers bathed in light.

One of these two Americans was Sharon Salzberg, and she was *very* young, barely nineteen at the time. The other was Joseph Goldstein, whom she had met not long before at her first ten-day retreat with the famous meditation master S. N. Goenka. Joseph had been in India for several years when Sharon arrived. Through another of his teachers, named Munindra, they met Dipa Ma, who had once been Munindra's student. Dipa Ma started practice quite late in life, after a series of great losses, and made remarkably swift progress through many advanced states of consciousness. Sharon describes her as "utterly empty. There's no one there." At the same time she is very powerful, with "the power of light."

Sharon spent several years in India and Burma, studying with a number of important teachers, including the great Tibetan master Kalu Rinpoche, about whom she speaks with love and veneration. But in some ways, Dipa Ma may have had the most profound effect on her life. For one thing, she told Sharon she would be a great teacher herself one day, and sent her home to put that process in motion (at a time when Sharon was feeling rebellious and unprepared). One of the results was the creation of the Insight Meditation Society, founded in 1975 by Joseph Goldstein, Sharon Salzberg, and Jack Kornfield in Barre, Massachusetts.

It was there that I first interviewed her for this book in the fall of 1983. I had talked to her before, as a student, at a number of ten-day vipassana retreats she had co-led with Joseph. Now at Barre the annual three-month course was in progress. The center was full (as it usually is at these times), and I was accommodated in a basement gymnasium that was fitted with partitions and platform beds—an entirely satisfactory arrangement, as it turned out. And except for the times I talked to Sharon, I kept the regular schedule for four days.

IMS is housed in a huge brick New England building that was once a Catholic seminary. There are several floors and wings where a newcomer can get lost. During the winter the building is very difficult to heat. But although it snowed while I was there, it did not get really cold. I remember a wonderful silent walk through scraggly woods, walking over layers of multicolored foliage, including star-shaped maple leaves, purple on one side and crimson on the other.

Sharon first discovered Buddhism at the age of seventeen, through Chögyam Trungpa's books *Born in Tibet* and *Meditation in Action*. She was a freshman at the University of Buffalo in upstate New York at the time. Two years later—by a series of what on the surface looked like "accidents," but which she now sees as the perfect unfolding of her life—she found herself in India on a junior year abroad. It was October 1970. She had never meditated before, but knew she wanted to learn. And by another series of "accidents" she found herself at a ten-day retreat with meditation master Goenka in New Delhi.

What she remembers most vividly of that early experience was pure, unremitting physical pain. It took seven months of undaunted effort for her to be able to sit still for one period of sitting (an hour in this tradition). Her determination, however, was absolute. Once she was embarked, she never wavered. Doubt about her direction never entered her mind. (She says today that although she has experienced self-doubt and questions about one particular practice over another, this complete lack of doubt about the path from the very beginning is sometimes a hindrance in dealing with students who do have problems with doubt.)

Sharon had experienced more than her share of loss and turmoil in her early life. Her father left the family when she was four and a half. Her mother died when she was nine. Her father returned briefly at that point, leaving again when she was eleven. By the time she reached India she was propelled by an intense wish to be free of suffering and all its causes. This conviction burned like a steady flame, carrying her through obstacles of every variety, particularly on the physical plane. When she became severely ill with hepatitis and had to return home for treatment, she remained in the United States only a few weeks before leaving again for Canada. There she did a series of retreats with vipassana teacher Robert Hover, and returned to India at the earliest possible opportunity. This time she remained one and a half years.

Now, remembering how naive she was during this early period, she is touched and amused. "I had no sense of boundaries," she says, "and I took things very literally. I didn't know what was possible for me and what was not possible for me." When Munindra explained practice was sitting until you awaken fully to the truth, she simply sat down to do it! "I was very malleable that way. It was very simple for me. Very unquestioned."

Simple doesn't mean easy. While she was studying with Kalu Rinpoche in Darjeeling, for example, she lived on the top of a hill in a potato shack without roof or even real walls. It had to be covered with plastic during the monsoon season, and the only water was in a stream at the bottom of the hill. Food was restricted to one meal a day. But she came to understand renunciation and—very deeply from Kalu himself—what it means to be a bodhisattva.

From Goenka she learned about pure, impersonal love. It was very clear that he wanted nothing from her. He accepted no money and was clearly not teaching for ego enhancement or power. This model of "tremendous purity" has been very important in the development of IMS (which, except for an incident involving a teacher from India, has never been plagued with destructive dramas of the kind that have occurred elsewhere).

The kind of protection and love Goenka provided made it safe for Sharon to look at the things in herself she had never looked at before. She began following him around from retreat to retreat in different parts of the country. After ten days of intensive concentration, suddenly she would find herself on a noisy, overcrowded, stifling train for three days, on her way to the other end of India. Then they'd be off somewhere else. Toward the end of her time with him, she was doing thirty-day retreats (or three ten-day retreats in a row).

By this time Sharon's practice had developed considerable strength and intensity. She was applying herself with the commitment of one who might die each night, with a one-pointed determination that after a while, however, began to feel unbalanced and twisted. Instead of her old pure motivation of release from suffering, she was now experiencing grasping and self-hatred, wanting to protect and repeat states of consciousness, wanting to be something or someone other than she was.

Then, as if created by her need, three influences came into her life which turned this process around. The first was Shunryu Suzuki's book *Zen Mind, Beginner's Mind,* which she read for the first time in India. In its gentle way, it shook her into awareness that the ego was not something she had to destroy: it had never existed to begin with! She saw that every moment she was not identified with it, she was free. Her practice began to soften.

Then, a short time later on a trip to Burma, Sharon met a teacher named Sayama, at a center where Goenka himself had studied long before. Goenka had spoken about her as "Mother Sayama," and Sharon was expecting to meet a saint. Instead she beheld a woman arrayed in diamond earrings, gold necklace, fancy silk brocade embroidered clothing, and makeup. "She was very real!" Sharon said. She was also an accomplished mimic, and given to teasing people and poking them in the ribs about their idiosyncrasies. When Sharon was seriously ill and feeling sorry for herself, Sayama coolly observed that her experience of illness was excellent preparation for death.

The third event was her meeting with Dipa Ma, sketched at the opening of this chapter, which Sharon described to me as "the culmination of a search for perfect love."

In very different ways, both Dipa Ma and Munindra especially helped her loosen her attachment to the states of deep and silent concentration she was achieving (a real danger of the retreat model, Sharon now feels). Dipa Ma taught by her very being—a perfect expression of integration and wholeness. Munindra would merely say, "Oh, come on, let's go shopping!"

When we talked in Barre, Sharon expressed concern about some of the dilution that may occur in transmitting the dharma to the United States. "Sometimes I have this nightmare," she told me, "that if we decide for the sake of American culture not to mention enlightenment anymore—because people get so goal-oriented and competitive here—in a hundred years the word won't be in our vocabulary. That's an exaggeration, of course, but we do have a responsibility to prevent anything like that from happening. I remember that some of the things we were told in India at first didn't please me at all—like how much effort practice takes. That's a real challenge to the expectation of instant gratification so many of us grow up with."

"Both of those are full of paradox," I said. "Enlightenment and effort. Do you really go for it, or does that just subvert the whole process?"

"It *is* a paradox, which is why it's so beautiful. It's not one or the other.

"Maybe that's what's important to transmit."

"I think that's right. That *is* what's important to transmit. And it's also all right to challenge people. When we taught the first parents' retreat here, some of them were quite upset about what their children were doing. And we did this funny thing. We decided to cater to their presumed prejudice, and I remember Joseph teaching about the truth of no self-image instead of the truth of no-self. We watered it down! What was really interesting was that they didn't need it—if you live long enough and go through enough suffering, you don't need the truth sweetened for you. Some of them had tremendous wisdom."

"So you were able to let go of 'catering'?"

"Yes."

"Good. That would have been cheating."

"I do get apprehensive sometimes that we teachers, having gone through our own epiphanies and struggles, want to spare others from having to go through them too. But these things have a life of their own. And we each have to work through our own conditioning. If I had met Dipa Ma at the beginning of my practice, it probably wouldn't have had the same impact. I had to go through all that delusion, that confusion about what I was doing. Yet I find myself wanting to say to people, 'Oh, don't do that, you don't need to do that, I did that!' I try to maneuver them a little bit so there will be more balance. But there's a natural balancing process that seems to take place, and you can't really spare people pain."

I asked Sharon if we could have a small practice interview at that point, because some of the issues that had come up were relevant to my experience both in recent weeks and in the past few days of sitting. She agreed.

Lenore: One of the things that seems to be shifting in me is a sense that nothing is really stopping me, that I can go as far as I want, and that I want to go all the way. In the past I felt I wasn't supposed to want that, and—isn't it amazing—that I should be satisfied with little crumbs. In a sense I *have* been satisfied with these small experiences that tell me what's real and that connect me with the universe. But now there's a deeper wanting—yes, a wanting, and I'm not inhibiting it—to know what's most basically true. Beneath everything, *what really is there?* And sitting here, I'm noticing a lot of energy during the day, and my concentration is deepening. There's also a kind of tension that has to do with striving and wanting—and I catch myself and don't know what to do with it. You'll probably say, 'Watch it,' but is that all?

Sharon: First, it's tremendous that you're not inhibiting this. When Dipa Ma told me I could be a great teacher, she said the only thing that would stop me is thinking I couldn't do it. Most of the trouble you're having, though, comes from the tendency to get into duality, which is what I did too. The striving, and trying to undo that, can become another duality, rather than realizing its essential emptiness. If you see the difference, it can't affect you. If we feel aversion toward the striving, we're in a double mess because we have the striving plus aversion.

Lenore: It's paradox again, isn't it? I need to learn how to work with it—obviously it's inherent in everything. I mean if you don't want enlightenment, then what are you doing here? And yet you're not supposed to want it. Okay, how do you want it without attachment? Is that helpful?

Sharon: Yes, that's very helpful. There are a few things. One is to first understand that what we tend to do in the West when we hear the Buddhist teaching is to take that concept of attachment, which he taught was the root of suffering, and translate it back into some kind of judgment: attachment is bad and wrong, evil and wicked—instead of realizing that it is simply the root of suffering. Because we get so judgmental, we don't see that to relinquish the attachment is like letting go of a burden. It's like abandoning that which is weighing us down and causing us suffering. That is the first thing that comes to mind.

I think you're right, that it's a question of learning how to want it without being attached—and yet not fearing attachment, not creating a whole new way of self-judgment around being attached or not being attached. If you can see that happening—the struggling and the striving—you can take that energy and turn it so that you're fully in the moment, observing. And that's all you need to do, again and again and again.

Lenore: I've been able to *half* do that, but the next minute I find myself becoming almost grim.

Sharon: I think the reason that the way out of paradox eludes us is because it's really very simple—which is just to return to the moment instead of trying to resolve it on a more conceptual or psychological level. Return that energy to being in the moment, again and again and again.

Lenore: So just the awareness of the process in myself is . . . enough.

Sharon: Is enough.

Lenore: It's so hard to believe that.

Sharon: I know. I know. It's hard to believe, but it's true. What we do instead is punish ourselves. In the beginning the things we see are gross—hatred, greed . . .

Lenore: Jealousy.

Sharon: Yes. Later we see more subtle things, like striving or ambition or comparing. But the tendency is the same, is to judge it and make it very solid and real. You may have had thirty thoughts, but this is the one you isolate out of the flow, as though it were not another changing event. And you say, 'This is me. I've got trouble. I'm a really striving person.'

The austerity of the practice is that whatever is going on, it's the same principle. There's nothing else to do but to be there with it and to let it go. There aren't many elaborations as one goes on. Basically we have to learn how to do one thing but we have to learn how to do it very, very well.

A short time later, the subject of reincarnation came up—it had been mentioned in the dharma talk earlier that morning. Though I'd heard it explained a hundred times, I'm always left with the question: If there's no self to continue after death, what then reincarnates? Sharon agreed it was slippery. She asked me what was the same in me now that was there when I was six. I replied that I didn't know. The teaching, she said, is that there is nothing the same, no substance or entity that has moved from then to now. But there has been a certain continuity to the process. One moment is affecting the next is affecting the next. It's not random or haphazard. There's a continuity "without any single thing being shlepped along through time." And the same is true of physical death. Just as we're being born each moment and extinguished each moment, in the same way there is a continual becoming, which is reborn.

"There's a stream of stuff that goes on," I suggested.

"That's close."

"What's wrong with it?"

"The word *stuff* is a little . . ."

"Oh, okay, it's like substance. There's a stream, then." (Or a *streaming*, I think now.)

"Right. There's the analogy of planting an apple seed and getting a tree which bears fruit with seeds which are not the same as the first. But there is a continuity, a stream. Joseph uses the image of a seal and wax. The seal leaves its imprint on the wax, but there's nothing of the seal in the wax."

"Well, I'm just going to let that brew," I said. "Karma is another really tough one for me."

"Let's talk about it."

"It's the suffering, the innocent suffering. I can't accept it at all. No matter how much one talks about past lives or cause and effect, it doesn't work for me. I also have trouble with the opposite end, which is cruelty. If karma works, then that's going to produce consequences and effects later on. But however much I try to grasp the largest possible picture, it eludes me there."

"It's very complex. The Buddha himself said that it can drive you a little crazy, thinking about karma too much."

"Do you think that with our ordinary minds we may not be able to really fathom it?"

"Oh, yes, I think that's true."

"So you can rest with its being unfathomable?"

"I can rest with its being unfathomable intellectually. But I have an intuitive sense of its rightness. Some of that is almost a kinesthetic sensitivity I've developed to my instincts. When I have more greed, more hatred, I can feel it. It creates an aura that I can perceive, and it sends out a certain kind of energy which attracts other energy. Something's been created in that moment that has a certain vibrational element, and I can sense the states of mind that creates. So I can see how I create my whole universe."

"Totally?"

"Yes. Not that I can control unpleasant things from happening. But my whole relationship to it."

"I know many people believe that everything we get, we've created. But my experience is that it isn't that simple. That there are other things going on. If there's a grand, huge design, then there are flaws in it. Do you know what I'm saying?"

"Yes. With my mind I don't believe I can understand it. But there's an intuition I have that things are not accidental, that I generate a certain kind of energy, and that that will come back to me. I've seen it. In the midst of misery, hatred, or greed, I can see the karma in the immediate suffering that comes from generating action based on those states. When I'm in a generous phase, I have a strong feeling of contentment—that I have enough. There's a rule of karma that if you're generous, you receive a lot. But it doesn't really matter, because what happens is that there's so much space created that, whatever I have, it *feels* like enough. Whereas when you're tight, nothing's enough. So I understand it in a very moment-to-moment sense. A kind of intuition of karma."

Before leaving Barre, I talked with two people on the staff there about their impressions of Sharon as a teacher. The first had been an art museum curator before becoming office coordinator at IMS. Her work with Sharon has been an important part of her practice since she started in 1977. And the fact that Sharon is a woman, she said, is definitely important to her. She appreciates the way Sharon combines gentleness and compassion with her intellectual power, clarity, and rigor of practice (which Sharon puts across very softly). She has a very special way of guiding metta (loving-kindness) meditation and generally has great spaciousness of personality. Her gentle allowingness and acceptance that everything is okay make space for anything that comes up. "She doesn't clench."

An important point this student stressed was that, in her seriousness, Sharon is empowering to women. Often the message is that "the real stuff, the deep stuff, is for men to do." Sharon's example is a vivid contradiction.

All the teachers at IMS, according to this student, share qualities of simplicity and lack of formality. At Barre, the concept of teachers as "spiritual friends" is an experienced reality. Nothing has to be glossed over or overlooked with them. There are no covert emotional or sexual dramas. Everything is out in the open. She sees this as part of the rigor that permeates everything. "It goes all the way—to emptiness," she said. They have nothing to protect, and this creates openness and trust.

A male student concurred on the importance of having female teachers. In his experience, women have a greater sensitivity and range of understanding, especially of subtle emotional exchanges. "There is less harshness and a softer quality that I feel is essential at certain times in practice," he said. "I feel more completely understood. Sharon's softness has made it okay for my own female qualities to be expressed."

He also agreed that female teachers are needed to demonstrate that women have equal potential in practice. "And it's important for students to have access to the whole range of possibilities in the mind. Males especially are normally restricted to a partial range," he said.

He recalled an important interview he'd had with Sharon sometime earlier. It was during a period when he'd been caught up in male competition with another student whom he perceived as developing rapidly, while his own practice felt stagnant and "plateau-ish." Because males are conditioned to be competitive, he feels a male teacher would not have seen this situation as clearly as Sharon did. What she told him was: "When you're competing, you're only competing against your own ignorance." He seemed to be remembering her exact words. And as we parted, he summed up: "Sharon's stability and equanimity are quite inspiring to people."

Six months after I talked to Sharon at IMS, an event occurred that, wholly unexpectedly, changed her life. It was May 1984, and the staff at Barre was expecting the arrival of a Burmese teacher named U Pandita, who was coming to teach a three-month retreat (he had never before traveled outside of Burma). Sharon had heard about him from others but had not felt particularly drawn to him. She was standing in the kitchen when he walked through the door—and the moment she saw him she felt "hit by lightning." Although she had had intense experiences with teachers in the past (for example with Goenka and Dipa Ma in India), she told me that she hadn't expected this to happen to her again in this lifetime.

· During that three-month course that she sat with U Pandita, their strong connection developed further. He was extremely hard and demanding with her, but she was overjoyed to be practicing with a teacher again for the first time in ten years. She described him as a "warrior type" who feels it is better to die in the effort to get free than not to try. Practice, the most important thing in life, is not to be done sloppily. He requires absolute moment-to-moment mindfulness, without a gap. If Sharon made one unmindful step during an interview, he would catch her and say, "Are you noting that?" Her movements began to slow down so radically that it took her an hour to get from the meditation hall back to her room. He would tease her and say, "You're walking so fast!"

For some, U Pandita's style is overly severe and harsh. He is able to raise an eyebrow and convey utter scorn. Some have felt fundamentally unmoored and devastated. For Sharon, however, his style was liberating. He took her relatively limited idea of what she was capable of and expanded it infinitely, she says. His teaching embodies the certainty that one can get free in this lifetime. Sharon never worked as hard in her life. Every moment of the day she felt challenged. It is not U Pandita's style to give much verbal encouragement, but Sharon felt no doubt or uncertainty. And in 1985, after a twelve-year absence, she returned to Burma to practice with him at his forest monastery for three months.

There she found his style utterly different. In his own monastery he was sweet and kind, like a "loving mother," she says. And the practice assigned her were the four *brahmaviharas*—recitations of loving-kindness, compassion, sympathetic joy, and equanimity. That part of the experience was "rapturous," she told me.

Physically, however, things were very difficult. The climate and conditions were much more severe than anything she'd experienced in India. There were rats and snakes and insects of every description. The last meal of the day was at 10:00 A.M., after which there was only boiled water till 5:00 the next morning. And Sharon finally became very ill.

Still, she expects to return. U Pandita is now sixty-five years old, and she feels a certain urgency to learn all she can from him before he dies. In the meantime, her work with him has significantly affected her teaching style at Barre. Especially at first, people felt the difference keenly. More recently, my impression is that there has been some rebalancing. Sharon explains it this way:

From her own experience with this teaching, and from sitting in on U Pandita's interviews with other students, she became impressed with the integrity and inclusiveness of the system. This makes it possible to follow people more closely and to guide them more confidently along the way. In contrast to her old approach, which assumed that everything would unfold naturally, now she can be more demanding and directive, recognizing signs in people's practice that allow her to be quite specific. Sometimes a very wide, spacious awareness is what is called for. Sometimes more focusing is better. She has become more sensitive to the sequential component of practice and has the technical competence to steer people accurately. ("Give up noting for a while and focus more on the body.")

Moreover, U Pandita possesses vast scholarly and theoretical knowledge to which Sharon hopes to have access. She is aware of the pitfalls of getting stuck within too narrow a frame of personal experience. At the same time she perceives what may be the limits of an Asian approach for students in America. The eradication of greed is primary to this teaching, and a common mode of transmitting the dharma in Asia. Here, Sharon has observed that greed may not be as predominant a mental state as anger, especially in the form of self-condemnation. Originally, rather than demand, "Uproot those hindrances!" (as Asian teachers might—an active, effortful, powerful message), she would say, "It's okay, just watch them—don't feel aversion." Now these are combined: "First know it's okay they are there. Then you can get rid of them."

U Pandita may not have perceived the self-judgments of students here or their aching self-hatred. In dealing with hindrances he would say, "Chop off their heads!" Sharon believes it takes a kind of grace—an ease as well as determination, and that it can't be done with anger or aversion. But now she also wants to take it "the next step."

Update: Winter 2000

In response to the questions I mailed her, Sharon sent back such concise and compelling answers that I can do no better than reproduce them here, mostly vebatim, with extremely few changes or editing.

"In 1989, Joseph Goldstein and I founded the Barre Center for Buddhist Studies, a sister center to IMS [Insight Meditation Society]. BCBS is dedicated to bringing together teachers, scholars, students, and practitioners who are committed to exploring Buddhist thought as a living tradition. Through conferences, workshops, classes, and research, we examine what it means to be faithful to the origins and lineage of Buddhist tradition and also to be developing an adaptable and alive response to the issues of the current world. The center's purpose is to provide a bridge between study and practice, between scholarly understanding and meditative insight. It encourages active engagement with the tradition in a spirit of genuine inquiry and investigation.

"In 1998, IMS initiated a project called the Forest Refuge, which will evolve into a long-term practice center situated in the forest between IMS and BCBS. This center will allow people to practice intensive meditation outside the structure of formal retreats, yet with ongoing personal teacher guidance. Over the centuries in Asia, centers and monasteries like this, where people could practice uninterruptedly and closely with a mentor, have fostered many of the great teachers. We believe that the establishment of the Forest Refuge is an important step for developing teachers of this caliber in the West.

"In the time since our interview all those many years ago, I've also written two books, created a correspondence course in meditation, compiled and edited an anthology of IMS teachers (which is being published by Shambhala [Publications] as a benefit book for Ram Dass, who suffered a devastating stroke in early 1997), and am now working on my next book, on the topic of faith. Oh—and taught any number of retreats!

"My first book was *Lovingkindness: The Revolutionary Art of Happiness* (Shambhala Publications). It focuses on metta, or loving-kindness practice, which was taught by the Buddha to develop concentration, fearlessness, happiness, and a loving heart. Metta doesn't require us to turn away from our path or pretend we are feeling something we are not. Rather, it helps us to open both to joy and to suffering. The consequence of this opening is knowledge of our innate goodness and interconnectedness with all beings. We realize we have never been separate or apart—that is why it is a revolutionary view, and a liberating way to live.

"My second book was *A Heart As Wide As the World* (Shambhala Publications). It contains several dozen short essays, mostly grounded in my own experience in meditation practice and in bringing the perspectives of mindfulness and compassion into my life. There are sections on classical Buddhist concepts along with stories about my losing my car and struggling with my computer. My meditation practice (since 1971) has continually shown me that our hearts are indeed wide enough to embrace all of life, all of our experiences, both pleasurable and painful. Here again is an emphasis on love and opening and on the real possibility of freedom in our everyday lives.

"The correspondence course mentioned earlier is called *Insight Meditation* (Sounds True Audio), and it mirrors a retreat experience. There are twelve audiocassettes, one side a talk by either Joseph or myself, the other side a forty-five-minute guided meditation led by one of us. There is also a workbook with inter-active exercises and ongoing correspondence with an instructor I supervise. This has allowed us to bridge a long-standing gap for those wishing a supportive structure for their practice in daily life outside of meditation retreats. Participants have included those raising small children, people with chronic ailments, prisoners (the course is distributed free of charge in prisons), cloistered nuns, people who are just beginning meditation practice, and also quite experienced practitioners looking for ongoing guidance.

"The anthology (*Voices of Insight*, Shambhala Publications, 1999) is the only collection of IMS teachers' essays that has come into being. The book is divided into three general sections: one on the Buddha (this includes stories of our own teachers, relationship to lineage, one's own Buddha nature, as well as the Buddha's journey); one on the dharma (this includes descriptions of mindfulness and loving-kindness practices, teachings on impermanence, suffering, emptiness, and liberation); and one on the sangha (which includes classical and contemporary meanings of community, and topics relevant to living in the world, such as everyday practice, family, and service). All proceeds of the book will go to benefit Ram Dass.

"My next book will be on the subject of faith. When I looked as deeply as I could into my own experience in meditation, both mindfulness and metta, I saw an underlying theme of faith. The Pali word that is usually translated as 'faith,' *saddha*, literally means 'to place your heart upon.' So I am currently exploring what it means for us to place our heart upon a path to freedom; how we recognize that, first of all, we have a heart; and then how we come to see that the offering or placing of our hearts is a genuine gift and should be greatly honored. Though one doesn't hear about faith too often in Buddhism, which is primarily a wisdom tradition, I believe that rightly understood, faith is a hidden thread throughout the path and is a tremendous support.

"From 1983 to 1989, I practiced the brahmaviharas (metta, compassion, sympathetic joy, and equanimity) almost exclusively, both on intensive retreat and in my daily life. U Pandita Sayadaw was my teacher for these practices. This fulfilled a long-held desire of mine to learn the meditations that mirror the heart of the Buddha. By wanting to practice the brahmaviharas, I was fundamentally seeking the ability to love myself, first of all, as I felt the Buddha would have—with clear seeing yet with undiminished compassion. I trusted (and later discovered through experience) that just as is stated in the texts, this was the basis for being able to truly love others, with both clarity and compassion. Cultivating these states fills us with faith in our loving hearts and in the strength of our connection with others. . . .

"Probably the most amazing moment that occurred while doing these practices intensively in Burma was when I recognized that, indeed, I was capable of this much love. I actually sat there dazed, thinking, 'Is this me?' In fact, we all are capable of tremendous love, but until we untangle our conditioning, our capacity for connection remains hidden or twisted and distorted. These practices widened my vision of what is meant by meditation immensely.

"In the years since then, I have traveled to many places in the world to teach the brahmaviharas. I am continually surprised that, no matter where I go, so many people consider these states of mind weaknesses. Students at a retreat will say, 'If I am loving and compassionate, I will allow myself to be abused and hurt.' Or, 'To me, those are just sweet sentiments, but it's not really possible to live like that.' Sadly, this attitude misses how genuinely strengthening the brahmaviharas can be, because they directly acknowledge and cultivate our deepest connection with life.

"Since 1971, my life has been pretty much singularly devoted to the dharma. By virtue of such long-term application and devotion (as well as of simply getting older), I'm now regarded as more of an elder in Buddhism in America, which often comes as a surprise to me. People sometimes say, 'Oh, you and Joseph and Jack must have had such incredible vision to start IMS in 1976, such prescience of how popular Buddhism would become.' But I always say, 'No, we didn't really. We made the decisions that were in front of us as best we could each day, made lots of mistakes, and continue to watch things evolve.' My life viewed from the inside is just my life, nothing special. Yet I feel very blessed. I have been practicing for almost thirty years now, and largely because of that, my mantra these days is, 'I am so lucky.' "

Gesshin Prabhasa Dharma

> She could be
>   a Japanese court lady
>   in soft gray silk
>   a secret love poem
>   crinkles her eyes
>   to the new moon
>   she whispers
>   calligraphy.
>
> Or
>   in the predawn light
>   in the silence before rain
>   her will a honed arrow
>   her hammered spine
>
>   you suddenly spy
>   the samurai
>   —Lenore Friedman

It is wartime. A ten-year-old girl is riding in a streetcar on her way to school. Everything is gray. People wear dark gray coats; the sky is gray, gloomy, threatening. Everywhere she rests her eyes, people's faces look hungry, sad, bitter. The little girl feels overwhelmed with grayness, with drabness. She feels that if she has to ride that streetcar one more day, she'll die. And then a brilliant thought flashes through her mind: why not imagine she has just arrived from another planet? That she knows nothing about the human world, does not speak its language? She has always had the sense that she came from somewhere else, from the Pleiades, perhaps. So it isn't hard to just let everything go. . . .

She opens her eyes and looks around. Everything is fresh, shining with life and color. She is seeing with "beginner's mind."

A young woman, small and delicate of feature and build, walks down to the beach from a cabin on a bluff high above the dunes. It is 1964, near Malibu, California. The young woman, a painter and a German by birth, has been living here for some months with her American husband, painting every day in the beautiful clear coastal light. Now she is slowly descending the hundred and fifty steps leading from the cabin to the sandy beach. There is a bench partway down where she sometimes sits, giving herself to the sound of the waves. Today she descends all the way, crossing the sand to the water's edge, aware only of the pounding surf. Suddenly there is an almost physical blow to the back of her neck, as if someone has struck her. But no one is there.

"I was really gone," she remembers now after twenty years. "I woke up wide, saw deep and far into the past. I saw a main road which, somehow, I had left behind. I was now on a detour, on a side road."

She realized that the main road was the spiritual path she had been on for many years, "for a long, long, long time." But she saw now that she had lately been in a dream world and that she had to get back to the main road.

Had her marriage been the detour? And was her art the way back to her true path? She separated from her husband and moved to a small studio house in Beverly Glen Canyon where she lived alone for some time, painting with renewed intensity. She found herself beginning to see all matter as interrelated. Choosing simple, single objects—for example, a cup—she discovered a technique for pulling it back and forth from the background, like matter coming into being and dissolving again. It became a process analogous to the truth she felt about things. The finished painting was not so important. It was the process that mattered.

She was still trying to find a way through art to communicate a message that was not conceptually clear to her yet—though it was crystal-clear on a feeling level.

Then, one day, after hours of intense painting, she stepped outside the studio to a deck overlooking the canyon. She sat down on a chair from which she sometimes looked at paintings from a distance. Today she had painted herself into exhaustion.

"As soon as I sat down it overcame me. I don't know how long I sat there. But when I awakened, an image came to me. It was a little card house, the walls made of four playing cards leaning against each other, with two more leaning against each other for the roof. Then there was a tiny *ping*, a little wisp of wind, and it all fell over. That's all it took. And then there was the vast openness of open space. And that vast openness was I, myself. Before, I'd thought I was inside the space, inside the house. If you think that's you, you have your shell on. But it took only that tiny breath of wind, and it all fell down. And then there was nothing."

In the moments that followed she perceived her whole life in a flash: it had already happened. She saw the purpose of the six senses, and the way living in space and time is like living in slow motion. "Now I'm living out the specific details of that one flash. When I began to study Buddhism a few years later, I discovered that that was the teaching of the *Diamond Sutra*: your life is but a flash of lightning."

The little girl on the streetcar and the young woman on the beach are both Gisela Midwer, known today as the Venerable Gesshin Myoko Prabhasa Dharma, Rọshi, founder of the International Zen Institute of America. When she is not traveling and teaching in Europe and in different parts of the United States, her headquarters are in Los Angeles, California, where I spent several leisurely days with her—talking, exploring the multiethnic neighborhood, and attending ceremonies at the Vietnamese Buddhist Temple nearby.

"I'm a lamplighter," Gesshin told me. "What I try to teach people is how to switch on their light. I don't consider myself a teacher. I'm just manifesting true self and enjoying life that way. And other people seem to enjoy that too and ask me to come and share it with them. When I was eight years old, I said that what I wanted in life was to shine, to shine like a star."

At that early age, a grownup had asked her what she wanted to be when she grew up. She had no idea, but thinking she ought to have an answer, she said the first thing that popped into her mind: I want to shine like a star.

"It wasn't anything I had thought of. It came from another place. When I heard myself say that, I wondered what it meant. These spontaneous, intuitive answers to questions surprised me throughout my life. Finally, when I was in my thirties, I realized that I wanted to get to that source. Spontaneous intuition. I wanted to function from that place at all times."

By the time she was ten or eleven, she was going into what she would now call meditative states. It was wartime Germany, with bombs falling every day, people in constant fear of being killed. She had seen her grandmother in her coffin, arms folded on her chest, and from then on she always went to sleep that way: hands folded, left over right, over the solar plexus. If bombs fell while she slept, she'd be in the right posture. But she also found she could induce meditative states this way. She would feel herself sinking, dissolving. Then she would stop, and hover, and then sink again into a deeper dimension, with greater expansion, until there was another hovering, and the whole process repeated four times.

"There was an interesting moment, like the bursting of a soap bubble: the slightest little *ping*—and I felt totally expanded. I felt I was everywhere. I always came out of these experiences knowing that there was something other than this heaviness of the body and the sorrow and the war. And I had such an urge to communicate this experience to others, but I didn't know how."

Even earlier, she had dreams of flying. In one dream, her classmates asked if she would show them how. So she took them out to a meadow, stood in front of them like a teacher, lifted herself up on her toes, and spread her arms wide like a bird. "Just stand like this," she said, "wait for the first breeze, and then lift yourself on top of it and glide along, letting yourself be carried." As she spoke, a breeze sprang up, she lifted herself on top of it, and she was flying. She sailed higher and higher, reveling in the sensation. But from very high up, she looked down and saw them all still standing there, like little stones. They were trying to get off the ground but could not. She was enjoying herself so much, and wanted only to go on and on. But seeing them down there, still on the ground, she thought, "Oh, I have to go back and show them one more time."

"A bodhisattva dream," I recognized.

"Yes," she replied. "It was already working in me."

Her wish to be free of "this heavy, clumsy body," also led to an early interest in ballet. She saw it as such a complete discipline of body and spirit that the body almost disappears. But her father refused her lessons because she was small and light, and he was worried about her health. But she had always had an innate desire for discipline, for conquering her limitations. She would attempt to duplicate difficult feats, like acrobatics seen at the circus, which would terrify her mother. One of her teachers offered to pay for her ballet lessons, but she refused, not wanting to hurt her parents.

Meanwhile, she had stopped praying. Since the war didn't end, no matter how hard she prayed, she just stopped one day. Instead, she depended more and more on the meditative states she had come to rely on. Toward the end of the war, when she was about thirteen, the family was evacuated to the country. At noontime, she would go out into the wheatfields when everyone else was resting. Since she was small for her age, when she sat down the wheat surrounded her like a forest. She would allow herself to settle into the heat and stillness, forgetting herself, surrendering to the sounds.

When the end of the war finally came, it did not bring an end to the terror. Sometimes, it could be worse. Under the occupying forces there was starvation, rape, and murder throughout the countryside. Once, when Gesshin was fourteen, only her acute intuition aborted a probable attack.

The village was occupied by American troops. They lived in camps up in the hills but would sometimes come down and break into people's homes. Most of the local men were gone, either killed or in camps, so the women were largely alone. Her mother kept the house barricaded. But one day she went out to get milk at a small farm up the road. It was midday, and very quiet. Usually there was an old grandmother inside the house, but on this day there was no one. There was no one in the barn either. Behind the barn was an old woodshed where the grandmother used to cook jam, a three-sided shed with one side open. She looked in, then suddenly felt there was someone behind her. Swinging around, she saw two soldiers. They carried guns and bayonets, and posted themselves in the entrance, trapping her. She was terrified, glued to the woodstack, but at the same time a calming energy came up and told her to wait, to do nothing. The two soldiers offered her chewing gum. She had been taught to accept nothing from such people, but her inner wisdom said, *Take it. Don't upset them.* She reached out very calmly, said thank you, and then they all chewed gum and grinned at each other. They started asking questions and she pretended she wasn't frightened. Her inner voice was saying, *Don't act. In time you'll know what to do.* And in a flash it came to her: a yell came out of her. She hadn't planned it, it was wholly spontaneous. She yelled very loud and pointed at the sky and they both swung round to look—and she dashed out between them. As she ran back down the road, she heard them shooting, though probably only to scare her. She made it to the house and fell to the floor, panting.

These experiences of spontaneous insight, Gesshin feels, are not unusual. Everyone has the potential for them, although mostly they're latent. "Perhaps for me it goes way back into my past, many lifetimes perhaps. But at an early age I stopped looking for external sources, stopped looking away from myself, and started looking inward. I found this inner place where I felt totally trusting and safe, and I could always go there."

She had often sensed this wisdom in older people. At holiday times, her mother had usually invited one or two to join their family dinners. Their weathered hands especially fascinated her, and as they sat at table, she could feel a kind of dignity radiating from their backs.

"My life is nothing special," she says, "just an example, to give people trust and faith in themselves, to see that that inner wisdom is really there. As soon as you awaken it, it's there. The reason I chose Zen is that I see it as the path that leads there most directly, and straight.

"From an outward point of view my early life was terrible. The whole country was a concentration camp. We lived the same way, starving, our lives threatened, the same fear of death everywhere. That kind of pressure can stir up something deep and profound, as if we were on our deathbed. It comes naturally then. But it would be so much better for us if we had that kind of death moment early in life. A crisis state—it can often be brought on in a sesshin—really squeezes you down to the essence."

It was during the period when she was painting intensively in the canyon house in Southern California that Gesshin first encountered Zen. For Christmas, a friend had given her Huang Po's *Transmission of the Mind*. She immediately identified with what she read. "I couldn't believe there was another human being who could speak right out of my heart." Not long after, a poet friend told her there was a roshi he'd like her to meet, and she agreed to have tea with him the next Sunday.

About ten in the morning they arrived at the little house in Gardena, just a bit late for the meeting, too late for any explanations. Gesshin was wearing a gray French knit suit, rather short and tight. A monk with shaved head and bright yellow kimono motioned peremptorily, and before she knew what was happening, she had been pushed through a doorway and placed at a black cushion on the floor.

"And I thought I was going to have tea with Roshi! None of the books I'd read had said anything about practice. But here I was. So I crossed my legs to sit on the cushion—and my skirt was halfway up my thighs! I was so uncomfortable and embarrassed that the monk took notice and brought something to put over my legs. He put me in the right posture, and there I was, sitting. But what was this all about? What were all the other people thinking about? What were they doing here?"

Then, in characteristic fashion, she turned the question onto herself. "What are *you* doing here?" And she tried hard to get into the posture. She became very still, and soon she had entered again that great spaciousness she had experienced in the past. The walls of the building began to dissolve, there was no inside or outside, the birds, the cars, her breathing—all was happening in one vast space. So deep was her concentration during that first sitting that, when it was over, she realized she would not have stirred even if a bomb had exploded right over her head. From that moment she had no doubt the practice was for her.

"I was hooked. I had to come back. That sitting was the best thing I'd ever done in my whole life." It had taken her to a place beyond this human condition where she felt utterly safe and totally aware.

Soon she was going to Gardena every Sunday to sit. A few months later—in October 1967—the center moved to Los Angeles, to the site that is now Cimarron Center. At the time it was very run down and in need of repair. It had been vandalized and vacant for some time. Since Gesshin was then still painting, and working on her own schedule, she was able to go often to help out. Soon she found herself there every day, at first working with other people, but after a while all by herself—fixing cracks, putting in new floors, doing repairs all over the building. During the day, Roshi worked and wrote in his room upstairs, coming down to cook lunch for both of them. Gesshin would sometimes cook dinner, stay for the evening sitting, and then go home to her apartment. In the morning she would be back for the sitting at 4:30 A.M. Finally Roshi said, "This is ridiculous. You spend all your time here, go home to sleep for a few hours, and come back. You should move in." And he added: "I want to train you to be a teacher."

Thus began a five-year period of the most rigorous training imaginable. Gesshin, to be sure, liked discipline by nature. But it was still hard to get up at four o'clock, to work hard all day and go to sleep late at night, to eat only white rice and a few vegetables, to endure all the pains of daily intensive practice. But she began to find her energy renewed through zazen itself, and soon was able to hold a koan so keenly in her mind that it was there when she awoke in the morning.

"You know how as soon as you open your eyes the thoughts rush in? They're just waiting for you to wake up! I would grab my koan right away before any thoughts could get to me. Holding my koan, I would go to the bathroom and brush my teeth. In the zendo, I'd sit down with it. When you start thinking about things, you destroy yourself. The koan makes it easier."

Early in her training she experienced her master's stick. Giving an answer during sanzen one day, she was hit, hard. Despite a large purple bruise on her thigh the next day, she bowed and thanked him for his kindness. She understood that the master uses the stick only when the time is right. "That's when I became his disciple."

There were three to five people in training during this period, but she was the only one who was there all the time. She cooked, took care of the center, answered the phone, did the shopping and driving. It was demanding, but she knew she was there to learn something she didn't yet know. From childhood she had been "after wisdom," but now she became aware of the impediment of ego and how it could trap her. One day she was preparing a meal for a large group when Roshi came in, tasted a dish, criticized it, and asked her to do it differently. Her ego flared up. She had cooked all her life! Who was he to tell her how to cook?

But instantly another voice inside her said: *You're here because you don't know anything. And he knows.* At once the flare-up subsided. And the moment that she saw her ego operating, saw it completely, in that moment she was transformed. "That's how you grow, and cultivate yourself." It's a ripening process that goes on for years.

Without her work with Joshu Kyozan Sasaki-roshi, Gesshin feels, she would not be where she is today. For five years they saw each other daily. In the early years they met for sanzen morning and evening, while she worked on koans. One morning during their first six months together, she did not have an answer. She had "lost" her koan.

"I was sitting and it just went away. Suddenly I felt drawn into this immense radiant energy inside my abdomen, which started rising and spreading throughout my body. I felt as if the sun were inside of me, not outside. So when the bell rang, I went to his room and said I had no answer. I was radiating warm feeling. He said, 'Now you are illuminating.'

"But then you fall into traps again. Get stuck, discouraged. That's why one really needs a teacher. He encourages you and holds you there and gives you confidence, and if you grow ego again, he cuts it off."

Furthermore, at every opportunity, he cut off her thinking.

Once, after a sesshin, they went for a walk together in a beautiful garden across the street from the center. It was spring, and the magnolia trees were blooming, and there were flowers everywhere. Gesshin noticed a perfect magnolia blossom that had fallen to the path at their feet. She smiled and was about to say something poetic or appreciative, when Roshi caught her: "Again you're thinking!" This daily kind of shaping and training was invaluable. And there was always his example, the way he lived each day. He was not saintly, but human, down to earth. His "saintliness" lay in being consistently there: he never missed a sanzen, for example, even when he was sick or in pain.

"When it got hard for me, my mind would say, 'If he can do it, you can do it.' And I would go on and do it."

One of the hardest things she did was supervise the creation of the new center at Mount Baldy. It was 1970 and she had been training only three years when Roshi gave her this responsibility. The site was an old Boy Scout camp at the top of a steep mountain road. There were twenty dilapidated cabins, no toilets, no heat, no windows or insulation. The fire department, the health department, and the national forest authorities all declared the place unfit for use. However, with great trepidation and no money, but four young monks to assist her, Gesshin went to work.

And one by one, with donated materials and dedicated labor, the cabins were renovated. The original plan had been that people from nearby Claremont would join them for practice. But at first, when they sat at dawn and after dark at night, no one came. No one wanted to drive up the mountain at those hours. In winter the road was treacherous with snow or ice. So while the work was still in progress, Gesshin conceived the idea of developing the site as a monastery, with training periods available for students during the summer months. She also saw that this would provide her with the opportunity to complete her own training, since Roshi would be in residence during the three-month training periods. In 1972 she was ordained as a teacher (*osho*).

During the period that followed, she spent one and a half years consolidating her training in Japan. She enrolled at Tenruiji Monastery, where she trained with Hirata-roshi. She also studied Japanese language and calligraphy with Morita Shiriyu, a world-renowned calligrapher. It was a time of richness and deepening; it was a time of turmoil and perplexity as well. There were strain and ambiguity in her communications with Roshi and her fellow monks in America. Even after her return, when she became head priest at Cimarron Zen Center, these were never wholly resolved. Despite efforts at reconciliation, negativity and misunderstanding persisted. The environment was no longer compatible. It seemed time to go her own way.

Cimarron, December 1969. Third day, Rohatsu sesshin. Practice from 3:00 A.M. to 11:00 P.M. Sanzen four or five times a day. Roshi has asked Gesshin to be the leader in the zendo. For the first time during Rohatsu, she carries the stick. Day three is often a crisis day. But Gesshin feels strong and full of energy. Standing up to carry around the keisaku, she feels enormous responsibility toward the fifty people sitting there. How should she conduct herself? All her role models have been males. In traditional Rinzai style, they yell great yells and whack with the stick at any sign of slackness in the zendo. But Gesshin is a woman. What would a woman do? Having no one to look to for help, she looks within herself.

At first, standing there with the stick in her hands, she feels totally helpless. Then, in peaceful clarity, it comes to her: firmness but kindness. Firmness and strength inside, gentleness and kindness outside. "You cannot let fifty people down on the third day when they all get crazy, confused, tired, or want to give up. You have to uphold them not with shouting but with your own awareness and spiritual strength": by nondoing rather than doing, by simply radiating energy.

And it works, she told me. Men and women both feel deeply supported, and she herself gains energy. "You burn up your pain. You burn up everything in the process." Men have developed one approach, she says. But a woman's rhythm is different. It is more like a wave, up and down. She allows for that because it's natural. Women and older people have difficulty with the traditional severe, high-pressure approach of the lineage in which she was trained, and which she now feels is inappropriate for Westerners.

In 1983 she resigned from the lineage and is now devoted to

working with Americans and Europeans to keep the essence of Zen alive.

"As a teacher I am open," she says. "I have no ideas. And when I go to give a talk somewhere, I never know what I am going to say. I sit there quietly for a few minutes, empty myself out, and then I absorb the audience. I look at them and then I begin to talk on their level. The purpose is not to teach them anything. It is to awaken them to their own inner reality."

To engage in religious practice, she says, means to go home, to return to original nature. Wisdom is innate, not distant from ourselves. It's what we *are*. That is the dharma, the process. Identifying with the process, you see there is no birth or death. That is what the Buddha taught, and people need these basic teachings. "I would do anything in this world, with hands and feet and my whole body, to get that across to people."

One of her role models in the history of Zen is the Chinese master Joshu. He was said to be very soft-spoken, never beating or shouting at students. Whenever he opened his lips, people said, gold flowed out of his mouth. With simple words he cut right through ignorance and emotion. "I feel very close to him and his way of teaching," Gesshin says. Until he was fifty-nine or sixty he was a disciple of Master Nansen. When Nansen died, he went on a pilgrimage for twenty years, encountering other priests and masters in dharma combat and sharpening his wisdom. Only when he was eighty did he settle down and begin to teach himself. Many were drawn to him, and he taught for forty years, dying when he was over 120.

Without intense effort, your practice cannot be deep, Gesshin warns. With shallow effort, your realization will be shallow. So she is grateful for the severe training she had both with Sasaki Roshi and later in Japan. Still, "this is not the only Zen there is!" There are Chinese, Vietnamese, and Korean Zen traditions too. She believes that for true enlightenment a traditional practice is necessary, but the particular style or combination must be right for each person.

She takes particular pleasure in working with beginning students. Something she told me in a different context echoes in my mind here. In a heightened moment of experience she had once seen the cells of her skin flying off with a great roar, "like a great fire." Dead cells were being flipped off at tremendous speed as she looked around her at trees, at flowers. "I saw everything connected, cellularly connected. I saw air almost like a substance, and I realized—tears came to my eyes—'My goodness, what people call beautiful is really just decay!' When you look at things, you look at the surface where the dead cells are. So what we call beautiful is already wilting. How much greater is the beauty that is underneath the surface. And the life of the spirit, just before it is formed, that's when it's most beautiful. To reveal that beauty became my path."

Since 1980 Gesshin has been traveling to many parts of the United States and Europe giving lectures and sesshins in all kinds of settings. She's become adept at creating her traveling monastery wherever she goes. Sometimes in the woods, sometimes in a city, she will set out cushions, candles, flowers, incense. "And I bring my bell, and we just sit together and start practicing. I explain that for seven days this is our monastery. And people are really great. They try so hard. It moves me when I see how much they put into it. Using force is not necessary. There is so much natural resistance that people have to deal with, especially in the first three days. The ego really rebels." If it's to burn away, though, it has to come up first.

"I feel like a great mother to all of them. That's what the Buddha taught me. When he was a monk, the Buddha said, 'I look upon all sentient beings as my children.' No matter how old they are, even if they're much older than I am, I see them as my children. I care deeply for each one, feel love and compassion for them, seeing that they are on a path. Some of them are lost, and some I can help find their way. It's not a matter of transmitting teachings, but of working unbounded, unhindered, free from traditions, directly with whatever you have. That is the essence of Zen—the awakening of Buddha-nature directly, heart to heart."

In all of Gesshin's groups these days, there are older people, seventy and eighty years old and over. "It is never too late," she says. Her sitting periods are usually twenty to twenty-five minutes long (possibly longer for advanced students), interspersed with very slow walking indoors or fast walking outdoors if people need movement. She sets the schedule after she meets the group, according to age balance and abilities. In the early afternoon there is usually a one-and-a-half-hour period of walking meditation outdoors or quiet sitting in the zendo. She also uses yoga and slow stretching at different times of the day. Her structure is clear and strict, but softer, accommodating different lifestyles and circumstances.

"You go with the nature of things," she says. "And women instinctively empathize."

One of her students wrote me that Gesshin's presence during a sesshin is remarkable, a model of clear-minded sitting and breathing. During formal meal service she can be tough but fair, correcting mistakes with a steady gaze. But, said the student, "somehow I did not take corrections personally (nor were they meant that way)." She understood they were in the spirit of benefit to all. Although this student found personal interviews terrifying, there was also "a warmth and understanding communicated. I was challenged in a way that has never ceased."

More than anything she was "struck with the fact that we all trusted Gesshin so deeply with our lives and spirits. The degree to which she understood our positions and our feelings—including doubts—was most evident during her talks. How could she speak so clearly to my present needs, and as I learned later, to everyone else's as well?"

Another student described her first encounter with Gesshin (at a Unity in Diversity conference in Seattle). "When this little woman, all in black, got up on the stage, the world changed." Their connection was immediate and intense, and they have worked together closely every since. Gesshin is a "good mirror," she says, reflecting her with such accuracy that she looks further, digs deeper. "She is a remarkable woman—courageous, determined, hugely compassionate.

"Zen—it isn't anything, is it? The dharma is conveyed to me just by trying to write this to you, and not to spill the tea!"

In April 1985, Gesshin received Dharma Mind Seal transmission from the Venerable Dr. Thich Man Giac, Supreme Abbott of the United Vietnamese Buddhist Churches of America. For several years she had been closely involved with the Vietnamese Buddhist community of Los Angeles, deeply appreciating their spirit of warmth and inclusiveness, and their respect and understanding for her own approach to the dharma. When she is not teaching and traveling in other parts of the world, she makes her headquarters there, at the International Zen Institute. She frequently gives Sunday lectures at the International Buddhist Meditation Center and the Vietnamese Buddhist Temple, both founded by Venerable Dr. Thich Thien-an, beloved Vietnamese Buddhist teacher and scholar, who died in 1980. In the past few years Gesshin has also conducted thirty-day retreats in the California desert.

THIS IS ALL THERE IS

the wind

two
jars
of
honey

the flight
of the pelican
—Gesshin Myoko

One day in the early sixties when she was still pursuing her artwork in the canyon house in California, Gesshin heard the telephone ring. Although she was working on a painting, for some reason she felt she had to answer it, and talked for some time. When she returned, with paint and terpentine dripping down her arm, she looked at the canvas with a shock. She had been in a totally different world. No wonder she could never finish a painting! Change occurred so swiftly that it seemed she had lost her connection to the work entirely. In a sense she could never return to that painting again. It was like a death experience. The person who had been working on that painting didn't exist anymore.

"Yes," she thought. "What if you had really dropped dead? Look at the painting, at what it is saying at this stage. Is it expressing what you want to say?" At that moment she felt poignantly the impermanence of life. She might really never again have a chance to work on that canvas. "So every instant has got to be *it*. Every brushstroke, every time you set down that brush, your total being has to be involved and revealed."

Her concentration increased. She strove to internalize the objects she was working with. In a life drawing class, she was closely observing the body of a female model. "She had a very unusual body. Everything was oval, her head oval like an egg, very beautiful, legs and arms very tubular. I drew and drew and drew, day after day, not thinking much at all. By the third day I thought I had become that body. I could do anything with it I wanted. I could put her in any pose or position I wanted to in my mind. Then I started painting without the model, just from that internalized experience. And I made a series of thirty small paintings that day. I was just flying. They were for me my best work. For the first time I came into my own way of working. I would do one and leave it, do one and leave it, not think about or change anything. That's the Japanese style of brushwork, putting it down and leaving it, which I came upon in this natural way. Very spontaneous, very direct, very concentrated."

Later, after the experience on the terrace when the walls of her ego fell away, a flood of poems came to Gesshin. In recent years she makes more poems than paintings. A beautiful collection of these, together with the poetry of Thich Man Giac, was published in 1983, entitled *A Sudden Flash of Lightning: Words Out of Silence.*

All the arts are practice, she believes. In fact, if we are really present with whatever our work may be, it is possible to penetrate deeply to the source. It takes a great deal of practice at first, and perhaps clumsy dependence on materials, but at last it becomes effortless, and then you let all the rest go and "just live."

CONTINUUM

life is a day

a passage

through green
where light is
more certain

than leaves.
—Gesshin Myoko

Thich Man Giac has written that his first meeting with Gesshin was "one of the most unforgettable events in my spiritual life."

Of her poems he says, "I find in them the mountaintop where I can look down on the moon and stars, and the surge of the mysterious sea." Here is a poem he dedicated to her in *A Sudden Flash of Lightning:*

THE ZEN MASTER

to Gesshin Myoko

the Master walks down the road
an oversized robe carries only compassion
time has no hold on her
who filled the night with laughter

Update: Winter 2000

At the time I talked with Gesshin for the first edition of this book, the International Zen Institute of America, which she founded in 1983, was a fledgling organization. Today, it has six branches, two in this country (in Florida and Colorado) and four in Europe: two in the Netherlands, one in Germany, and one in the Basque country of Spain.

When I talked to her for this update in 1998 and early 1999, Gesshin had been very busy, *over*busy. In order to accommodate all the students who had sought out her teaching as well as to reduce the pressure of traveling, her first training center for European students was established in 1996 in the Netherlands. It is called "Noorder Poort," which means Northern Gate, and is located amid beautiful countryside in the district of Drenthe "in a large farmhouse with a huge thatched roof, surrounded by green fields and a healthy herd of cows," Gesshin told me in a phone interview. Here, she offered her annual summer training for students from all over Europe and the United States as well.

For fourteen years, Gesshin also held an annual Desert Spring Retreat in Joshua Tree, California. All her retreats are international and interreligious, explicitly welcoming people from all over the world and from all religious traditions. In her gentle, musical voice, she told me that this was the realization of a dream from her early life in wartime Germany—"to bring people from all nations together in a peaceful and joyous way."

Although I spoke with her thirty years after her ordination as a Rinzai Zen nun, Gesshin was "increasingly aware of the limitations of traditional Rinzai training," especially for people with careers and families. To bring the practice and teaching of "enlightened life" to laypeople, she began making real changes. First, she trained a group of "dharma workers" to introduce new students to Zen practice and prepare them for more intensive practice with the master. "In the Rinzai tradition, we distinguish very clearly between a Zen teacher and a Zen master," she said. Zen teachers who wish to become masters require long years of practice and ongoing study with the Zen master.

Retreat programs for families were another interesting innovation. These are specially designed to introduce children to the dharma. So far, family retreats have taken place in Germany, the Netherlands, and Spain.

Gesshin also experimented with starting retreats with two gentle, nonstrenuous days so that people can be initiated into dharma study in a relaxed setting. This allows a gradual entry into the deep silence of sesshin and into "the experience of basic mind and the true nature of the self."

Even though the strict simplicity of Zen structure is usually retained, sesshin participants are permitted to determine their own appropriate level of practice intensity. For example, once in a while, instead of zazen, they might substitute a period of walking or lying-down meditation outside the zendo, to which they return for the next period of sitting. Gesshin was touched by the sincere motivation of most of her students and by the degree to which this more flexible practice makes the dharma accessible to more and more people.

To my delight, Gesshin also reported that ten years ago, she held a "bicycle sesshin" in Holland. In a beautiful part of the countryside crisscrossed by miles of bicycle paths, she and her students cycled for a week, mostly in silence. Sometimes they'd stop by a lake, stripping off their clothes and diving in, later meditating together on the shore. Each evening, there would be formal meditation and sometimes a talk by Gesshin.

Later, Gesshin condensed this weeklong adventure into a sin-

gle day in the middle of a seven-day sesshin. Bikes were rented at
a train station, transported by rail to a picturesque starting point,
and thirty or forty people took off for the day. Sometimes, the
sixth day became a "free-form" day, when people could sit or
not sit, even "lie on their backs under a tree all day if they
so choose." One result is that on the traditionally structured
seventh day, people tended to really appreciate the old forms
again. They're also better prepared, Gesshin believed, for the
problems they're likely to encounter at home in their ongoing
practice.

At the end of sesshins, she sometimes also added a "sangha
day," when participants can celebrate together with their families, including many children who often come to "pick up their
mommy or daddy." All these innovations reflect the care and
nurturance that added a special flavor to Gesshin's otherwise rigorous presentation of Zen.

"I see the whole of society as the 'sangha,' " she said. "It
would be wonderful if every member of society could live this life
in the only truth there is: great love and great compassion for all
beings."

An accomplished poet and calligrapher as well as a Zen master,
Gesshin was particularly interested in the interface of art and spirituality. For five years or more, she offered courses in zazen and
dharma study combined with the writing of prose and poetry
(including haiku). In ancient China and Japan, advanced practitioners were required to express their experience of enlightenment in the form of a haiku accompanied by a prose commentary.
They were judged not only on their words, Gesshin said, but on
their calligraphy as well.

In 1991, Gesshin learned that she had ovarian cancer, which by
that time had already progressed to stage four, a very serious
diagnosis. "They never expected me to live." But seven years
later, after surgery and several rounds of chemotherapy, she was
still traveling and teaching in different parts of this country and
Europe. Her three series of classes for women cancer patients at
the Rhonda Fleming Clinic at UCLA have brought her a new

kind of joy and gratification. Not a support group per se (although that component can certainly develop), these are classes in Zen meditation taught by a Zen master who is also a woman living with cancer. "I received so much from people at the clinic that I was very happy to give something back." In the beginning, there was a six-week course, then an eight-week course, which had to be interrupted because Gesshin fell ill again. Then a third course started up with thirty new women wanting to attend as well as old ones wanting to continue. It's quite different working with people who are sick, she says. "But I've been there myself. I know what they can and can't do.

"What they learn from me is how I live with cancer in the Zen way, the Buddhist way. The most important thing for a person faced with terminal illness is to learn how to live in the moment. That's what I practice with them. Simple things. Chanting. Short meditation periods. Walking meditation. I encourage them to practice at the beach, in the fresh air. Very practical down-to-earth things that really work, that anyone can do, without books or tools. Just seeing your body, and your mind, as they are. I enjoy these classes. It's a great thing to be with these women and to be able to take away some of their burden. From one week to the next, you can see changes. Some darkness disappears: the fear, the anxiety, the anger. You can undo so much by just looking at the moment. After an exercise, I'll ask, 'Is the cancer here now? Is there a thought of it, or a notion of it?' And there isn't! The mind doesn't need to go that way. You can work with your mind the same way you wash dishes or the kitchen floor—without adding a soap opera to it."

Gesshin also introduced these students to "laughing Zen." Once, she told them about her mother, who awoke from an afternoon nap and, still partly asleep, answered the phone in a loud, clear voice: "Hello. I'm not here now." Laughter erupted spontaneously. But we can also *initiate* laughter, at any time, she taught them. "Start with your feet apart, hands behind hips, bending slightly backward. Then reach into your hara with your breath and come back up. It will be forced at first, but then it will just roll out. And you won't be able to stop laughing."

As we work together to bring the dharma to the West, Gesshin concluded, "we continue to learn from each other and love each other, realizing that we are nothing but 'fellow travelers in the moonlight.'"

Venerable Gesshin Prabhasa Dharma, Roshi, died on May 24, 1999.

Sonja Margulies
Yvonne Rand

Sonja Margulies

When I first heard about Sonja Margulies, I conceived the fantasy that she might be a modern-day "tea lady" in the tradition that I have described in the Introduction. The picture that I formed from the few details I was given was of a teacher of an untraditional bent, relatively invisible, whom people sought out in her apartment in the middle of San Francisco, who ordained students in her living room, and who was most likely to manifest the dharma while cutting vegetables, arranging flowers, or dodging city traffic. Now that I've found my way to her door, my original fantasy has shifted a bit, but the basic notion I think still holds.

Sonja lives on the second floor of one of the large rococo apartment buildings on upper Broadway. On the phone earlier, she had likened it to a white-frosted Italian confection, and I had no trouble spotting it. Upstairs the odor of Japanese incense greeted me as I walked down the carpeted hallway. Sonja's door was ajar, and she was waiting for me in a bright silk shirt and comfortable black pants in which, she told me later, she's been sitting zazen for twenty years.

We did drink tea together, in the living room that becomes a zendo at least once a week, and in which she did indeed ordain three people in 1985. "Your zendo is where you sit," Sonja said. Although historically this may be unusual, her particular sangha has a tradition of sitting zazen in each other's homes. Her teacher, Kobun Chino, started his own center, now known as Bodhi, in a Los Altos living room, and Sonja joined it in 1969. In 1975, she received ordination. What this means, she said when

I asked, is simply that "things are the way they are, and you are confident about your practice." Doing zazen is meaning-free, she says.

Similarly, the precepts (which she has both taught and translated) are the natural action of a natural state of mind. You recognize that you "have" the precepts and then you ask for ordination. "They exist and are not separate from you." With regard to the precept "I will wear the Tathagatha's teaching," she commented, "That is just zazen. That is the robe."

Sonja was born in Minnesota in 1931 to a Lutheran family. She completed a B.A. in history, married "a Jewish agnostic," and had two children. In the 1960s, in California, she studied the psychology of religion with Abraham Maslow and Anthony Sutich, with whom she worked on the *Journal of Transpersonal Psychology*. During her research into Asian religious literature, she was especially delighted by the injunction in a Tibetan text not to believe anything without first testing it out in one's own mind. When she discovered Zen, she felt particularly drawn to this tradition "outside teachings, beyond scriptures, and concerned with seeing into one's own nature." She began Zen practice in 1968 when her children were six and eight years old.

In the years that followed, Sonja began looking closely not only at what Buddhism *said*, but at what actually took place in Buddhist history, in Buddhist countries, and in modern Buddhist lives. Although she and other women were being trained along with men, it was clear to her that the forms their training took had been devised by celibate male monks for male trainees. But she says she put her feminist doubts aside in order to practice single-mindedly. The genuine gratitude in her voice toward her teachers was unmistakable when I spoke with her. However, she also remembered that many times, while chanting the names of teachers in her lineage and realizing they were *all* men, her throat would close, her eyes would water, and her breath would disappear. How could she support the transmission of another patriarchal form?

Then, in 1982, at a Berkeley Zen Center women's group meeting, while many of the listeners were moved to tears, Sonja chanted in her powerful voice her own *female* lineage: the names of all the women who had supported her from childhood.

And on her forty-seventh birthday, she found herself writing:

> Today the patriarchs
> not taken in by
> historical situations
> grew breasts
> gave birth
> and stayed home
> to celebrate
> (forty-seven years
> of undivided life)

One of the people who was ordained by Sonja, after months of precepts study in her living room, is a psychologist who had been sitting zazen off and on since the early seventies. A year ago he decided to work with her intensively to strengthen and formalize his practice. Now, along with other important female figures in his life, he feels grateful to her for helping him develop values that he calls "horizontal"—such as interconnectness and relatedness—which he feels are basic to practice. He is impressed by Sonja's warm practicality, in her life and teaching. He was struck years ago by her emphasis on developing and encouraging gratitude in ourselves. "We're teaching each other constantly," she would say. An attitude of gratitude allows us to accept all sentient beings as our teachers. Sonja emphasizes the present moment, always, and that everything that comes our way is our teacher.

He also remembers how she stressed the basic, bodily aspect of zazen: "Meditation is really practice in *just sitting*," she would say. Very, very simple. Yet this one sentence had a powerful impact on him. He added that he is often moved by Sonja's emotional availability, by the intensity of her feelings, and by her giving herself permission to express them. She has experienced great loss in her life (including the death of her husband in 1981) as well as some more recent gratuitous physical violence. Her personal courage has been extraordinary throughout, he told me, but in the very same measure she enjoys life, is fun-loving, and delights in the things of this world.

That Sonja *lives* her Buddhism was stressed equally by a woman writer and psychotherapist who was also one of the three people ordained last year. There is no split at all between Sonja's life and what she teaches, this student said. She doesn't set herself up as a personality or charismatic figure, "doesn't hit you over the head with how spiritual she is. There is no 'stink of enlightenment' here!" In fact, if anything, Sonja has more of an attachment to "invisibility."

The student told me about Sonja's special relationship to Tony Sutich, founder of the *Journal of Transpersonal Psychology*, who was paralyzed for many years and who died in the mid-seventies. While he was alive, and while he was dying, Sonja had a remarkable capacity to be truly present for him with equanimity, matter-of-factness, respect, and reverence. Although she has in many ways lived a "traditional" life, she has a depth of understanding and compassion that makes her extraordinary—and yet ordinary at the same time. At the journal, Sonja is an exceptional editor with a "sharp, well-honed mind." Yet she has remained co-editor by choice and has mostly stayed behind the scenes. "As soon as you make something special of it, that's not *it*," Sonja says. She sees through, cuts through, illusion and appearances to the core of things.

Sonja received the teaching stick from her own master in 1983. It is a short, simple wooden staff with a curved top and an orange tassel, which in the old days was a horse's tail, she told me. There was lightness and humor in the way she handled and talked about it. *No big thing,* her voice and gestures were saying. She told me about her interest in ecumenicalism, about an informal group of Christians and Buddhists who meet in her living room each month to sit zazen and talk together, and about a Buddhist-Christian dialogue conference at which she was scheduled to speak the following week.

"Emptiness is no *special* thing," she said. "It's not so important to be a Buddhist, though it's *very* important to know who Buddha is. Practice is just to get confidence. It's not dependent on a particular form.

"When you are not thinking about who you are, who are you?" Sonja wants to know.

Update: Winter 2000

Although her living-room floor is now to be found inside a house in Santa Cruz, California, rather than in her old apartment in San Francisco, Sonja Margulies still meets there with experienced Zen students with whom she delves into koans and other Zen texts. Her primary goal is still the deepening understanding of this very moment, this life, and how we meet (or *are*) it.

Sonja is still a "noninstitutional" teacher who is drawn to examining the secular, nonaffiliated version of Zen practice that she believes is the most common one in our country today. Suzuki Roshi once described followers of this path as "not quite monks, not quite laypeople." Their questions interest Sonja: Without external supports, without a daily schedule or a sangha, how do I practice? Will it be *real* practice?

But since I first met with her in the early 1980s, I've learned that Sonja has lived through some enormous life challenges. Shortly after moving to Santa Cruz in the late eighties, she discovered that she had breast cancer. She had a mastectomy in 1987. Afterward, she told me recently, during a thirty-eight-mile drive to a postoperative medical appointment, she noticed the fluid-filled tubes sticking out of her chest, and she started to laugh. In that moment, she says, she began to deal with her situation. "I knew I had to get real, I had to face death, I had to find the humor."

When she directly faced the pain, the exhaustion, the loss of energy, the real possibility of dying sooner rather than later, her whole "angle of vision" changed. "We have to embrace all of it—things as they actually are."

And then there was more. Four years after her first surgery, Sonja's thirty-one-year-old daughter, Robin, was also diagnosed with breast cancer. Robin's prognosis was more serious than her own, and harder to accept. She had to say to herself again, "Things as they are."

From 1991 until late 1998, she and Robin shared their "cancer-treatment life" literally side by side. Sonja had one recurrence of the disease and one more operation, while her daughter's cancer spread to the bone. Robin underwent exhaustive treatment regimens, Western and alternative, and later experienced a serious decline, which finally required hospice care. But inexplicably, she rallied and even "graduated" from hospice. With her body still ravaged by the disease, she lived her life from her bed, doing healing regimens and studying Zen texts with her mother. In the midst of serious physical decline, they still laughed together at the absurdity of it all.

Robin, whose Buddhist name means "Ocean of Truth," found breathing practice and "don't know mind" to be the most helpful parts of her meditation during this period. She frequently quoted a Chinese Zen master whose main teaching was: Expect nothing. "Dying or living," he said, "the way is straight ahead."

Sonja was spending so much time with her daughter that she stopped teaching beginning students, who, she believes, "want and profit from more structure and company" than she could provide. But she tried to be available for dokusan to people who had left formal practice settings behind or who were reentering the secular world after a period of monastic life.

"Sometimes, with luck, we draw some fresh spring water from our very old Zen well. When it happens, it's hard to say who's teaching whom, but it's not so hard to realize, once more, that every day is a page of our common sutra of everyday life."

A few months ago, I learned that Robin had died—on November 17, 1998. Sonja wrote me that in the moment of death, it was obvious that "death itself had become the teacher and that the teaching stick had passed to Robin, as it does to all who die among us. Robin had asked for no funeral, no memorial service. Complying with her wishes, I was left to watch in amazement as the news of her death spread. The threads of her life that connected so many friends and loved ones developed into a spontaneous wake in the hours we kept her with us before cremation. A path of flowers and candles appeared, leading to her front door. Almost a hundred people passed through to say their good-byes with tears, laughter, Robin stories, flowers, and love to share. A few of us chanted her out at the end with the *Prajna Paramita Sutra* she had heard throughout her life.

"The events around Robin's death confirmed for me the truth that the teaching already, and always, exists. As a teacher, I can only 'pay attention' and hopefully be of some help to others to do the same."

YVONNE RAND

For twenty years, ever since she met Shunryo Suzuki-roshi in 1966 and became Zen Center secretary four months later, Yvonne Rand has been intimately involved with the San Francisco Zen Center. She has held virtually every administrative office one can hold there, as well as working closely with Suzuki-roshi in a hundred ways for the rest of his life. Most recently she has lived and worked at Zen Center's facility in Marin County, Green Gulch Farm. Yvonne is an articulate, forthright, down-to-earth woman with whom it is invigorating to talk.

Among her most important teachers, she told me, have been a series of older, ill, and dying people—both ordinary and extraordinary—with whom she's worked closely over the past fifteen years. The first was Suzuki-roshi, who died in 1971. Two years ago it was Lama Govinda, the renowned author and scholar of Tibetan Buddhism. Before he died, he said to her: "Be willing to give up all the forms we've been accustomed to following, and go back to the original teachings of the Buddha." Yvonne was struck by this advice and it has guided her ever since. As a result, she has been incorporating into her own practice and teaching a variety of methods originating not only from Zen, but from the vipassana and Tibetan traditions as well.

For her personally, two of the most important have been the practices of breath-walking and of the "half-smile," each of which she learned from the gentle Vietnamese Zen master Thich Nhat Hanh. "Learn to walk as a Buddha walks, to smile as a Buddha smiles," he says. "You can do it. Why wait until you become a Buddha? Be a Buddha right now, at this very moment!" Yvonne now practices the half-smile at stoplights and in grocery lines. Having breath-oriented practices that can be done for one to three breaths in the midst of activity has helped her experience a connectedness between the states of mind that arise in formal meditation and those arising in everyday life.

Other practices, especially with the precepts (or rules for conduct), have been useful in examining deeper levels of herself, levels beyond action and language and thought. Layers of resistance and denial had to be plumbed, but now she experiences a much wider range of connection with other people. A vipassana forgiveness meditation, for example, has been useful in working with her "fierce, judging voice"—that voice so peculiar to American and Western minds, which Yvonne perceives as a wall or hindrance to being awake.

The precepts are "absolutely necessary ground" for her. "I can't be calm if my behavior is 'off.' " Sometimes she will use one precept as a mantra. Or she will hold, in the background of her mind, the image of a sieve, each of whose wires are the precept, through which she passes everything she does or thinks or says during the day. This "creates a grid—large holes or small—depending on the gross or subtle material which I intend to pass through it." This image came out of her working in her garden and noticing how different gradations of sieves determine the soil one can make. Images have more liveliness, she believes, if they come out of concrete experience.

Yvonne respects the way "practice grabs us. One of the precepts often jumps off the page at me, from an intuitive, barely conscious awareness of exactly where an 'edge' is at any moment." For instance, the precept about not stealing, or not taking what is not given (a translation Yvonne prefers), has expanded for her into an acceptance of things-as-they-are, which has been "very, very powerful." She says the precept acts like a rope along a pathway, and has allowed her to move through and be done with old patterns more effectively than any other single practice she has done up to now.

With its constant reminders of impermanence, she says, Buddhism helps us cultivate nonpossessiveness toward everything, including our personalities, or "who it is we think we are."

Mindfulness practice, with its emphasis on being awake to *whatever* arises, teaches us to relate to our "stickiness and corruptibility" as grist for the mill. Aversion is an obstacle to seeing things as they are. *Seeing* leads to the possibility of transformation.

"We're all corruptible," she says. But the degree to which we *know* our capacity for corruptibility (that is, the roles and masks we wear that cause disharmony or harm to ourselves and others) is the degree to which we don't act on it.

There is a Tibetan practice called the "inner offering" that Yvonne finds very useful here. Imagine, she said, a bowl carved out of a human skull. (She recently brought one back from India.) Fill it with whatever stands for the "dark side" in you: blood, bones, shit, instruments of mayhem and torture, whiskey, demons. With a chopper, chop it all into tiny bits until it is transformed into nectar—which then can be an offering. In the same way we can chop up our corruptibility and transform it into an offering, says Yvonne.

Working with these different approaches from other schools of Buddhism has brought her back, refreshed, to traditional Zen practice. She is now interested in reexamining some of its formal aspects, such as dokusan and certain rituals in the zendo. She asks penetrating questions about power, authority, dependency, and relationships within the community of practitioners. How can we cultivate interdependence while, for example, we are doing retreats and giving lectures?

"Over and over, in meditation centers all over the U.S., issues of authority and projection are coming up. In our understanding of the Zen tradition as coming from Japan, we include robes from Tang-dynasty China, shaved heads, formality in meeting, hierarchy in the authority structure, and a tradition which, in its ideal form, includes long periods of living a daily monastic life with one's teacher. If I give a lecture in my traditional robes, I can feel an increase in the degree of authority which the people listening to my lecture attribute to me. They edge toward accepting what I say as true, without really examining and questioning it. Subtle changes, but they go deep, begetting a kind of handing-oneself-over. This is sometimes useful in one's learning process, but it is also dangerous to student and to teacher alike if not really conscious and within clear boundaries.

"Each of us needs to be in a feedback system. Without that we can fool ourselves about what we are actually doing to ourselves and to others. I find a deep resonance with the Buddhist tradition of being a spiritual friend. I can be on the path with another and offer what I have found in my practice. If my experience can be helpful to another, that is great. And if it is not useful or helpful, that is all right too. We can, in any event, walk this path together."

Some very specific, bold, and concrete questions have been surfacing. For example, Yvonne wants to know, "How do those of us in teaching positions get others to shed light on our shadow side so that we ourselves can see it?" She's been encouraging students to do this recently, but that's not enough, she feels. It needs to be done with peers as well. "We need to hear what our peers have to say, no matter how discomfiting." One suggestion she makes is for weekly peer consultation groups for people at Zen Center who conduct practice interviews with students. What, she wonders, would constitute an environment safe enough for looking at our shadow side? The group would have to be small, but not too small (five people would be the perfect size, she believes). There would have to be agreements about process—for example, a commitment to self-revealing and real contact with each other, a shared interest in each other's development, a willingness to attend each other's lectures and interviews and to share critiques: in other words, a totally open process that would be revolutionary in most traditional Zen settings, and certainly at Zen Center.

Yvonne's teaching activities at present include Sunday lectures at Green Gulch once every four or five weeks; leading a day of mindfulness once a month (including zazen, breath-walking, half-smile, and simple physical work); periodic workshops and weekend retreats on Zen and mindfulness practice at Green Gulch and elsewhere; retreats on death and dying, and workshops using pain as a teacher; and profession-specific retreats for people in the helping professions, lawyers, nurses, and doctors. She is primarily interested in working with "householders"—lay people practicing in ordinary life.

Since she was a child Yvonne has felt a special affinity for adolescents and old people, when "developmentally things are up for grabs, challenging and yeasty," and she wants to continue working with these age groups. In the future she also wants to work with people in mainstream work situations, giving longer, more intensive retreats in business and industrial settings. She says she wants to explore "visible versus invisible practice," and her trajectory seems to be to extend herself farther and farther into the ordinary world from the intentional community that has been her base for twenty years.

Update: Winter 2000

In response to my "updating" questions, Yvonne Rand wrote me the following letter, which I have lightly edited:

"Dear Lenore,

"You ask me where is my life right now? Where is my practice?

"My home path continues to be Soto Zen, with significant amplifications from the stream of the Elders and the heart-centered practices of Himalayan Buddhism.* Beginning in the winter of 1985–86, I was fortunate to meet and begin studying with His Holiness the Dalai Lama and the Venerable Tara Tulku, then the abbot of the Tibetan monastery in Bodh Gaya, India. Over the years, until Tara Tulku died, I was able to study closely with him and, most important, to study him and his life. I learned more than I probably yet know from his great and deep mind and heart and especially from his continuous expression of boundless compassion. He supported me in staying with my home path in a way that now seems remarkable. He took interest in teaching me about how and what to teach. And with him, I had a taste of what a truly androgynous person looks and feels like.

---

*Yvonne prefers the term *stream of Elders* to *Theravada* and *pre-Theravada* because it carries less sectarian overlay. "Himalayan" Buddhism encompasses Nepal, Bhutan, Ladakh, and Mongolia as well as Tibet.

"I have been teaching at Redwood Creek Dharma Center in Marin County since the late eighties. Our center is small and eccentric, set in the midst of a beautiful garden with places to meditate both outdoors and in. Developing this center has given me a chance to express my artistic inclinations to create a place filled with beauty and fun. The situation has grown slowly and organically and is small enough so that I can know the people I practice with quite well.

"I also have the great good fortune to be studying with a Zen teacher who is a real yogi, Shodo Harada, Roshi, from Sogenji Temple in Japan.

"Since the early nineties, I have met regularly with a number of teachers from various Buddhist schools and traditions. The contact and friendship that have grown out of these meetings help me keep an eye on my own capacity for self-deception and other pitfalls that lie in wait for anyone occupying a teaching seat. I value the company and feedback from colleagues and friends willing to speak up when they notice something I might need and want to notice myself. We discuss our teaching lives and give each other suggestions and inspiration.

"In the fall of 1997, I was diagnosed with a cancer and subsequently had surgery. The entire journey from diagnosis through recovery was a great teaching and a chance to go deeply into breath practice of the most ancient and reliable sort. I found affirmation that dharma practice is exactly the resource I have always known it to be. The challenge of this time was learning to receive help, to be helpless with grace, and to taste the extraordinary experience of being prayed for.

"I am now old enough for the teachings on impermanence to have become more than theoretical (as though they were ever other than what is so). My mother died last year, in her nineties, after a long and unhappy life. Despite all the experiences I have had being with people as they die, I found her passing remarkable and difficult.

"Today, I lead retreats, both long and short, give dharma talks fairly often, enjoy working both individually and in groups with all sorts of people, cultivating an authentic spiritual life. I continue to lead a ceremony for children who have died through abortion, miscarriage, and sudden infant death. I do this ceremony once a season and find that more and more people, as they hear about it, respond to the container it can provide for the grief and suffering that otherwise may linger unresolved for years.

"In the past several years, I have been invited to teach in situations that are not identified as Buddhist and have found the forays into the larger American secular world quite stimulating. A long-standing interest for me has been to find ways of talking about the Buddha dharma in language and with images that arise out of our own cultural context and to find ways to make Buddhism accessible to people in the mainstream. I am currently writing a book on right speech. I find writing as another form of teaching quite enjoyable, and at the same time, the process of writing is teaching me.

"Recently, I have been exploring how to live a life that is less busy and less scheduled and has, consequently, more opportunity for spontaneity. The long time I had for recovering from surgery taught me a lot about the high price we Americans pay for our dense and busy lives. I have worked all of my life since I was thirteen years old. This is the first time I have truly 'just stopped' for an extended period of time. I notice a vast difference in my life, inner and outer. For example:

"I am meeting individually with a rather small number of students these days, and I notice that with few appointments, I have large blocks of time that I can now spend writing or studying or working in the garden. I have time to sit in the morning sun or to watch the birds. I experience creative energy arising often and in ways that leave me surprised and delighted. For years, I have aimed to do more of less. Now I am beginning actually to get the taste of what this way of living feels like. There is an enriching of the day's experiences that seems to come without any special bidding or expectation on my part.

"And my teaching is different, goes deeper, as a result. There is a price to pay for this shift, but I think a simpler lifestyle is exactly what is needed to cultivate the heart/mind deeply. And I like it. In addition to writing, I am drawn back to my old friends, clay and stone. I do not know what will become of this shift toward quietness, but I do know I am very much enjoying my life now."

12

Jacqueline Mandell
Colleen Schmitz
Ayya Khema

JACQUELINE MANDELL

In Rangoon, Burma, on the day of the full moon in January 1980, to the accompaniment of rhythmic chanting by hundreds of devout onlookers, a small thirty-two-year old American woman whose long dark hair had just been shorn received ordination for three months as an eight-precept Buddhist nun. She had been practicing vipassana meditation intensively for eight years under the guidance of eminent masters in India and Southeast Asia, including Sri S. N. Goenka and the Venerable Mahasi Sayadaw, who in 1979 had given her formal authorization to teach. For some years she had been practicing and teaching in the United States, particularly at the Insight Meditation Society in Barre, Massachusetts, where she had become one of the principal guiding teachers. Now, having returned to Asia for the renewal and deepening of her practice, wearing fresh saffron robes, she was led through the ceremony of renunciation by her preceptor, Mahasi Sayadaw.

The newly ordained young woman was Jacqueline Mandell. Today she remembers, "I was joyous when I had my head shaved. Nothing was extraneous. I was right there in full being. There was nothing to pay attention to but the present moment." For two months she practiced intensively at the Thathana Yeiktha meditation center in Rangoon and then was provided with a translator for a three-week pilgrimage through upper Burma, visiting affiliated monasteries and traditional Buddhist holy places.

In tiny villages she would find herself surrounded by clusters of nuns living a simple, meditative life.

Less than two years later, back in this country, at the invitation of Venerable Taungpulu Sayadaw, another Burmese master then living in the United States, Jacqueline ordained for the second time. At the Taungpulu Kaba-Aye Monastery in Boulder Creek, California, she took ten precepts, and once more in robes and with shaved head she practiced intensively for two months. At the end of her stay, Jacqueline was asked by Taungpulu Sayadaw to teach a retreat at his monastery the following year. She did so in the spring of 1981 and is the only Western woman to have received such an honor.

Jacqueline taught full-time at IMS for six years beginning in 1977. During this period she studied with many of the important teachers who visited there, including Dipa Ma, Achaan Cha, and Rina Sircar (with whom she also co-led a number of retreats). She also attended many Zen sesshins, working intensively with Joshu Sasaki-roshi on koan practice for several years.

It was therefore no small matter that, when I first met her in the fall of 1983, Jacqueline had just resigned from her teaching position at IMS. She told me, "I can no longer represent Theravada Buddhism because it oppresses and discriminates against women. At birth, women are already seen as lesser, not equal. Within the monastic tradition, a woman who has been a nun all her life, and fully enlightened, must bow down to a monk of one day. In the scriptures, women are primarily seen either as seductresses or as lesser suffering beings who have to give birth. In the *Therigatha*, descriptions of women's lives seem pretty horrible.

"Part of the reason I could leave was that I could also stay. I felt I had completed my own process. But I personally had never been discriminated against by my own teachers. The teachings themselves were freely given, and I had utilized them to the utmost. But the Theravada tradition is a little tricky. They say a woman can get fully enlightened, but she still would not be given full power in the hierarchy.

"In order to be totally honest in what I'm doing, coming into my own as a woman, I can't represent a tradition that says women can't come into their own unless they're *arahats,* or fully enlightened. Even if they're fully enlightened the structure will keep them limited."

"You're referring to the social and political level?" I asked.

"Yes. On the spiritual level, there is never any barrier to receiving or practicing the teachings. But, for example, in Burma, going into lunch, the monks walk in first, then the laymen, then the nuns, and then the laywomen. Every step of the way it's very visual, very out in the open. During high ceremonies the men sit in front and the women in back, if they're allowed in at all."

"How did you feel about this subjectively at the time?"

"These kinds of issues didn't affect me at the time. I was looking at everything from the level of ultimate reality. But the fact is you live in relative reality. You know the Zen saying that when you begin there are mountains and rivers, then no mountains and no rivers, but you have to come back to mountains and rivers. So here we are. And there are lots of women, and they're just not given equal respect as females. That whole shadow has not been gotten rid of in the Theravada tradition because it fits right into the shadow of the people."

"The shadow, in order to be integrated, needs to be conscious."

"Yes. That's why I want to drop any identification with androgyny—so that other women don't use it as a cover or denial of the oppression and inequality that do exist."

To live *in* the world, free of the constraints of an external structure, to express her spirituality, and to help other people do likewise—these are Jacqueline's goals today as an independent teacher. For years she had channeled her vitality into the realm of spirituality and meditation teaching: "I could be serving and giving and growing and meditating, but it was also a safety zone. I didn't have to show my own power. Part of what happened is that I outgrew my safety zone." During a Yucca Valley vipassana retreat in the spring of 1983, she had announced a special sitting for women only and gave a talk "just to women, on women." It turned out to be a preliminary step to the first conference of women teachers at Providence Zen Center that summer, where she spoke in a less personal vein to a larger group of both men and women.

Her main message to women was to honor who they really were, rather than put their primary energy into a relationship with any other human being or organization or teacher "where their own intuition or beauty has to be put aside."

In Providence she said, "Listening within ourselves to what is being said is our first step toward empowerment; that is, taking the authority back into ourselves. . . . We must always question and investigate the authority, teacher, and tradition—as ancient or experienced as they may be—in order to begin honoring our own personal experience and to find our own path as the Buddha shows us."

Some of the things she said may have been unsettling to many women at the time, she told me. Within a context that does not traditionally empower women, her stepping forth in that way may have been difficult but also, she thought, nourishing. "When I was younger I wanted everyone to be okay, to feel good, to be taken care of. Now I feel that it's the truth, presented in the clearest way, that really gives the greatest care."

Jacqueline's "truth" at that point was essentially to live unfettered in the present moment, free to experience or question any situation that arose, to perceive it without conditioning from the past, and to move on without residue to whatever came next. She had let go of history. In the past she might have said, "Isn't it wonderful that we're doing a practice that's twenty-five hundred years old?" Now, she would say, "Isn't it wonderful that we're here? *Here* is what empowers." What was most interesting and relevant to her was not that there were women teachers or bodhisattvas in the past. What interested her most was the possibility in the present time for a woman to really be herself. Whether a particular woman had ever meditated before wasn't relevant to her either. "What is relevant is the ability of a woman or man to be open to an ever-changing age and to really move with it. Life is in motion. Life is in movement. An ever-changing openness to wisdom is the result of a willingness to move, not from trying to clarify or qualify anything from the past."

She stressed the importance of woman-to-woman empowerment—not because she wanted to exclude men but because female relationships, as a real contribution to spiritual growth, have not always been honored before in Buddhist tradition. "Part of the conditioning of our time," she said, "is that many women really trust men more than women. And they trust men's opinions even more than their own about themselves."

"I think that's changing," I said.

"Intellectually it's changing. On a being level it hasn't changed yet. When it comes right down to it, women are still participating in giving up their power to men. And thinking that they need to hear men express something before they can validate their own perceptions. The opening of women into their fullness and into their own integrity as women, as far as I can tell, has not taken place yet except with some individuals."

She made it clear that she didn't believe men repress women or that a system represses anyone. "Everyone is doing it together," she said. And all aspects of conditioning have to be looked at.

Our discussion then moved into the realm of teacher-student relationships. Jacqueline felt strongly that most people still project a great deal of authority onto teachers, women teachers included. "The word *teacher* exists in an old context. I want to freshen it up! All I know as I'm talking to you is that there's no notion of teacher in my mind. That feels important to say. Along with that, I don't represent anyone. And I don't represent anything. I'm a human being on the earth who is in touch with myself and willing to be with another human being."

She was not repudiating her past. She felt great love for all her teachers and her old colleagues at IMS. But having any associations now, carrying anything along with her into the future, would limit her energy and freedom. "Love is without conditioning," she said, "without history. The past is the past, and I'm really in the present. If we can only be aware, the whole context of spirituality is right here."

In recent years Jacqueline has lectured at the World Health Organization in Geneva, Switzerland, at Brandeis University, and at Harvard University Divinity School. She is including a broader audience and a broader conceptual basis for her work, in meditation courses (open to both men and women) and in women's retreats as well. At first she was primarily concerned with the Buddhist community. That has expanded to include other religious groups, such as Christian and Jewish. To women's retreats people were coming with specific issues that had surfaced in meditation centers, churches, or synagogues. Then, in a shift to "women and spirituality," she let go of traditional religious distinctions in favor of a more basic commonality.

When she first started speaking about women's issues, people began plying her with stories about women hurt in affairs with male teachers. Soon she began to see that it was almost always the same story—a common pain, a common situation, a common difficulty between male and female. "I saw it everywhere I went." But it's not black and white, she says. Each of us plays our conditioned role. "It's two people doing a dance together. I both want to respond compassionately and to help women ask, What has allowed this to happen? I don't work with blame, but to help women find out what part they play and to start to remedy that. How can you empower yourself? How can you heal the hurt? How can you avoid this situation again? Not just avoid, but complete whatever it is you need to complete, so this doesn't happen again.

"What that led into," she goes on, "was looking at certain qualities and patterns in women's lives, and examining them. And beyond that, recognizing that there is a fallibility in all systems. Whether it's a Buddhist belief system we're looking at or the most compassionate Christian setting, conditioning is still manifesting, and we have to look at it.

"So I'm not as interested in 'issues' anymore—though if a woman were to come to me with a problem, I absolutely would deal with it. I don't need to deny or judge it. It's very important to notice where denial is operating, because it can block any movement. I saw that in the Buddhist system. What I'm working with now is some kind of evolution. A lot of times there is fear, because we're working with the unknown. For thousands of years it's been patriarchy. Now we're in a time when there can be change, there can be a shift. But it means letting go of certain kinds of behavior, of standards that don't need to be accepted anymore."

Later she reiterated, "I'm still evolving. A lot of what I feel is the pulsation of life. It's not just me as a woman or me as a teacher or me on a physical, mental, or emotional level. It's a more inclusive approach to myself and to others. It's reciprocal, give and take. Maybe that's why I feel more energy. There's a flow both within myself and with others and the world."

Update: Winter 2000

In the past ten years, a fundamental shift has occurred in Jacqueline's life as a Buddhist teacher. When I first knew her, she was an independent vipassana teacher, working especially with women and developing her own style and form of teaching. In previous years, she had also studied Zen, including numerous sesshins with Joshu Sazaki, Roshi. But today, having been steeped by turns in the Hinayana and Mahayana traditions, she finds her primary affiliation and deeply felt alignment to be with the Vajrayana tradition of Tibetan Buddhism.

The seeds of this turning were planted many years ago when she first heard His Holiness the Dalai Lama speak in Bodh Gaya, India, in 1972. In subsequent years, she returned often to hear his annual teachings under the bodhi tree. An incident during that time stands out for her. In the winter of 1973, as she was meditating alone inside the Bodhi Temple, two figures entered the room and sat down quietly in front of the Buddha figure on the nearby altar. She "could feel the energy shift," Jacqueline says. One of the figures was a young monk, the other a very large older man, who she later learned was Dilgo Khyentse Rinpoche, one of the most revered Tibetan Buddhist teacher-scholars in the contemporary world. His effect on her was so palpable that when he stood up, she felt herself pulled up along with him. When he left the temple, she felt herself pulled to leave. "When he circumambulated the temple, I was pulled in his wake."

In the following years, Jacqueline met with many other Tibetan masters, including Dudjom Rinpoche, Chatral Rinpoche, Kangur Rinpoche, Kalu Rinpoche, and Sakya Pandita, the sixteenth Karmapa. As a result of these experiences, her "amazement with the subtlety of training only increases." But "moving into Vajrayana took an enormous amount of faith," she says.

"My inspirations to delve in were the kindness of the Tibetan masters and their generous spirit. In the beginning, I could never have predicted this complete shift in my practice." To finalize this transition, in 1996–1997, Jacqueline offered a two-year teacher-training program in which she passed on the teachings of her earlier years. She says this freed her to be "even more wholeheartedly" committed to Tibetan Buddhism.

There has been a second major "commitment of the heart" in Jacqueline's life. It began with the birth of her twin daughters in 1987, an experience so arduous at first that it felt like a protracted Zen sesshin. In fact, she attributes her ability to survive those seventeen months of cold early mornings and middle-of-the-night feedings, nursing first one baby and then the other, to her rigorous Zen training years before. "All of my Buddhist practices have been vital in helping me do the best that I can do in parenting my twin daughters," she says. "I love bringing them into a positive environment and creating a home where kindness is the most important thing. What supports them most, I believe, is openheartedness." She feels lucky to have completed so much meditation practice before they were born.

Jacqueline considers her daughters to be her best teachers. They encourage her to develop patience and to practice "spontaneous dharma." During one of her mother's classes, one of the then four-year-old twins defined mindfulness this way: "When you're on the playground, you know you're on the playground."

To describe what she is teaching today, Jacqueline uses the term *transformational Buddhism*. She relates the following story: "I woke one morning at Ridzen Ling during the 'Heart Advice' teachings with Chagdud Tulku Rinpoche. It was a crowded retreat, so I meditated and slept in the shrine room. I awoke before 4:00 A.M. hearing the very clear words in my mind: 'New and unbounded ways of the dharma.' The words were unmistakable and distinct, and have profoundly impacted my work."

She stresses the importance of speaking colloquially rather than formally and of listening really carefully to anyone with whom she is conversing. These were admonitions passed on to her by some of her earliest Theravadin teachers, like Venerable Mahasi Sayadaw and his close disciple Usujata, of Thatzana Meditation

Center in Rangoon. "The activation of dharma day by day is what I find exciting," she says. "How will I meet the experience of this very day?"

In her classes and workshops, Jacqueline uses guided meditation to lead people into reflective work. Her meditation instructions have traditional roots but "may not follow a restrictive form." She makes use of calming and stabilizing practices "to guide people into their own inner awareness. To be centered in our lives means to be able to shift our focus from object to object, from sensation to sensation, from getting the kids to school to focusing on work. Letting go and keeping flexible is a key to daily happiness."

Another powerful technique that Jacqueline teaches is an ancient meditation on "The 32 Parts of the Body." She was trained and instructed to teach this meditation by Venerable Taungpulu Sayadaw, of Meitilla, Burma, who considered it his central practice. Jacqueline presents it as a vehicle for deepening our awareness of impermanence and death and thereby illuminating life's true purpose. "In bringing such an ancient practice into the twenty-first century," she says, "I think it's necessary to allow our prejudices and attachments to flow through us like water rushing to the sea."

In 1996, Jacqueline made another pilgrimage to Tibet. "I did not go seeking a realized master," she says, "but I found one." His name is Adzom Choktul Paylo Rinpoche, and at his stone-and-adobe dwelling in Chimpu, Jacqueline received teachings from him on the true nature of mind. "Each day, he asked me questions and gave me precise instructions. I followed these teachings with my whole attention. I experienced no language barriers, no culture barriers, only the teacher giving precise instructions and the student receiving profound wisdom."

Colleen Schmitz

A delicate, slender young woman of thirty-four with a hint of a British accent (she was born in New Zealand), Colleen Schmitz talks with obvious respect and affection for her teacher, S. N.

Goenka, Indian master of vipassana meditation. She first met him when she was twenty-three years old and traveling in India, searching for something that was not yet clear to her. But when she arrived in Bodh Gaya and heard of a meditation course in Dalhousie, she immediately decided to attend. The teacher was Goenka-ji, and "that was it," she said. "It was the answer to everything I was looking for."

Colleen remained in India for sixteen months, traveling and attending meditation courses whenever she could. Then she spent some time in Japan, earning money as an English teacher to support her continuing with work Goenka in India. She came to this country after marrying a fellow student, an American, with whom she currently teaches vipassana meditation in California. But she still returns to India every year to do a course with Goenka-ji.

The essence of this vipassana technique (which originated with Gotama the Buddha and was passed on from teacher to pupil, from generation to generation, Goenka-ji having received it from his teacher, Sayagyi U Ba Khin of Burma) is to develop a mind that is balanced and equanimous in all situations. This is accomplished through meticulous observation of bodily sensations. By experiencing them in their true nature of impermanence, egolessness, and unsatisfactoriness, one develops wisdom.

After the taking of five precepts (against lying, stealing, killing, sexual misconduct, and use of drugs), a typical ten-day course begins with three and a half days of anapana practice, or mindfulness of breathing, in order to calm and concentrate the mind on a single object. "This develops our samadhi," Colleen said. "We choose this object [of awareness] because it's *real*. We want to learn to observe the truth of ourselves, free from any imagination, speculation, or visualization."

On the afternoon of the fourth day, vipassana is presented. (*Vipassana* means to see things as they really are.) The focus of attention now moves throughout the body. For five days, students observe bodily sensations as well as whatever comes up in the mind. By observing sensations, one is able to observe the totality of oneself, Colleen says, because (according to the Buddha) whatever arises in the mind flows with the sensations of the body. When "impurities" such as anger arise, if they are not fed or fueled, they will tend to lose force and dissolve. This comes from experiencing the sensations with equanimity, by appreciating their impermanent nature. Students' awareness may move sequentially throughout the different parts of the body; it may encompass the body as a whole; or it may move back and forth between these two modes.

On the tenth day, metta (loving-kindness) is practiced. "After purifying our minds to some extent, we try to fill the sensations in the body with feelings of love and compassion for all beings. A fountain of love springs naturally from a body/mind freed of tensions and impurities. This develops naturally as one walks the path."

The meditation technique presented in these courses is based on the Satipatthana Sutta (Pali). According to this teaching, human consciousness is by nature completely pure. In the course of our lives, however, we generate defilements (for example, greed, craving, aversion). But through the practice of awareness with wisdom, a purification process is set in motion by means of which the mind naturally purifies itself. As one experiences impermanence, one realizes there is nothing to cling to—and equanimity develops.

Goenka's teaching encourages "zestful ease"—effort characterized by ease rather than tension, according to Colleen. Vipassana, she said, means attention to the ever-shifting reality in the body. With a mind free from craving and aversion, one accepts this reality from moment to moment, seeing it as it really is. The mind is freed of push-and-pull, of holding on to what one likes and pushing away what one dislikes. Uprooting these tendencies from the very base of the mind brings happiness and tranquillity, she said.

The most faithful transcriptions of these original teachings of the Buddha—while ultimately lost or corrupted with other influences in India—were preserved in particularly pure form in Burma. However, until this century, they were transmitted only to monks (that is, male monks). Today, we are seeing the fulfillment of the ancient prophesy that 2,500 years after the Buddha's death, the dharma would spread to unprecedented numbers of followers in far-distant lands. But for Goenka and his students, the purity of the tradition is still of paramount importance. "The power is in the purity. Nothing should be added or subtracted from the technique." This spirit comes through clearly when Colleen speaks: her own personality neither intrudes nor colors what she says.

Yet interestingly enough, it is modern technology that is carrying the original form and essence of these teachings to courses all over the world. By means of audio- and videotapes, Goenka himself presents daily instructions and discourses (which generally remain the same over time). Assistant teachers follow students closely in individual meetings each day.

Since 1982, Goenka has appointed fifty-six assistant teachers worldwide, twenty-seven of whom are women. Twenty of these are teaching with their husbands; seven teach independently. Within this network, there is a preference for couples teaching together, Colleen said, because "we're presenting this practice to laypeople, and by teaching together, we encourage people to become ideal householders." The idea of women teachers is probably not an innovation in our time, she pointed out, since complexes of superiority and inferiority are merely games of the ego that dissolve as one walks the path.

During meditation courses, however, male and female students are completely separated—in dining and sleeping quarters and in the meditation hall—to "minimize distractions and make it easier to restrain one's sense doors and look within." Absolute silence is maintained between students. The techniques presented are considered to be universal, scientific, down-to-earth, nonmystical. The teacher is only a guide, and students must do their own work, but anyone with an average intellect can do it. People of all ages, races, nationalities, and religions have studied with Goenka-ji (including Tibetan Buddhists, Christians, Jews, Hindus, Jains, Parsis, and Muslims). Conversion is not required. "The only conversion is from impurity to purity, from unhappiness to happiness," according to Colleen.

"We can change ourselves. Our nature is not fixed. We can come out of blind reaction, come out of agitation." The technique opens up the unconscious, so that the entire mind becomes conscious. Normally, ignorance creates a barrier between conscious and unconscious. In our subconscious minds are stockpiles of past reactions that color our perceptions throughout the day. But by steadfastly observing bodily sensations, one penetrates more and more deeply into the entire mass of the mind. "At the level of sensation, we create 'sankharas'—knots, or reactive thoughts. At the level of sensation, we can dissolve these knots." The goal is equanimity—experienced through all the vicissitudes of daily life. Action then comes out of a balanced mind, from a base of positivity. And when one is happy and healthy, Colleen said, one has a positive effect on everyone else.

This practice puts considerable emphasis on *sila* (morality). *Sila, samadhi* (right concentration), and *panna* (wisdom) all support each other. It is possible to develop a certain degree of concentration without morality, according to Colleen, but if you want to develop wisdom, morality is essential. Immoral actions always create agitation within the mind, and if one continues to practice, following the precepts becomes increasingly natural and spontaneous. "Not to suppress, not to give free license—this is the middle way taught by the Buddha." The more one purifies the mind, the more one is content with things as they are. Happiness comes from within, and external pleasures are not craved for stimulation. The true art of living, Colleen concluded, is "to live life with awareness and equanimity, moving from gross to subtle till we reach ultimate reality."

Update: Winter 2000

In Asia, Europe, and America over the past fifteen years, Colleen has seen a steady and heartening rise in interest in the vipassana teachings of her beloved Indian teacher and meditation master S. N. Goenka. Residential centers have mushroomed to forty-five worldwide, five of them in North America. During this period of growth, nearly five hundred people (half of whom are women) have been authorized to teach meditation courses; each year about fifty-thousand people worldwide attend these courses—in Europe and the Americas as well as farther-flung places such as Russia and Mongolia.

"It's wonderful to see so many people around the world appreciating the universal nature of the dharma," Colleen says.

In California, a similar kind of growth required the California Vipassana Center to relocate to larger quarters—to a 110-acre plot of land in the Sierra Nevadas at an elevation of three thousand feet, thirty minutes from the south entrance of Yosemite National Park, with wildflower-covered meadows, orchards, pond, seasonal streams, and wooded acres of oak, pine, cedar, and manzanita.

Each month, the center usually holds two ten-day courses that can accommodate up to 140 people. There are also intensive courses for people who have been practicing for a long time—*Satipatthana Sutta* courses and three- and twenty-day courses. There are also plans to build a "pagoda complex" with rooms for individual meditation. When this complex is in place, the center will begin conducting thirty- and forty-five-day retreats.

A fascinating development in recent years is courses conducted for prisoners, first in India, but now increasingly in the United States and elsewhere. The first such course was conducted in November 1997 by Goenka-ji in Delhi's Tihar Jail, Asia's largest prison. After it ended, the jail director, Kirin Bedi, widely known for her progressive views, dedicated an entire building exclusively to vipassana courses, which have been held there on a regular basis ever since. Other Indian jails have now followed suit. A remarkable film on this subject, *Doing Time, Doing Vipassana,* produced by two Israeli women filmmakers, has been released by Karuna Films. In 1998, the film won the San Francisco International Film Festival's Golden Spire Award and ran for many months at San Francisco's Roxie Theater. The BBC has also documented the project.

Colleen likens the Buddha dharma to the ocean: "It is so vast, so deep." Her enthusiasm for practice, for her own personal retreats, has not diminished. The dharma "keeps leading me on, step after step, each leading me a little deeper, teaching me a little more, inspiring me to keep walking on. It is so clear that the results you get are in line with the effort you make and that the more you practice, the more your understanding grows."

Colleen sees herself as a guide along this path. As people progress, she believes, the dharma, rather than an external person, becomes their teacher. "There has been no change in my view of this."

She and her husband have been given the position of oversee-ing the California center, "but it is not 'our' or 'my' center." Courses continue to be provided on a donation basis, without remuneration for teachers or other staff members.

AYYA KHEMA

With her shaved head and yellow robes, Ayya ("Venerable Lady") Khema is a shiny berry of a woman, both tart and sweet, who vibrates energy and is propelled by absolute conviction. If one wants to get from here to there, and one has the means at hand, then one doesn't waste any time getting down to it. That's what she seems to be saying, and that's what she seems to be *doing*, all the time. Where Ayya wants to get is nirvana, or *nibbana*, in the Pali usage she employs. Nibbana means freedom from the mires and traps of our thinking mind and all its attach-ments. It means absolute inner peace that comes from penetrat-ing into the truth of the matter, which is endless, inevitable, eternal change.

"The universe is moving," Ayya has said. "It is contracting and expanding all the time. Within that movement, what is there to hold on to? Which star would you like to hang on to? Which one looks better than the next? They're all moving. There is nothing solid at all."

To see this for one moment is a moment of liberation, she says. And such moments don't come by grace from above, "like a golden mantle of bliss." Not at all. She maintains that nibbana is the result of long, hard work, "until the last speck of impurity has been removed." What she means by "impurity" is craving and clinging, and we *can* have moments without them. When we do, we need to attend to them with great care. "One has to know what one has done so that one can repeat it again and again." This is the hard work she is talking about—the hard work of awareness. Without awareness, unfortunate mind states prolifer-ate. And that's why we see so few happy people, she says, underscoring her own words with those of the Indian sage Ramana Maharshi: "Happiness and peace are not our birthright. Those who attain it do it by constant effort."

Ayya was born in Berlin in 1923. Her family was Jewish, and when she was fourteen she fled from the Nazis to Scotland, rejoining her parents later in China. She attended high school in Scotland and college in Shanghai, was married twice, has two children, has lived in many countries, including India and the United States, and in 1964 moved to Australia. Her first experience of a spiritual practice was at the Sri Aurobindo Ashram in Pondicherry, India. But ultimately she was strongly drawn to the pragmatism of Theravada Buddhism and spent some time in Burma, Thailand, and Sri Lanka studying with several eminent meditation masters. In 1978, at Wiseman's Ferry, New South Wales, she established a forest monastery in the Theravada tradition called Wat Buddha Dhamma and spent five years living and teaching there while giving courses in many parts of the world as well. In 1982 she established the International Buddhist Women's Center near Colombo, Sri Lanka. One of her most important teachers over the years has been the Sri Lankan master Venerable Nannarama Maha Thera of Mitirigala Forest Monastery. She was ordained there as a nun by Venerable Narada Maha Thera of Vajirarama Temple in Sri Lanka in 1979.

"I didn't know it at the time," she says now, "but it was the best thing I have ever done. The moment I put on these robes and got rid of my hair, I felt, 'Whew! Wonderful!' And it's been like that ever since." It represented a letting go of all the final obstacles to her living completely within the spiritual world of the dharma.

"This is the kind of love affair that cannot disappoint one. This is the kind of love affair where the lover does not run away or pick someone else. . . . It is not dependent on a human being who will undoubtedly die, who is undoubtedly imperfect." It is a relationship that does not require us to be loved. It only requires us to try to *see*, to open our entire perception to what is happening with us right here in our lives. When we see completely, clearly, "then this loving devotion will arise."

Ayya's enthusiasm and energy these days are primarily directed toward Parappuduwa, an international Nun's Island she established in Sri Lanka in 1984. It is situated in the middle of a beautiful lake on land donated by the Buddhist government. Women from Europe, Asia, and the United States come for periods of three months to a year or more to live the life of bhikkhunis. They can ordain as nuns or practice as *upasikas,* taking eight precepts. All community members keep the same schedule, starting at 4:00 A.M. each morning, meditating six hours a day, working, studying sutras, chanting, listening to dharma discourses, and participating in discussions.

Every day at 8:30 P.M., after evening meditation and chanting, Ayya presents a talk on some aspect of the Buddha's teaching or the life of the community. One evening she talked about right effort and said, "There is only one single moment that exists, and that's this one. The future doesn't exist. It is a figment of everyone's imagination. . . . It's all happening in one day, and if effort doesn't happen in that one day, we've wasted the day. If we're wasting a day, we're liable to waste a good human life.

"Effort has its own reward. Just by making it, the reward is there. If the effort is just a little bit more than before, one stretches the mind, and if one keeps stretching it, the mind stays expanded. If one continues making the effort, then it will eventually stretch to the point where it cannot snap back, where the mind becomes pliable, malleable, extended, where it can see the whole rather than these tiny little specks of the universe that each of us occupies, like a pinhead."

But the effort must be constant and steady, she went on. And it's not what one does that's important; it's how one does it. If an action is performed with total mindfulness and a letting go of ego, then it's done correctly. At the end of the day Ayya recommends we check on ourselves: have we done a bit more than the day before, or have we wasted our time? If so, no blame. The next morning a new life begins. Each day then has a buoyancy, a lightness, a joy. "The holy life cannot work without joy. It's as if it were the yeast in bread. Without joy the holy life cannot rise to its full height. So enjoy every moment and especially the effort," says Ayya.

On another evening she spoke about stretching the mind to the impossible. The universe is full of possibilities of which we have no inkling, she said, and without considering these possibilities, we limit ourselves. But in our hearts and minds there is an innate knowing that there's more. "So why not be a little more caring toward your heart and mind? Be a little more considerate toward them. Watch them more carefully, treat them like a very precious jewel. Pack them into cotton wool, as one would a precious jewel, so that it doesn't get buffeted and scratched. A scratchy mind can't meditate.

"Our minds are baby minds," she went on. "They need a lot of protection." And she said we are the guardians and cultivators of the mind. We need to cultivate the good seeds, the positive states of mind. We also need to realize that the ordinary mind has no place on the meditation pillow. "The ordinary mind can be left outside. On the meditation pillow there has to be an understanding that the impossible is possible." Only this will allow the inner vision that there is only flux and flow, that there is no core anywhere.

"There is nothing to get. Nobody has anything to give away. You've got to let go," Ayya admonished. "The mind needs to come to the pillow totally unaffected, like a child. Just sit down and do it." You need to be completely open and completely convinced that you can do it, she said, like a child who takes things on trust, without doubt or suspicion. "There has to be that child-like trust in the impossible." Cleverness doesn't work. It's tangled up in ideas and mind convolutions, and all of that must be chucked out. There's no room for the Buddha's teaching if anything is left in the mind at all.

"One can intellectually understand every single discourse of the Buddha and still nothing has happened yet. The mind has to expand to the extent that we understand the universality of all existence, and then the relative reality in which we live will not have the impact it used to have."

Ayya often says that the whole of the spiritual life is a process of letting go, a process of seeing what arises in oneself and letting it go. Seeing and letting go. "There's no other choice. It's easier when there are no other choices. If peacefulness is one's aim,

renunciation is the way." So drop whatever you're hanging
on to, and see its impermanence, she urges. To experience a moment of freedom, drop whatever is in the mind. We don't have
to worry about what happens after death, only about now and
the moment of death. "These are accessible to us. All of them
can only be experienced truthfully if we keep on shedding, dropping, more and more. Every day, one little thing. . . . This
whole life is intended for penetration into wisdom. Every day is
our whole life."

Update: Winter 2000

Ayya Khema died on November 2, 1997, after having been ill with
breast cancer for fourteen years. She told almost no one until she
required surgery in 1993, when the pain began to interfere with
her teaching. Her right breast was removed. "It was a big operation," her dharma successor, Reverend Nyanabodhi, wrote me
from Germany, "but she recovered and gave us four more years,
probably the deepest."

In 1989, several years after I last saw her, Ayya created Buddha-
Haus in the German countryside southwest of Munich. It had
originally been a farmhouse, which, in short order, was converted
into a center for seminars and meditation courses. Here, thousands of students over the following years were able to hear
Ayya's unique, clear voice elucidating the heart of the dharma.

"She taught the whole teaching," Nyanabodhi continued,
"not only the insight, the 'male' part, but also the calm, the
'female' part. And this was very extraordinary in the Western
Buddhist world." Encouraged by her own teacher, the Venerable
Nannarama Mahathera, who had said to her, "Go to the West
and teach the Jhanas. They are becoming a lost art," Ayya had
indeed begun teaching these meditative absorptions with a precision and detail not heard before in the West.

"Her genius as a teacher lay in her ability to present the essence
of the Buddha's teaching in simple, accessible prose," according
to Sandy Boucher in her foreword to Ayya's recently published
autobiography (*I Give You My Life*, Shambhala Publications,
1998). "This she did without notes or sources of any kind, quot-

ing frequently from the sutras, speaking distinctly, in a strong voice, as her large eyes assessed her audience."

Her teaching of the Jhanas was "the most amazing, remarkable, and controversial aspect of her teaching," I was told by Leigh Brasington, an American student of many years who was among several whom Ayya authorized to teach before she died. "I seem to be the only one in North America, though, who is crazy enough to actually try and teach the Jhanas." It was mostly during private interviews that detailed information on how to navigate these states was imparted, he says. "Ayya could listen to us describe what occurred during our sittings and point out what was useful and what was a dead end or waste of energy."

(In a conversation on the Jhanas with the editors of *Inquiring Mind* in the fall of 1996, Ayya had been asked about the frequently heard bias against "absorption" that associates it with being "spaced-out" or hypnotized. Ayya replied that "in absorption, we are no longer projecting our ego onto reality. We are tasting an experience of the emptiness of self. . . . And the only way we can be enlightened is when we *feel* or *experience* that there's nobody at home.")

Ayya was "truly in her element," according to Leigh Brasington, on the longer retreats of a month or more, which she began conducting in 1989. "She could take a sutra and go into it in great detail." For example, in July 1991, she spent twenty-five days expounding on a sutra that can be read in about an hour, because she considered it one of the most important in the whole Buddhist canon.

"These long retreats were also wonderful," Leigh says, "in that we had such long, frequent interviews with Ayya. We could see her every third or fourth day for forty-five minutes, and this is where her real teaching happened. She wasn't the least bit interested in our psychological hang-ups. Her only question was, 'Tell me about your meditation practice.' "

In May of 1994, Leigh registered for Ayya's twenty-four-day retreat in Santa Cruz, California. When he arrived, he was told to see Ayya immediately. He was shocked to see the toll the cancer had taken since last he saw her, to hear that she no longer felt able to do all the interviews and that he was being requested to do some for her. "This was the retreat where Ayya taught me to be a teacher," he says, "a hard but wonderful learning experience." It was also at this retreat that Ayya decided not to come back to the United States because "she was tired of our preoccupation with our own psychological processes." Later she relented, and there was a last U.S. retreat in July 1996 at Green Gulch Farm, in Muir Beach, California. Leigh and another longtime student did all the interviews, but even though her health had clearly failed even more, Ayya's talks, he says, were as powerful as ever.

"I visited her in Germany three weeks before she died," he told me. "She was obviously in pain but never mentioned it. Her whole attitude was, 'Well, my body has given out; it's time for me to go.' She wasn't the least bit concerned about dying. Her mind was as remarkably clear as it always was. It was a very upbeat visit, even though I knew I would never see her again."

Most of all, Leigh remembers Ayya's clarity as well as the emphasis she placed on metta (loving-kindness) practice. At retreats, she would lead beautiful metta meditations each evening, believing that without a heart capable of metta, real progress on the spiritual path would be difficult.

A week before she died, Ayya founded the Order of the Western Forest Monastery Tradition and ordained the first woman ever to be ordained in the German and Pali languages. According to the Buddha long ago, the dharma will take root in a country only when its people can be ordained in their mother tongue.

In her lifetime, Ayya wrote more than twenty books (with new ones still coming out) and gave more than twelve hundred taped dharma talks in German and more than a thousand in English. In her talks, Nyanabodhi has said, Ayya presented "the way to the final goal from many different angles, including all the details one might wish for, steeped in the power of her own experience."

In the final chapter of her autobiography, Ayya wrote in her no-nonsense way: "For me death is a matter of course. I am prepared to disappear." No longer having any desire to continue as a separate self, she was ready to have nothing happen next, to let go entirely into the absolute peace of nirvana. "The last great absorption," she wrote.

13
Tsering Everest
Joanna Macy

TSERING EVEREST

In a splendid room overlooking the full expanse of the San Francisco Bay, surrounded by handsome Oriental paintings and rugs, and immense vases of gracefully arranged fresh flowers, a craggy-faced man with a topknot, in a faded red cotton *chubba* (a long skirt worn by Tibetan men and women), sits with his legs crossed under him on a small rust-colored couch facing the large, quiet room. His eyes are closed, and he moves his lips to a silent mantra as prayer beads slip through his fingers. Turned slightly in his direction, from the low seat of a high-backed wooden chair a few feet away, a young woman in her mid-thirties sits without moving, a large leatherbound book in her lap. She has a serene, oval face with gray-blue eyes set far apart, her brown hair pulled tightly back from her forehead and held in place with an ebony chopstick. People are filling the room, sitting on cushions or against the walls, waiting silently or talking softly. They have come to hear the man on the couch—the Tibetan lama, Chagdud Tulku Rinpoche—preach the dharma.

When he opens his eyes, placing the beads on the pillow next to him and smiling slightly, a glance passes between him and the woman on his left—a glance of unequivocal trust and understanding, tested by time and tempered with humor. As the evening progresses, this first impression deepens. The people in the room witness an extraordinary collaboration between teacher and student, who, in antiphonal form, convey the full depth and compassion of ancient Tibetan Buddhist doctrines to this heterogeneous American audience.

Chagdud Rinpoche speaks very little English, and what he speaks is incomprehensible to many. But his student, Tsering Everest, understands his words exactly. She understands more than his words. From long association and perfect attunement, she perceives the context, intention, and spirit behind the words, and she articulates these in a natural, refreshing linguistic style of great clarity and richness. While Chagdud Rinpoche is speaking, she writes without pause in the large book that she holds in her lap (although when she speaks later, she hardly refers to it at all). Sometimes she will interrupt him for clarification. Her concentration is one-pointed and unwavering, and entirely relaxed. From time to time, Chagdud may joke with her playfully about one of her queries, or she may reveal a wry or comical detail about him. The atmosphere is permeated with kindness and good humor, and with an absolute devotion to the transmission of the dharma for the sake of all beings.

Tsering means "long life." The name was given to her by His Holiness Dudjom Rinpoche at her first initiation into Tibetan Buddhism in Ashland, Oregon, in 1979. She was then twenty-five years old—a single mother who had grown up in Helena, Montana, had married there at the age of nineteen, and had left her husband after five years to move California. During her childhood she had experienced a deep natural faith and sense of ultimate truth, but it was elusive, she told me. Her first real teacher was an elderly Rosicrucian, the owner of a used-book store in Los Angeles, who gently guided her reading and advised her never to "guru-shop." After a while she moved to Oregon where one of her two sisters was living, explored a number of esoteric teachings, including astrology, but realized that she "wasn't getting the essential point" and needed a teacher. Without really knowing whom to pray to, she put out a prayer to the universe—and about a week later was invited to a lecture given by "a young man with a British accent. I didn't know he was a Buddhist. I didn't know he was a Tibetan."

He was talking about absolute reality—how to taste, see, catch, and feel it. From the very bottom of herself, she recognized a truth she already understood. "My whole life had been a process of trying to find something completely accurate, something worth investing myself in totally." She felt a compelling desire to discover all she could about the totality of absolute truth, and felt impelled to ask who this man's teacher was. Still without the essential information that what she had encountered was a form of Buddhism, she learned that his teacher was His Holiness Dudjom Rinpoche and that he would soon be conducting an initiation in Ashland, Oregon. She traveled the short distance without delay, and there, on a high throne, was "this wonderful old man" announcing through an interpreter that people who wished to take refuge in the Buddha should remain, while those who did not should please leave the room.

"I was totally shocked." Until that moment she had associated Buddhism with idol worship and with cows overrunning India. But she saw instantly that if what she'd been experiencing over the past few days was real, then her naive ideas could not be correct. "I was on the doorstep of becoming a Buddhist. How could I live my life saying 'I *should* have'? So I did it, and have been involved without hesitation ever since."

On the day of her initiation she also saw Lama Chagdud Rinpoche for the first time. He was serving at the shrine, carrying the incense and bowls, and he looked very powerful to her. She thought, "That must be what a yogi is!" The next day she told Dudjom Rinpoche that she wanted to study seriously and asked if he would send a teacher to the Eugene area where she lived. In response, His Holiness Dudjom Rinpoche asked Chagdud Rinpoche to become the resident lama for the newly forming sangha in Eugene. With him, Tsering immediately went "right to the core." His mode of teaching, she told me, at every step "contains and maintains absolute truth." Had it not, she confessed, she would have had more difficulty, her mind being so "essence-oriented."

A small number of people from that original initiation are still Chagdud Rinpoche's students, and many others from all parts of the world have joined them over the years at their center in Cottage Grove, Oregon. Tsering remarried in 1982, and her son, Joseph, is now ten years old.

When I asked about her remarkable connection to her teacher

and the lucidity with which she grasps and expresses his precise meaning, she said: "To begin with, I just adored what he meant. I adored the essence. I adored the dharma. It's like my blood somehow. So when he came from that place that I adore, I had no trouble communicating. At first it was almost a matter of listening with my skin. He couldn't speak English, and I wanted to know everything. He'd move his hand a certain way or he'd laugh a certain way, and I looked through these things to find the meaning. Now I do it with images. He's a painter with words. He makes pictures, like a haiku. His English is like haiku. If you see the images around his words, then you can understand the meaning."

"Last night the image that came to me was that you were making tapestries."

"Exactly, exactly. He'd make one stroke on the page and I knew from that stroke what the whole picture looked like. So I'd fill in the details and paint the rest of it. That's what makes me so happy. His mere stroke on the page contains the whole meaning, so if I can fill out the view for other people, it gives me great happiness."

"Were you able to do that from the beginning? Did you give him the tapestries in your mind?"

"I think I might have stimulated the teaching because he knew I really wanted it. You push, and then it starts to come, and then it's a matter of catching it. For years all I did was push a little and catch. It was a matter of doing that for a long time."

"So you never knew Tibetan and he never really talked Tibetan?"

"No. But he did have a translator for a short period. And it was like a dam bursting. Rinpoche finally had a mouth, and the teachings were unbelievable. He would talk for eight hours at a time. I was thrilled, because it gave me all the details I needed."

"By now you must have heard it all many times. But from where I sit, it seems absolutely fresh, as if it's the very first time."

"It is, in my mind. It's like fresh air. I try to stay at that point where it's exactly what I need to hear. It's exactly the missing piece for what I need to know. Then it's fresh, then it's real, then it's something I can give to people because it means something to me."

"It's not learning in the sense of incorporating knowledge but of being alive with it and of having it be your life."

"That's right. It's total. It's the breath of it. It comes in, it comes out."

"Is there anything else you want to do?"

"No. I don't want to do anything else. I don't have any other kinds of ambitions. This is something I must have prayed for a lot. It's hard for my family sometimes. I'm away a lot. And sometimes it's hard for me—just the hustle and bustle of the travel. Always in a different room, in a different car, in a different train station. Everything is constantly changing. New people, new faces. But the benefit is immeasurable because Rinpoche lives the truth. He gives me a constant example of how you live it. We all lurch in our practice, but he has a smooth consistency that never stops, never starts. It's pervasive, it's permanent, birthless, deathless. Plus he pushes me. Oh, yes, he pushes me when I want to be lazy, when I want to go to the beach."

"You don't mind?"

"Sometimes I mind. But it never goes very far because what I really want to be is what he's causing me to be."

"Is there anything about which you sometimes feel, 'Oh, let me have a little of that'?"

"Movies. He thinks they're a terrible waste of time and money. But I go. I need it to stay in touch with reality. But there's something else I've been learning. I used to think, 'If I can just get through this, then I can collapse and regenerate.' But it's that very idea that causes exhaustion. Being 'on' is being 'on.' It's not any different than being 'off.' I've been watching my mind for years and I can see that the quality of real practice is the fact that it's 'on.' It isn't ever 'off.' The sun doesn't decide to turn off or take a break. So I've been working with just continuing. If you can, you don't get exhausted."

"Rest is somehow there anyway."

"Right, in the midst of it. Sometimes someone will suggest that Rinpoche take a vacation. But for him it would be three days lost and nobody's heard the meaning of Being!"

"This is a unique kind of thing, don't you think—these two people from whom the dharma flows? It seems that it's something between you, that it's both of you together that make it possible."

"I support what he does, and then I have the power to do what I do. I channel what his meaning is. He ignites the meaning in me and then I can expand it, using any word I can catch. I'm able to do it because of the mere force of his being, and the vast realization he has. I benefit most by recognizing him as the source. The more I serve that, the more I support and encourage and create my own development. It's most useful to me to think of him as the Buddha, the living example, to which I listen, which I absorb and serve. Because he's the Buddha doesn't mean there isn't the essence of the Buddha in me, or that the nature of my own mind isn't the Buddha. That's how it works when we're dualistic beings."

"And when we're not?"

"And when we're not, no words."

Update: Winter 2000

For a while, it was difficult for me to catch up with Lama Tsering. She was moving around so quickly—from Oregon to Arizona to Brazil to El Salvador and back to Brazil—that we kept missing each other, finally resorting to E-mail, which at last put me in touch with her husband, David Everest, also a lama, who was able to fill me in on the details of her life since our last meeting.

Tsering continued in her role as Chagdud Rinpoche's translator from 1981 to 1991. On her birthday, September 1, 1990, Rinpoche told her she should begin preparations for a traditional three-year retreat. Tsering and David and their son had already moved from Oregon to California, where they had begun building a retreat center in the Trinity Alps. A site for their house had been cleared, and with the sangha's help, they completed enough construction for Tsering to begin her retreat on July 11, 1991 (the day of a solar eclipse). As the retreat progressed, construction continued all around the rocky flats outside, so she regularly did her meditations to the accompaniment of hammers and bulldozers. Her family was able to visit her during this time, and Rinpoche came periodically to give instructions. He also asked her to begin teaching even before the retreat was over, so she began to speak from behind a screen through a small sound system so that people could hear her. In December 1994, Rinpoche was delayed by flooding in the Napa Valley and requested that Tsering assist in a monthlong retreat already in progress at the center. So they quickly rigged up a bigger sound system, and the retreatants, many of whom had never seen her, according to David, "were captivated by her voice and sincerity." Anyone who has heard Tsering speak will understand the truth of his observation.

Among the participants at this retreat was a Brazilian man named Manoel Vidal, an attorney from Sao Paolo, who was so impressed by her teaching that he proposed she come to Brazil for a teaching tour—and he himself would be her sponsor and translator. So when her retreat ended in February 1995, Tsering already had her next assignment in place. Rinpoche presented her with a suitcase and said, "You, me, same, suitcase going." He recognized her as an emanation of Tara, a realization holder of the Red Tara Lineage, and ordained her on March 2, 1995.

Tsering now has three centers under her care: Odsal Ling, in Sao Paolo (her primary residence); Dorje Ling, in Curitiba, Brazil; and Mingyur Ling, in Ashland, Oregon. Although she still travels extensively in this country and worldwide, her primary focus—for now, at least—will be on her work in Brazil.

Tsering and I finally caught up with each other on the telephone during her visit to California in December 1998. Her voice sounded as young and vibrant as it had all those years ago, long before she had been ordained or had taken on all this far-flung responsibility. She said she had no idea back then "what it was about, what it was going to be." Now she's in a different country and culture, at the "first moment" of introducing new people to the dharma, and it feels "like an experience of *déjà vu*. I've been here, I've done this—only I'm in a different position. Before, I was sitting there listening; now, I'm the one telling."

This experience of the dharma's coming to a new country feels timeless to her, almost as if the same people who gathered in the United States years ago are gathering now in Brazil: people connected to the dharma coming to meet the teachers and listen to the teachings, people with the heart and character to practice with love and compassion for the enlightenment of others.

"I can imagine it being in any country, any place. It's very beautiful to me." I asked her whether she felt at home in Brazil, and she said, "Yes, I do. But you know, Rinpoche trained me really well about home. I was never able to stay 'home' very much, because all my years of dharma activity have been traveling. You have to be at home wherever you are." I reminded her of something she told me years ago, about finding "the quiet in between things." She said, yes, it's there all the time, in between things, until finally "things" simply exist in the midst of silence.

We looked at two other compelling issues together: first, the reality of anger and hatred in ourselves and the world, and how to work skillfully with them; second, the crucial importance of wholly opening our hearts to our mothers (a widespread difficulty among Western practitioners). Tsering distinguished three possible approaches to working with anger, derived from the three Buddhist traditions of Hinayana, Mahayana, and Vajrayana. In the first, anger is *abandoned*, along with other negative tendencies. In the second, it is *converted* into something positive— through love or compassion, for example. In the third, it is *liberated* through seeing that its essence is energy and already perfect. You need not change or convert anything but simply expose its essence. Anger is inseparable from enlightened energy, she said, even though it's occurring in a distorted way. By liberating this fundamental energy, anger's "mirrorlike wisdom" can be seen.

What makes this possible, according to Tsering, is simply learning to relax. "It's the effect of effortlessness, the effortless process." But it's easy to get confused conceptually here, she cautioned. "It's not so easy to practice Vajrayana."

Later, moving to the second issue mentioned above, she told me about an "amazing moment" in which she understood that dharma practice begins naturally with learning love and compassion for one's mother. "She's not a perfect person, just a human being with a lot of conditioning. But she gestated us, gave us the actual moment of birth. Sometimes, our parents don't have the karma even to support sanity," she said. "But it's particularly important to come to terms with and love one's mother, even if she made lots of mistakes, to appreciate her and understand that she just wants to be happy. You're not going to get a lot of points, you're not going to get a lot of praise, but here's this woman who gave you a body, and how can you help her?"

There is a structured Vajrayana practice, she told me, for understanding the "kindness" of a mother in a very direct and visceral way. "Here's this woman on the way to dying," she said. "There's only so much time. What can be done?" By means of this practice, we acquire the insight, love, compassion, and wisdom to benefit this woman who gave us this body. "Every joy you have is dependent on the fact that she let you be born. Further, dealing with our mothers in this way gives meaning to the teaching that all beings have once been our mothers. She is the first in line but is a link to all the others who have mothered us, been kind to us, held us and nurtured us throughout limitless time and space and cyclic existence. Many remarkable experiences have come from this work," she said. "It opens your heart, breaks your shell."

I told her about my own work with my ninety-six-year-old mother and how, as I blanch at the weight of conditioning that still causes her suffering, I keep doggedly trying to help her "see the truth." In my bones, I know that this is wrongheaded, that I need to let it all go and just love her. But I'm caught.

Tsering pointed out that "the expectation is that she's going to understand. And who knows if she's going to understand? You have to get past needing her to appreciate or understand or excuse you. Or to let you teach her. She's not going to listen! But if your power were greater, if your love and compassion were less limited, it would move in a different way." (Indeed, I thought.)

"This teaching is basic dharma," Tsering added. "It's first-step dharma, and it's the whole step. Rather than skip on to real heady stuff, people need to look at this woman who gave them life." If we cultivate love and compassion and wisdom toward our mothers, Tsering believes, when they die, their connection to us is their strength.

In our culture, we do not have the concept that simply giving us birth is an act of kindness. We have a hard time recognizing this kindness, she said, "because nobody gets under our skin in quite the same way. It's why everyone needs to start there."

Toward the end of our talk, Tsering returned to her early experience with Chagdud Rinpoche. He was then literally always there, sitting in the room while she translated the dharma. Now, although he's not physically present, it feels the same, she said. The stories she tells are her own stories now, not his. But the teaching is timeless. "There's a stream of meaning that comes through. It goes into different cups, is expressed slightly differently by different people, but the nectar is the same."

I told Tsering I was smiling. I could hear the happiness in her voice.

JOANNA MACY

One evening in June 1986, a roomful of people in Boulder, Colorado, in a matter of minutes turned into a Sri Lankan village. The event was part of a Strategies for Peace Conference cosponsored by Naropa Institute and the Buddhist Peace Fellowship. By absorbing the details of a fifteen-minute guided visualization led by Joanna Macy and simply by sharing in the human condition, as Joanna expressed it later, the participants had all the information they needed for the transformation to take place. For three hours they became farmers, laborers, mothers, officials, and children collectively grappling with grass-roots issues half a world away.

Joanna's intimate knowledge of the Sri Lankan people and countryside grows out of a year's experience living and working there in the late seventies. For the workshop participants, she set the scene in loving detail—the colors, the sounds, the smells. When it was time for people to choose their roles, they even knew what clothes they were wearing. Then Joanna's voice led them up a hill to the Buddhist temple under an early evening sky, gravel crunching underfoot, the air smelling of jasmine. She herself played the part of a community organizer from Sarvodaya (the Buddhist social change movement founded in Sri Lanka by A. T. Ariyaratne) and led them in chanting the Three Refuges and a loving-kindness meditation, the traditional opening of all Sarvodaya meetings. Then for two hours people were totally immersed in their roles—serious, intense, practical, funny—children scrambling around in front of the room listening and adding their news as their parents tackled the most pressing local problems. Time was foreshortened so that into one evening they compressed three meetings usually separated by two- and four-week intervals. By the end of the allotted time, they had formed working committees and had planned a village-wide work project known as *shramadana*. The participants had experienced firsthand how Buddhist principles apply to processes of social change, and the often overwhelming issue of Third World development had been demystified. Joanna believes that feelings of guilt and overcomplexity often confound people here. But by enacting roles we overcome guilt, we learn these are people just like ourselves, that they're smart and wise, and barriers melt. There can be an experience of collective consciousness that is almost awesome, she says.

At 10:00 P.M. that night in Boulder, there was so much energy in the room that no one wanted to leave. People were excitedly applying the principles to their own lives and communities as they were shooed out the door. But a good shramadana, according to Joanna, takes at least six weeks—and usually six months—to prepare. "The point is not to do the job so much as to change people. 'We build the road and the road builds us' is a Sarvodaya saying."

The two major themes underlying this work—the spiritual and the social-political—have played back and forth or side by side throughout Joanna's life. Born in 1929 in Los Angeles, she grew up mostly in New York, attending the Lycée Français in Manhattan. At Wellesley College she majored in biblical history: "I was fascinated by the religious questions our species asks," she recalls. At the same time she became politically radicalized and received a Fulbright grant to study nationalism in the Third World. She was married in 1953 and had three children, and in the sixties her husband became administrator of the Peace Corps. The whole family moved to India for two years, and it was there, at age thirty-five, that she had her first encounter with Buddhism—an audience with His Holiness the Dalai Lama with a group of Peace Corps volunteers.

At the time she was working with a community of 100 Tibetan lamas and 300 laypersons who, under their leader, Khamtrul Rinpoche, had fled to India from the land of Kham in eastern Tibet at the time of the Chinese occupation. They had a distinctive culture, rich in dance, music, and art, as well as ancient yogic tradition. Khamtrul Rinpoche had brought out with him six or seven *tokdens,* or advanced yogis who dressed all in white, their long hair arranged in an unwashed pile on their heads. They appeared at once savage and mystical, and they practiced one of the most esoteric forms of yoga and medicine in the world. Joanna became closely bonded to this community—"We mutually adopted each other"—and spent weeks at a time as well as summers with them in Dalhousie near Dharamasala, India. It was like being in a corner of Tibet, she recalls. With the assistance of Peace Corps volunteers, she organized grass-roots projects (such as a cooperative marketing venture) to help promote community self-sufficiency.

From time to time other Westerners arrived, looking for "instant Buddhism." But Joanna held back. She valued the ordinariness and concreteness of her day-to-day associations, and it was only in her last few months with this community that she decided to ask for spiritual teachings. In the meantime she had met and become close to Sister Palmo, a remarkable Englishwoman who had married a Sikh and moved to India in the thirties, had been arrested with Gandhi as a *satyagrahi,* had studied meditation with Mahasi Sayadaw in Rangoon in the early fifties, and in 1959 was asked by Prime Minister Nehru to organize camps for the thousands of Tibetan refugees who were fleeing from the Chinese to northern India and Nepal. While carrying on this work, Sister Palmo had close personal contact with such major Tibetan Buddhist leaders as the Dalai Lama and His Holiness the Gyalwa Karmapa, and one of the consequences was that she recognized them as her teachers and Tibetan Buddhism as her true tradition.

It was Sister Palmo who introduced Joanna to meditation and became her first dharma teacher. Sister Palmo had established a Tibetan Buddhist nunnery, and Joanna spent some time there, practicing and receiving instruction in the vipassana tradition. Afterward she received teachings from the lamas of the Khamtrul community. She still feels deeply connected to these Tibetan teachers, although she does not practice in the Vajrayana tradition. Her primary practice is vipassana, but her relationship to Buddhism is still strongly colored by her Tibetan friendships and by the qualities of humor and absolute compassion that permeate these people's lives. They express no bitterness toward the Chinese invaders, for example. "Poor Chinese," they will say. "They make such bad karma for themselves." Their remarkable spirit opened Joanna's psyche to a dimension of generosity she had not imagined possible.

During the 1970s, when she was in her forties, Joanna went back to graduate school, completing a doctorate in religion from Syracuse University in 1978. Her area of concentration this time was Buddhism, and her dissertation dealt with early pre-Theravadin scriptures (sutras and vinayas). She was particularly interested in the central teaching of causality and in questions about the relationship between mind and body or mind and nature. These ancient teachings posit a nonlinear, reciprocal causality, which Joanna later found precisely echoed in contemporary Western systems theory. This vision has been fundamental to Joanna's work ever since. She says that most scholars feel that "dependent coarising" weakens the ethical thrust of Buddhism, their assumption being that a persuasive morality requires a foundation that is unchanging and absolute. Joanna, by contrast, was intrigued by the possibility of a cohesive worldview and social ethic based on radical relativity.

Such a position she finds in fact to be "very pragmatic," especially when working with issues of planetary survival and personal empowerment, the issues that especially engage her today.

In 1979, Joanna received a Ford Foundation grant to study the Sarvodaya movement in Sri Lanka. She wanted to see firsthand how Buddhist teachings were used to motivate and mobilize people for social change, and what she might learn about methods that would be relevant to our own country and culture. "I believe in reverse technical assistance," she says. "*We* can learn from *them*." She found that the dharma permeated the movement on all levels, shaping its goals as well as its tactics, from central head-quarters to remote villages. She became acquainted with people from every corner of society during her year's stay, and continues to be very close to the Sarvodaya movement and its leadership. Her first book, *Dharma and Development* (1983; revised edition, 1985, Kumarian Press, West Hartford, Conn.), was based on this experience.

But it was her growing perception of the depth and universality of repressed despair and psychic numbing in our time, in response to the unimaginable possibility of planetary extinction, that inspired most of Joanna's most recent work. "We are now an endangered species," she wrote in a 1981 booklet entitled *Despairwork* (Philadelphia: New Society Publishers). "The greatest danger to human survival is not nuclear holocaust or destruction of the biosphere, but our massive denial of these threats, our blind immersion in business-as-usual, and our culture's taboo against expressions of despair." In response, she began to develop workshops, based in part on Buddhist insights and practices, that help release and validate feelings of rage and grief and then empower people to act. She recognized that these feelings are universal and spring from concerns extending beyond our individual egos, and that they vividly confirm our interconnectedness. Without necessarily talking about Buddhism, she was finding ways to communicate the dharma experientially.

For example, in a group workshop on Despair and Empowerment, she would present a meditation on compassion, adapted from a Tibetan *bodhicitta* practice. First she would invite people to give themselves permission to imaginatively experience the suffering of other people, as vividly and concretely as possible, and then to take these sufferings into themselves with their breath, visualizing them as a dark stream drawn in with each inhalation into and through the heart. There is nothing to "do" about these sufferings; one simply allows and experiences them. The focus is on feelings, not ideas. "By breaking taboos against despair and permitting it to be openly expressed in imagery, ritual, tears, rage, and plain talk, these workshops release blocked energy. In that release and communication comes stronger commitment to our common task of humane survival."

In the past six years, with enormous focused energy and warmth of heart, Joanna has brought a Buddhist perspective to between ten and twenty thousand people through hundreds of workshops in the United States, Canada, England, Scotland, Australia, and New Zealand. In the fall of 1986, with the help of an interpreter, she conducted a dozen more in Germany, Norway, and Sweden. Her book *Despair and Personal Power in the Nuclear Age* (Philadelphia: New Society Publishers, 1983) describes this work in detail. Most recently she has begun leading workshops on Deep Ecology called "The Council of All Beings." Through highly interactive exercises and rituals, she extends our identification beyond the human species to all beings everywhere. Part of her inspiration has come from the Vietnamese Buddhist monk and Zen master Thich Nhat Hanh. And recently she has been drawn back to Hua-yen Buddhism, a form of Mahayana that presents what appears to be a holographic vision of the universe. In the *Huayen* (Flower Ornament) *Sutra,* Joanna has found hints of meditative practices that foster the kind of unitive identification that she is most interested in developing.

Her belief in the power of interpenetration is very deep ("It's true!" she says). But it needs to be named, and people need experiences that confirm it. "That is the shape my work has taken."

Once in a while, though, she has questions. Some years ago, she approached Chögyal Rinpoche, one of her Tibetan dharma brothers and teachers, in Tashi Jong in North India. With some trepidation she told him she was using techniques borrowed and adapted from Buddhism with people from other religions—with Christians and Jews—sometimes in secular settings, sometimes in houses of worship. "Do you think this is wrong?" she asked. He laughed, she told me, and his eyes filled with love. "Oh, Joanna," he said, "the Buddha was not a Buddhist!"

Update: Winter 2000

Two major forces, Joanna told me in her very particular, passionate voice, have shaped her work over the past decade. The first has been the coming together in our consciousness of the political and spiritual realms. "It's much more obvious to people now that they belong together," she said. But in the early eighties, her workshops guiding people to confront political issues from a spiritual perspective "took a tremendous amount of chutzpah. "Now, they say, 'Of course!' "

A second insight that has directly affected her work (and been affected by it) is the recognition of how deep and how structural the dysfunction of our society is—and how devastating and suicidal are the forces this dysfunction has generated. "The accelerating divide between rich and poor, with fewer and fewer people more and more obscenely rich, and more people destitute, below subsistence level—I don't think anyone really imagined it could get that bad." The ecological crisis also far exceeds what we could have visualized a decade ago.

So on the one hand, there has been a flowering of wisdom, and on the other, an "acceleration of peril and stupidity." Holding these simultaneous truths, Joanna has felt supported by both Buddha dharma and systems theory. "They nourish each other; they dance with each other; they use different parts of my mind-heart and stimulate insights that keep me from slitting my throat."

It seems that our system is spinning out of control, in what has been called "systems runaway." Yet in her recent work, Joanna more and more emphasizes gratitude. "Being human now means that we can take part in the most significant chapter in the human story." She realizes, of course, that "there is no guarantee, that we could fail. So we embark with a kind of lightheartedness, willing to wager everything, thankful for the opportunity to taste the full measure of our courage, to use everything we've ever learned about interconnectedness, to see the beauty and valor in our human hearts."

At the same time, Joanna has also been confronting anger. Using meditations from both the vipassana and Tibetan traditions, she has "made friends" with her anger. Anger and rage can arise in response to injustice and the harrowing suffering in the world. One of her Tibetan teachers told Joanna, "Such great anger—it comes straight from the heart of compassion."

We are in the midst of a transition, she believes, from an industrial growth society to a life-sustaining society, an period that future generations ("if there *are* future generations") may call a Great Turning. In her latest book, *Coming Back to Life* (with Molly Young Brown, New Society Publishers, 1998), she combines passionate theory with nuts-and-bolts practicality, giving us "brain food" to perceive and confront the global crisis as a crisis in perception. Instead of separate entities in endless competition, she insists we are "flows of relationship," inseparable from the living body of earth.

In her workshops around the world, in the courses she teaches as adjunct professor at the Starr King School for the Ministry in Berkeley, at the California Institute for Integral Studies in San Francisco, and at the University of Creation Spirituality in Oakland, Joanna speaks with both great urgency and great appreciation of the crisis we are in and of our capacities to create such a turning.

In her advanced trainings, for example, students come together for twelve days, and Joanna brings "everything I can pass on from what I've learned, in as usable a form as I can, as if I were going to die tomorrow." She doesn't insist on the label "Buddhist," wanting instead to bring the teachings into every modality, to touch people *now*.

"As things fall apart, as systems break down, people begin to scapegoat each other, and fear grows. I want to give people resources to cope with panic and fear and social hysteria so we can get through this time without turning on each other, but with the full dignity and majesty of our journey on earth until now. As we go back and look at how beautiful our evolutionary journey has been, then this current crisis is a big one all right, but we realize how much we've got going for us in terms of our own adaptability and in terms of the mysterious adaptability of life. This, too, can help us move beyond fear, because fear is a contraction of the heart."

Epilogue *

To paint an accurate, comprehensive picture of the changes that have occurred in the world of women and America Buddhism in the past decade would, I believe, require a whole new book (I hope it will be written soon). The following account, by its very nature, will be quite condensed, with necessary omissions and possible errors of emphasis or interpretation. My intention is to provide an evocative overview of developments within the Zen, vipassana, and Tibetan Buddhist communities, and also a few snapshots of women acting courageously (or, it could be said, inevitably), manifesting this ongoing shift of consciousness, the loosening of ancient barriers, and the opening of fresh possibilities.

ZEN

To start with a little fanfare, in the Zen tradition we now have a flurry of new abbesses installed in different parts of the country. San Francisco Zen Center was among the first, with Blanche Hartman in 1996. Now it has a second abbess, Linda Ruth Cutts, whose Mountain Seat Ceremony took place on February 13, 2000, as described in the preface. Los Angeles Zen Center installed Wendy Egyoku Nakao as abbot in 1999. Minnesota Zen Center, after the death of Katagiri Roshi in 1992, spent consider-

*For generous help in gathering material for this epilogue, heartfelt thanks to Sandy Boucher, Linda Ruth Cutts, Anna Douglas, Sunyana Graef, Anne Klein, Lee Lewis, Sue Moon, Lama Palden, Diana Rizzetto, Maylie Scott, and Joan Tollifson.

able time deciding who would be the best person to continue leadership there. Should it be a seasoned and established person from outside or one of Katagiri's own dharma heirs? Deliberations took almost six years (during which time an interim priest was hired), but in the end, dharma heir Karen Suna became abbess in 1998.

Other abbesses include Mitra Bishop at Mountain Gate, a monastic community in New Mexico, who is also spiritual director at Hidden Valley Zen Center in San Marcos, California; Dai-en Bennage at Mt. Equity Zendo near Williamsport, Pennsylvania; as well as two more abbots: Diane Rizzetto at the Bay Zen School in Oakland, California; and Ni-Osho Sherry Chayat at the Zen Center of Syracuse, New York.

Zen teachers in other important leadership roles include Jan Chosen Bays, a dharma heir of Maezumi Roshi, and a wife, mother, and pediatrician specializing in cases of child abuse, who directs the Zen Center in Portland, Oregon; Sunyana Graef, head teacher at the Vermont Zen Center in Shelburne, Vermont, at the Toronto Zen Center in Ontario, Canada, and at Casa Zen in Santo Thomas, Costa Rica; and Tai Taku Pat Phelan, who will be installed as abbess at the Chapel Hill Zen Center in North Carolina in October 2000. The center is an affiliate of San Francisco Zen Center in the tradition of Suzuki Roshi.

A striking circumstance at the time of this writing is that all major leadership positions at San Francisco City Center, at Green Gulch Farm, and at Tassajara Mountain Center (the three affiliates under the umbrella of San Francisco Zen Center) are filled by women. These include two abbessess, the board president, and three tantos (heads of practice).

But at all levels, and in many places, there is a virtual explosion of women who are taking leadership roles. After years of practice and study, some are starting circles and meditation groups where none have existed before. In California, Mary Mocine, longtime student and ordained priest at Berkeley and San Francisco Zen Centers, established the Clear Water Zendo in Vallejo, California, in the fall of 1998. Layla Bockhorst, dharma heir of Norman Fischer, conducts the Mill Valley Zen Circle (sitting group). Fu

Schroeder, dharma heir of Reb Anderson, teaches tea ceremony, has a sitting group in Tiburon, and is tanto (head of practice) at Green Gulch Zen Center. Wendy Johnson, who received dharma transmission from Thich Nhat Hanh, works with his Community for Mindful Living, does outreach work with families and children, and is writing a book on the spiritual practice of gardening at Green Gulch Farm, where she has long been head gardener. And in Minnesota, Joen Snyder O'Neil, dharma heir of Katagiri Roshi, works with students in a style influenced both by Jon Kabat-Zinn and the mindful living principles of Thich Nhat Hanh.

This patchwork overview may suggest the scale of recent developments, but I also want to convey some individual particulars, personal and specific. The following teachers are not necessarily the most eminent or representative, but they are, I think, arresting in their variety.

I've known Maylie Scott for more than thirty years, not intimately, but from a near distance: we were both English department faculty wives at the University of California at Berkeley in the sixties. We started Zen practice around the same time, but Maylie sat down on her zafu and never strayed, while my course was much more erratic. I attended her jukai (lay ordination) ceremony in 1976 and remember tears welling up in my eyes as she entered the zendo with a shaved head. Her tokudo (priest ordination) ceremony was in 1988, and ten years later she received dharma transmission from Mel Weitsman, abbot of Berkeley Zen Center. Now she has her own center in Arcata, California, where she moved six months ago after ten years of commuting back and forth for teaching and sesshins.

The move shouldn't have been easy; there were many obstacles, like a ninety-seven-year-old mother who lived with Maylie and was cared for by her. She considered taking her mother to Arcata, which would not have been simple, but then three of her children announced that their grandmother should stay, and they would move back home to take care of her.

"It was as if the sea parted," Maylie recalled. Finding, buying, and remodeling a new house in Arcata was easy, too; everything that was needed appeared at the right time. Now zazen takes place there every morning except Saturday, and two evenings a week. A garage has just been remodeled into a spacious new zendo. There are twenty regular participants, nine of whom are sewing rakusus in preparation for lay ordination, in addition to about a hundred on the mailing list. People often drive up from the Bay Area (three hundred miles) for monthly one- or three-day sesshins.

"Right now, we're going easy with forms," Maylie told me. (One of her students terms it "Zen lite.") She has been using forms as a means for cultivating mindfulness, but gradually people are developing an *appetite* for them.

Maylie's vision for the center is that it be a place of contemplation as well as action. She was a pioneer of engaged Buddhism in this country, and her profound integration of spiritual practice and social change work has been an inspiration to many. In the past five years, she's taught meditation (often with a Christian flavor, she told me) in jails and prisons around the Bay Area. She plans to work with an interfaith team to do postrelease work at the Eureka County Jail. "Our hope is that this jail becomes a focus for ongoing interfaith community action," she said.

Katherine Thanas, for twenty years a resident and then an ordained priest at the San Francisco Zen Center, moved down the coast to Santa Cruz twelve years ago to become head teacher at both Santa Cruz and the newly organized Monterey Bay Zen Centers. It was a "tremendous learning," she told me, "to come out of the monastic environment, especially Tassajara, into these two lay communities, each with its own culture and demographics." She had to adapt her long-honed practice and understanding for new practitioners who were reaching for something immediately and directly applicable to their lives. Today she presents traditional teachings as "nothing other than one's body and mind." Using experiences from her own life in her talks seems to be the "juice that brings the teaching alive." She has allowed herself to become more and more exposed. "Revealing the undeveloped parts of myself seems to encourage my students and stimulate their own inner teacher," she said.

Dai-en Bennage, formerly a classical ballet dancer, first moved to Japan with her husband in 1963 and stayed three years. She had been entranced with Japanese art, especially brush painting, since childhood and had studied both spoken and written Japanese at Princeton. So after a divorce in 1969, she returned to Japan and remained there for twenty-one years. She practiced Zen Buddhism intensively with a number of teachers during this time, applying the energy and discipline of her ballet training to this new practice.

In 1978, she came to "a big fork in the road," she told me. She had completed a rigorous pilgrimage around the island of Shikoku, visiting eighty-eight temples and offering the Heart Sutra at each. It was "a seminal experience," she said, and it solidified her commitment. She was ordained as a celibate nun by Noda Daito Roshi, whom she described as a "fly-by-the-seat-of-your-pants sort of teacher," whose zendo was a bus with a beautiful yellow carpet. "If you are a true teacher, no other accoutrements are needed," he told her. As a test for ordination, she lived for three winter months in a hermitage made of an overturned soy-sauce vat and then completed twelve years of rigorous monastic practice. During this time, she received transmission and completed roshi training.

Today, at Mount Equity Zendo in north central Pennsylvania, she has two nuns training with her, one American and one French, who are both her ordained disciples. Twenty-odd people have taken precepts, and thirty-odd students attend daily sittings and sesshins. She has also established five prison sanghas, two in maximum-security prisons, and has given precepts to five inmates who asked to receive them. After teaching meditation in prisons for seven years, she told me that people with multiple life sentences often come to Zen because they "have run out of mind games."

The fact that American Zen is mostly a lay practice she thinks is "wonderful but scary. Who's reading the whole encyclopedia?"

she wants to know. "We need a few who will go the whole nine yards." If Buddhism in this country is not built by ordained men and ordained women as well as laymen and laywomen (as the Buddha taught), then "American Zen won't get past Wonder Bread."

In 1995, Charlotte Joko Beck (see Chapter 4) and her first three dharma successors established the Ordinary Mind Zen School to manifest the practice of everyday Zen. Within the school, there is no hierarchy, and each dharma successor determines the teaching approaches and structure for his or her individual practice places. Its members acknowledge that they are ongoing students and that the quality of their teaching derives from the quality of their practice.

Diane Eshin Rizzetto, one of these early dharma successors, has been abbot of the Bay Zen Center in Oakland, California, since 1994. The center has a full schedule, with daily practice and sesshins, and Diane works closely with individual students both in person and on the phone. She uses approaches from other disciplines that "help us see the truth of our life just as it is." Often people work on koans arising from events in their daily lives. As a wife, mother, and grandmother, Diane cannot help but bring these experiences into her teaching. She asks: "Can we hold our wrath, our terror, our sorrows like a baby in our arms? Can we witness in silent stillness the frustration, bitterness, or panic the way we sit patiently next to a screaming child, witnessing the tears as they run their course? All our experiences are a vital force in learning to live an awake life, even hot flashes in the zendo, monthly migraines, or surging sexual energy. These are not burdens or interferences but the fuel flaming our awareness."

Roko Ni-osho Sherry Chayat received dharma transmission in the Rinzai tradition from Eido Shimano Roshi in 1998. The feminization of Buddhism in America, she believes, is one of the strong points in its transmission from East to West. Because she came out of the early women's movement, she feels sensitive to identity issues—as well as to the identitylessness of Buddhist practice. "Dwelling in the contradictions and paradoxes can be a source of fruitful revelation and understanding," she said. She believes that her involvement in the liberation struggle *and* her Buddhist questioning of fixed identity make her particularly sensitive to students' issues around sexuality, gender, abuse, power, and authority.

VIPASSANA

To get a sense of changes within the vipassana Buddhist community, I talked with Anna Douglas, a founding teacher of Spirit Rock Meditation Center in Marin County, California. She told me about a moment that occurred three years ago, during a one-day women's retreat she was teaching there. "It was a little epiphany," she said. "Looking out at the circle of seventy or seventy-five meditating women, I suddenly realized that most of them don't know there was ever a problem with women and Buddhism. New practitioners at Spirit Rock are accustomed to seeing women teachers, a female Kwan Yin next to a male Buddha in the meditation hall, women in leadership positions, women everywhere!"

As the number of women teachers has increased, Anna has noticed that they are becoming more differentiated. That is, some teach very traditionally, following the established male model. Others are introducing a more female style (one that is more intuitive, spontaneous, inclusive, relational). "It's one thing," Anna said, "to have more women teachers. It's another to bring an awareness of the feminine into the form." Old patriarchal models are still there, she observed, as they are in the larger culture, and they change slowly. She believes a feminine way of being and of running dharma centers is a key question for American Buddhism today. "Are women going to take on leadership in a traditional way or bring a more feminine consciousness into our institutions?"

I asked about the newer teachers in the vipassana tradition and will offer a sampling here:

Catherine Ingram was one of the founding teachers of the Insight Meditation Society. Later she studied with a number of non-dual (or Advaita) masters, including Poonja-ji in India. Now, unaffiliated, she teaches a technique of open inquiry in workshops called Dharma Dialogues.

Sylvia Boorstein, author and teacher at Spirit Rock for many years, currently is interested in integrating Buddhism with Judaism. In addition to her regular classes at Spirit Rock, she has been teaching mindfulness to rabbis and other spiritual leaders.

Deborah Chamberlain-Taylor is one of the younger generation of vipassana teachers. She and her husband of many years, George Taylor, both of whom are experienced therapists, are now conducting retreats for couples that incorporate relational issues into meditation practice.

Anna Douglas's own teaching currently focuses on meditation and the creative process. She has been painting for fifteen years, meditating for more than twenty, and is now bringing the two together. "I teach painting from the perspective of the play of form and emptiness," she said. "It is nonclinging in action!"

Julie Wester has been active for years in the administration of Spirit Rock, is currently on the board of directors, has been very involved in the family program, and is mothering a young daughter.

Mary Orr has established a vipassana center in Santa Cruz as well as leading retreats in many parts of the country.

Carol Wilson lives near IMS and travels all over the world teaching traditional vipassana retreats. Despite a chronic illness, she is "totally dedicated" and maintains a daunting schedule.

Tara Brach established the Insight Meditation Community of Washington, D.C., where she teaches classes and retreats.

Lucinda Green, a student of Ruth Denison and the late Ayya Khema, created the Rocky Mountain Insight Meditation Center in Colorado Springs.

Because of the unique nature of her contribution to vipassana practice in America, I also interviewed Arinna Weisman.

Arinna was born in Johannesburg, South Africa, where her parents were jailed as political activists under the apartheid regime. They left the country in 1961, and her subsequent experience of political exile fueled a hunger for freedom that permeates her teaching to this day. She was trained in the lineage of U Bha Khin and Ruth Denison, which emphasizes direct access to our body experience through mindfulness using breath, scanning the body, and movement.

Arinna founded the Dhamma Dena Meditation Center in Northampton, Massachusetts, in 1998. She conducts classes and retreats there for the general community as well as annual retreats for lesbians. In Seattle, Spirit Rock, Washington, D.C., and New York, she gives annual retreats for the lesbian/gay/bisexual/transgendered community. There is something "very special" about these retreats, she says, a "particular energy of being together that is very lovely."

She emphasizes coming together as a community and stresses loving-kindness, the ability to love ourselves and to leave negative messages behind. "We all have the possibility of becoming increasingly free."

Arinna's new book, tentatively called *A Guide to Insight Meditation,* will be published by Random House in the fall or winter of 2000.

TIBETAN BUDDHISM

In the Tibetan Buddhist tradition in this country (often referred to as Vajrayana), there has also been a blossoming of women's energy among new teachers. With it has come a new interest in feminine deities like Tara and Yeshe Tsogyal and in questions like, "What does it mean that in the Tibetan tradition wisdom has always been associated with the feminine?"

Before citing some of the newer women teachers in the Tibetan tradition, I want to acknowledge Tsultrim Allione, who unfortunately was not included in the first edition of this book, but who was the first American woman to be ordained as a Tibetan nun, and one of the first American women to teach Tibetan Buddhism in this country. After studying in India and Nepal with many high Tibetan masters, she began teaching here in the early seventies and was associated with Chögyam Trungpa in establishing the Naropa Institute in Boulder, Colorado. For twenty years she has been training with dzogchen master Namkai Norbu and now teaches under his guidance. Her center, Tara Mandala, in Pagosa Springs, Colorado, offers retreats every summer. Tsultrim's teaching schedule takes her all over the world and she leads pilgrimages to sacred Buddhist sites in India, Tibet, and Bhutan.

Lama Palden Drolma (Caroline Alioto) is a forty-seven-year-old native Californian and a longtime student of the late Kalu Rinpoche. She lived for two years in Bhutan, also spent time in Sikkim and India, and was designated a lama in the Kagyu lineage. After teaching Vajrayana Buddhism for fourteen years in northern California, three years ago she established a dharma center in Marin County called the Sukhasiddhi Foundation. There she teaches Vajrayana, mahamudra, and dzogchen practices from a perspective deeply grounded in feminine spirituality. She has a deep devotion to Tara and often teaches the practice of Green Tara. The feminine side of things, she believes, is nonconceptual and nonstriving. It may be difficult to articulate verbally but is very accessible through experience.

"I honor each individual's own process," she told me, and she tries to facilitate the emergence of each student's particular inner wisdom. She will suggest practices and ways of working spiritually that are tailored to each individual, trusting that his or her path is self-revealing. Her own male teachers worked this way. "I feel blessed and empowered by them."

This is a nonauthoritarian, "shared process," that emphasizes kindness and "joyful participation."

The foundation is growing slowly but strongly. Individuals' well-being "comes before the organization!" Its structure is nonhierarchical, based on concentric circles. The board and committees literally sit in circles, but more important is an attitude of mind. Everyone's input is valued. "Energy flows toward the center, back and forth from one circle to another, and then out into the world."

Traditionally, Tibetan Buddhist institutions have been hierarchical, feudal, and patriarchal. Still, in the monasteries where she studied in the Himalayas, Lama Palden never encountered sexism. She reminded me of the long history of highly realized and revered women practitioners in Tibetan Buddhism, one of whom was Kalu Rinpoche's mother.

Lama Palden is also a trained psychotherapist and believes strongly that for spiritual practice to thrive, psychological issues often need addressing. Instead of "just striving" against all odds toward an elusive goal (so common in other spiritual settings), she encourages students to work with themselves on all levels: spiritually, emotionally, psychologically, and physically.

Venerable Robina Courten, of the Gelugpa lineage, is the editor of *Mandala* magazine, founded the Maitrya Prison Project, and was featured in the Australian-made film *Chasing the Buddha,* recently shown at the Sundance Film Festival. She teaches throughout the world in a down-to-earth way, which one of her students described to me as "fiery, direct, clear, wrathful, and compassionate."

Anne C. Klein is professor and chair of the Religious Studies Department at Rice University in Houston, Texas, where she teaches courses in Buddhist thought and Tibetan language. In 1995, her book *Meeting the Great Bliss Queen: Buddhism, Feminism, and the Art of the Self* was published by Beacon Press. She is a founding member of Dawn Mountain, a Tibetan temple, community center, and research institute in Houston, and for the past few years has also been leading pilgrimages to sacred sites in Tibet and Nepal, most notably to the birthplace of Yeshe Tsogyal (the "Great Bliss Queen"). With Phyllis Pay, an intuitive counselor and Tibetan Buddhist practitioner in the Sakya lineage, she has developed a program called "Buddhism in the Body," which connects energy awareness work with traditional Tibetan practice.

Julie Henderson, after nine years in Australia—teaching or on retreat with her Tibetan masters, the twelfth Gyalwang Drukpa and his father, the Nyingmapa Lama Vairochana Tulku—returned to the United States in 1993. With their approval, she teaches in a nontraditional way in Europe, Australia, and the United States. Her books include *Embodying Well-Being: How to Feel As Good As You Can in Spite of Everything; I Ching: Revealing Story, Training Mind;* and *The Hum Book.*

For the following teachers, I've given only Tibetan names, but all of them are American.

Lama Inge, whose root lama is Chagdud Tulku, Rinpoche, is the resident teacher at Padma Ling in Spokane, Washington. She travels extensively to teach in places like Canada, Alaska, and many other parts of this country.

Lama Yeshe Wangmo is Hawaii's resident teacher for the Vajrayana Foundation. She is based at Orgyen Dechen Cho Dzong, the retreat center of dzogchen Master Lama Tarchin Rinpoche, on the big island of Hawaii. She teaches regularly throughout Hawaii and the mainland.

Karma Lekshe Tsomo, who is also based in Hawaii, is a nonsectarian Buddhist teacher trained in all four schools of Tibetan Buddhism as well as in the Burmese, Korean, and Chinese traditions. She directs eight education projects for women in India (in Dharamasala, Spiti, Ladakh, and Kinnaur) and teaches Buddhism and world religions at Chaminode University in Honolulu. She is secretary of Sakyadhita: International Association of Buddhist Women, and is in the process of establishing a retreat center on the island of Kauai.

Venerable Thubten Chodren, in the Gelugpa lineage, teaches at Dharma Friendship Foundation in Seattle, Washington.

Sangyey Khantrul, student of Gyatrul Rinpoche, teaches all over the West Coast, especially the Bay Area and Portland, Oregon.

Lama Shenpen Drolma was ordained by Chagdud Tulku, Rinpoche, teaches primarily in Arizona and New Mexico, and can be reached through the Chagdud Gonpa Foundation.

Chagdud Khadro, wife of Chagdud Tulku, Rinpoche, has taught in many parts of this country and is currently teaching mostly in Brazil.

Finally, I want to cite three other features of the past decade in the world of women and Buddhism. Whether these are gender-related or purely general trends that transcend gender is very hard to say. In any case, they have occurred in the same period that women have become increasingly prominent in the Western Buddhist world.

Epilogue

First is the phenomenon of cross-fertilization, both between Buddhism and Western religions and among the various Buddhist traditions themselves. Buddhist-Christian dialogue is not so new. But the budding connections between Buddhists and Jews seem fresh and surprising. Jewish Buddhist teachers like Sylvia Boorstein (Vipassana) and Norman Fischer (Zen) are reaching out to rabbis and the Jewish community for mutual explorations. And the burgeoning new Jewish meditation movement has been hosting conversations with Buddhist meditators and teachers.

Within Buddhism, Zen students have been doing vipassana retreats and vice versa. Tibetan students show up at both. Zen students attend retreats with Toni Packer, who has not considered herself a Zen teacher for years (see Chapter 1). Her own students attend a wide assortment of other retreats. And many vipassana practitioners and teachers have been studying with Tibetan dzogchen masters as well as with the non-dual masters of Advaita-Vedanta.

Second is another important change (sometimes subtle and sometimes not so subtle) in the structure and ethos of many American Buddhist institutions. It has been described as democratization, feminization, process or consensus orientation. More and more, hierarchies are loosening or disappearing, and decision-making processes are becoming open and flexible. The Ordinary Mind Zen School of Charlotte Joko Beck and her dharma heirs is entirely nonhierarchical and open to innovation by any member. The San Francisco Zen Center has an elaborate system of mediation for resolving disputes, and abbots are no longer elected for life but for four-year terms with a renewable three-year term. Lama Palden's Sukhasiddhi Foundation is based entirely on circles, for doing business as well as spiritual work. Everyone is equal; every voice is important. Tsultrlm Allione and Anne Klein also teach in circles—a very different story, Anne pointed out, from the teacher sitting on a throne.

Last, and very important, I want to acknowledge the tremendous strength and vitality of the engaged Buddhism movement in this country. A recent book, *Engaged Buddhism in the West*, edited by Christopher S. Queen, chronicles this movement in a very comprehensive way. In her chapter in that book, entitled

"Activist Women in American Buddhism," Susan Moon asks: "How does feminism fit in" here? Her answer speaks to the issues discussed in the previous paragraph as well:

> Because we are women, we know what it is to be marginalized, and this knowledge can help us to be truly inclusive. We have a leg up, as women, at recognizing the patriarchal structure that is so often embedded in our Buddhist institutions, and knowing it is not the ultimate truth. So we tend to be flexible in terms of doctrine. As women we also know something about the suffering caused by oppression, and we feel a moral imperative to redress this. . . . [W]omen have lived their lives close to tears, their own and other people's. So now they go right to the heart of suffering.

Maylie Scott told me that "social engagement is now *usually* regarded as an aspect of practice. Some of us feel it is the most important practice edge: how do you express what you have learned on the cushion? There is internal practice and external practice. The Dalai Lama said you need both."

I believe the impact of these developments on the evolution of Buddhism in the West cannot be minimized. They are changing the lineaments and character of our institutions and sanghas, and clearly there is no turning back. Western Buddhism is becoming a different animal than Eastern Buddhism (as Buddhism has historically done whenever it moved from one part of the world to another). Still, many of us continue to deeply value the presence and contributions of traditional women teachers like Dai-en Bennage, many of them trained by Asian masters. Other teachers are straddling the line, adhering to traditional modes while incorporating feminist values. In the Zen tradition, Dianne Rizzetto and Ni-Osho Sherry Chayat come to mind. Within Vajrayana Buddhism, Lama Palden and Tsultrim Allione, while treasuring their Tibetan heritage, have introduced new feminine forms in a sensitive, respectful way that is at the same time revolutionary.

To end this epilogue, I would like to present the words of Wendy Egyoku Nakao, abbot at the Zen Center of Los Angeles.

Epilogue

They first appeared in *Turning Wheel,* the journal of the Buddhist Peace Fellowship, in spring 1999.

> What are the forms that we as women will create? What practice structures will come out of our own lives? What skillful means will we bring forth out of our being? People say, "Don't throw the baby out with the bath water." And I say, "What's the baby? What's the bath water? Throw it *all* out and let's see what arises from the vast unknowing."

NOTES

1. R. H. Blyth, *Zen and Zen Classics,* vol. 5 (Tokyo: Hokuseido Press, 1960), p. 53. See also *Zen and Zen Classics: Selections from R. H. Blyth,* compiled by Frederick Franck (New York: Vintage Books, 1978), p. 172.

2. Rick Fields, *How the Swans Came to the Lake: A Narrative History of Buddhism in America* (Boston: Shambhala Publications, 1981; revised and updated, 1986).

3. Gary Snyder, *The Real Work: Interviews and Talks, 1964–1979* (New York: New Directions, 1980), p. 106.

4. I. B. Horner, *Women under Primitive Buddhism* (London: George Routledge & Sons, 1930; Delhi: Motilal Banarsides, Delhi, 1975).

5. Diana Y. Paul, *Women in Buddhism* (Berkeley: Asian Humanities Press, 1979).

6. T. W. Davids and C. A. F. Rhys Davids, trans., *Dialogues of the Buddha,* 5th ed. (London: Luzac & Co., 1966).

7. Frances Wilson, "The Nun," chap. 3 in Paul, *Women in Buddhism,* pp. 78–108.

8. Sulak Sivaraksa, "Buddhist Women, Past and Present," *Kahawai: A Journal of Women and Zen* 6, nos. 1 and 2 (Winter/Spring 1985): 3–11.

9. Ayya Khema, *Can Women Attain Nibbana?* (Sri Lanka: private printing, 1984), p. 5.

10. J. Hughes, *Buddhist Feminism* (Main Circleville, Ohio: private printing), p. 1.

11. Ibid., p. 3.

12. Susan Murcott and John Tarrant, trans., "The Therigatha" (Selections), *Kahawai* 1, no. 3 (1979): 1–14.

13. Khema, *Can Women Attain Nibbana?,* p. 14.

14. Frances Wilson in Paul, *Women in Buddhism,* pp. 98–102.

15. Quoted in Paul, *Women in Buddhism,* pp. 175–176.

16. John Blofeld, *Bodhisattva of Compassion: The Mystical Tradition of Kwan Yin* (Boulder: Shambhala Publications, 1978).

17. Tsultrim Allione, *Women of Wisdom* (London: Routledge & Kegan Paul, 1984), p. 12.

18. "Women in Kamakura Buddhism: Dogen's Raihai Tokuzui," translated by Deborah Hopkinson, *Kahawai* 1, nos 2 and 3 (Spring/Summer 1979): 9–13

and 2–4. Another translation, by Francis H. Cook, appears in *Women and Buddhism,* edited by Rev. Teacher Komei Larson, O.B.C. (Mt. Shasta, Calif.: Shasta Abbey Press, 1981), pp. 45–53.

19. "Kahawai Koans," translated by Robert Aitken and Thomas Cleary, *Kahawai* 3, no. 3 (1981): 1–18; vol. 4, no. 1 (1982): 14–16; and vol. 6, no. 2 (1984): 16–23.

20. Thich Nhat Hanh, *Zen Keys* (Garden City, N.Y.: Anchor Press/Doubleday, 1974), p. 96.

21. Elise Boulding, *The Underside of History: A View of Women through Time* (Boulder: Westview Press, 1976).

22. Iris Murdoch, lecture at the University of California, Berkeley, 1984.

23. Peter Haskel, trans. *Bankei Zen,* ed. Yoshibo Hakeda (New York: Grove Press, 1984), p. 8.

24. Interview excerpted in *Karuna: A Journal of Buddhist Meditation* 3, no. 2 (1986): 11–14; and in *Inquiring Mind: A Journal of the Vipassana Community* 3, no. 1 (1986): 8–9.

25. Allione, *Women of Wisdom,* p. 18.

26. Carol Ochs, *Women and Spirituality* (Totowa, N.J.: Rowman & Allanheld, 1983), p. 19.

27. Ibid., p. 104.

28. Carol P. Christ and Judith Plaskow, eds., *Womanspirit Rising: A Feminist Reader in Religion* (New York: Harper Forum Books, 1979), pp. 9–10.

29. For further information on Women-church, a grass-roots movement among Roman Catholic feminists and theologians, including Rosemary Radford Ruether, contact WATER (Women's Alliance for Theology, Ethics, and Ritual), 8035 Thirteenth Street, Suites 1 and 3, Silver Spring, MD 20910.

30. Charlene Spretnak, ed., *The Politics of Women's Spirituality* (Garden City, N.Y.: Anchor Press/Doubleday, 1982), pp. xv–xxiv.

31. Blyth, *Zen and Zen Classics,* p. 53 (Franck edition, pp. 173–174).

32. Informal statement reported to me from a vipassana teacher-training workshop, March 1986, and later confirmed by Jack Kornfield.

33. Robert Aitken, "The Body of the Buddha," *Parabola* 10, no. 3 (Fall 1985): 26–31.

34. In partial amends, I would like to acknowledge Judith Simmer Brown, Judith Lief, and Lila Rich, all of whom, under Chögyam Trungpa, Rinpoche, are teaching or have taught at Vajradhatu or the Naropa Institute in Boulder, Colorado.

35. Philip Kapleau, *The Three Pillars of Zen* (Boston: Beacon Press, 1965).

GLOSSARY

abhisheka (Skt.): Literally, sprinkling. Consecration or initiation.

anapana (Pali): Attending to the breathing, in and out. One of the fundamental exercises of mindfulness practice, common to all schools of Buddhism.

Avalokiteshvara: One of the most prominent bodhisattvas in Mahayana Buddhism, "he who looks down with compassion on the human world."

bhikkhuni (Pali), bhikshuni (Skt.): Buddhist nun. (Masc.: bhikkhu, bhikshu)

bodhicitta (Skt.): Wisdom heart. The aspiration of a bodhisattva for supreme enlightenment for the benefit of all beings.

bodhisattva (Skt.): One whose being or essence is "bodhi," i.e., wisdom resulting from direct perception of Truth. A "Buddha of Compassion" whose aim is the enlightenment of all, without distinction of self and not-self.

brahmavihara (Skt.): The four divine states of mind or spiritual abodes, methods of meditation in which the mind pervades the universe with thoughts of loving-kindness (metta), compassion (karuna), sympathetic joy (mudita), and equanimity (upekkha).

buddha (Skt.): Title, rather than proper name, meaning "enlightened one" or "awakened one." The historical Buddha, Gotama Shakyamuni, founder of Buddhism, was born in 563 in Lumbini, India.

Chakrasamvara (Skt.): Literally, the binding or union of the chakras (primary centers of the illusory body). A yidam having to do with discriminating awareness wisdom. A masculine energy principle of anuttara tantra.

daisan (Jap.): Individual meeting of student with teacher (sensei) in the Zen tradition, similar to dokusan with a teacher who has attained the rank of roshi.

dharma (Skt.): Truth, doctrine, essence, teaching. Can also mean phenomena or ultimate constituents.

dokusan (Jap.): Private, face-to-face study with a roshi, the spirit of which penetrates the essence of life.

dukkha (Pali): Suffering.

gassho (Jap.): A gesture of respect in which the hands are held, palms together, at the chest.

guru yoga (Skt.): The fourth ngondro practice, having to do with the receiving of blessings.

Glossary

hara (Jap.): Deep center of gravity in the body which develops during zazen; technically an area three centimeters below the navel.

inka (Jap.): Literally, seal of approval. In Rinzai Zen, equivalent to dharma transmission from master to student, bestowed upon the completion of formal study.

Kagyu (Tib.): One of the primary Tibetan lineages through which oral transmission of the teachings take place.

karma (Skt.): Law of cause and effect by which one reaps what one has sown either in this or in a past life.

kensho (Jap.): Seeing into the essential nature of things; an experience of opening or understanding. The first experience of satori, or nondiscriminitive consciousness.

kinhin (Jap.): "Sutra walking." Formal walking in a single line around the zendo between periods of zazen.

koan (Jap.): Teaching formulation, baffling to the logical mind, pointing to a truth beyond intellect.

Kwan Yin (Chin.): Feminine aspect of bodhisattva Avalokiteshvara.

kyosaku (Jap.): Also keisaku. Long wooden stick applied to the shoulders to offset sleepiness and/or stiffness as well as generally to encourage people's zazen practice.

mahamudra (Skt.): Great seal, symbol, or gesture. Meditative transmission handed down especially by the Kagyu school. In this state, all experiences are transformed into transcendental knowledge and skillful means.

Mahayana (Skt.): The Northern School or School of the Great Vehicle, embracing Tibet, Mongolia, China, Korea and Japan. Emphasizes heart and intuition over intellect and the compassionate being-in-the-world of the bodhisattva.

Maitreya (Skt.): The Buddha to Come. Most popular bodhisattva in Buddhist art. (In Japan he is known as the fat, laughing figure of Hotei.)

mandala (Skt.): A magical or ritual circle. In Tibet, a diagram used in invocations, meditation, and temple services.

mantra (Skt.): Formula or invocation used in Tantric Buddhism in Tibet and in the Shingon School of Japan. Based on the science of the occult power of sound.

metta (Pali): Loving-kindness, active good will. The first of the four brahmaviharas.

Mu (Jap.): A koan, often the first assigned to beginning students in the Rinzai Zen tradition. The meaning of Mu is both inexpressible in rational terms and designed precisely to shatter rationality. The story with which it is associated is simply a monk's question ("Does a dog have Buddha-nature?") and Zen master Joshu's answer: "Mu!"

ngondro (Tib.): Four preliminary practices of Vajrayana Buddhism, consisting of 100,000 prostrations, mantras, mandalas, and guru yoga.

nirvana (Skt.), nibbana (Pali): A state of supreme enlightenment beyond intellectual conception, in which ego discriminations are dissolved in union with ultimate reality.

Glossary

osho (Jap.): Title accorded to the head monk in a Zen monastery.

rakusu (Jap.): Square apron hung from the shoulders over the monastic robes of Zen monks.

Rinzai (Jap.): Ninth-century Zen master, pupil of Huang Po, who founded the Rinzai or "Sudden" School of Zen Buddhism. His sayings, collected in *Rinzai Roku,* are considered a supreme example of Zen literature.

roshi (Jap.): "Old teacher." Name given to a Zen master who gives personal instruction to lay and monastic students.

sadhana (Skt.): A type of Vajrayana ritual text as well as the actual meditative practice it describes.

samadhi (Skt. and Pali): A state of concentrated even-mindedness devoid of dualistic thought in which distinctions between self, object, and relationship are transcended.

samatha (Skt. and Pali): Tranquillity of mind.

sangha (Skt.): "Assembly." The monastic order founded by the Buddha. Community of practitioners. The third of the three Jewels: Buddha, Dharma, Sangha.

sankhara (Pali), samskara (Skt.): Collection of mental contents including complexes, conditioned reflexes, subconscious habits, and memories. Psychic material that influences consciousness and is influenced by it.

sanzen (Jap.): Intense interview between a roshi, or Zen master, and a monk or lay person in Zen training. May take seconds or minutes and, during sesshin, may be scheduled daily or several times a day.

satori (Jap.): A state of consciousness beyond the plane of discrimination or differentiation, beyond description, and incommunicable. Considered the beginning rather than the end of true Zen training.

sesshin (Jap.): Intensive Zen meditation retreat.

Shakyamuni: The historical Buddha.

Shambhala (Skt.): A mythical kingdom in which all citizens were kind and learned and practiced meditation. Also used as a symbol of wakefulness and sanity that exist as a potential for each human being.

shunyata (Skt.): Void, emptiness—but also empty of the concept of emptiness.

sila (Skt. and Pali): Moral precepts.

Soto (Jap.): School of Zen Buddhism founded by Dogen in the thirteenth century. Soto utilizes gradual methods (e.g., shikantaza, or deep meditation) by contrast with the "sudden" or direct methods of Rinzai Zen. Since all *is* Buddha, we need only to realize what we are.

suto (Viet.): Master. Similar to the Japanese title "roshi."

Tathagata (Skt.): A fully realized being who has become one with the absolute. Title used by Buddha (in reference to himself) and by his followers.

Theravada (Skt.): Way of the Elders or Southern School of Buddhism, previously called Hinayana or Lesser Vehicle by Mahayanists. Widespread in Southeast Asia (Burma, Thailand, Cambodia, Sri Lanka).

tonglen (Tib.): Practice of exchanging oneself for others. The practitioner breathes in the suffering of others and breathes out warmth and generosity.

tulku (Tib.): The appearance-on-earth body of a Buddha. The reincarnation of a holy man in the body of a child, subject to diligent inquiry and strict rules of proof.

upasika (Skt. and Pali): Feminine form of *upasaka*—a lay disciple who strives to keep five or eight precepts at all times, to follow the Eightfold Path while living in the world.

Vajrayana (Skt.): Tantric school of North Indian and Tibetan Buddhism.

Vajrayogini (Skt.): A yidam representing the feminine principle of prajna, or knowledge, involving the transformation of ignorance and passion into emptiness and compassion.

vinaya (Skt.): Rules of discipline governing the monastic order.

vipassana (Pali): Insight; intuitive knowing. Also refers to a Theravadin meditation practice (satipatthana) for developing right mindfulness.

yana (Skt.): Vehicle; vehicle of salvation from the wheel of samsara. Thus: Mahayana (the larger vehicle), Hinayana (the smaller vehicle), and Vajrayana (the diamond vehicle).

yidam (Tib.): A personal deity who embodies the practitioner's awakened nature.

zabuton (Jap.): Meditation mat.

zafu (Jap.): Meditation cushion.

zazen (Jap.): Zen sitting; Zen meditation.

zendo (Jap.): Room or hall, often in a separate building, used for zazen.

APPENDIX

Addresses of Teachers and Centers

Charlotte Joko Beck
Zen Center of San Diego
2047 Felspar Street
San Diego, CA 92109
(619) 273-3444

Pema Chodron
Gampo Abbey
Pleasant Bay, Cape Breton
Nova Scotia BOE 2PO
Canada
(902) 224-2752

Ruth Denison
Desert Vipassana Center
Route 1, Box 250
Joshua Tree, CA 92252
(760) 362-4815

Lama Tsering Everest
AL. dos Araes 117
Planalto Paulista
Sao Paolo S.T.
CCEP 04066-000
Brazil
E-mail: tscring@chagdud.org

[Gesshin Prabhasa Dharma, Roshi]
International Zen Institute of
    America and Europe
1760 Pomona Avenue, No. 35
Costa Mesa, CA 92627
(949) 631-0323
E-mail (at Noorder Poort):
    kanromon@euronet.nl

Appendix

Ven. Karuna Dharma
International Buddhist Meditation
 Center
928 South New Hampshire Boulevard
Los Angeles, CA 90006
(213) 384-0850
E-mail: karunadh@wgn.net
Web site: www.wgn.net/~karunadh

[Rev. Jiyu Kennett, Roshi]
Order of Buddhist Contemplatives
Shasta Abbey
3724 Summit Drive
Mount Shasta, CA 96067-9102
(530) 926-4208
Web site: www.OBCON.org

[Ayya Khema]
Buddha-Haus
Uttenbuhl 5
87466 04-Mittelberg
Germany
08376/502
fax: 08376/592
E-mail: buddha-haus@t-online.de

Joanna Macy
2812 Cherry Street
Berkeley, CA 94705

Jacqueline Mandell
Leadership from a Pure Heart
P.O. Box 2085
Portland, OR 97208-2085
(503) 790-1064
fax: (503) 790-0602
E-mail: leadership.pure.heart
 @worldnet.att.net

Sonja Margulies
205 Seabright Avenue
Santa Cruz, CA 95062

Toni Packer
Springwater Center
7179 Mill Street
Springwater, NY 14560
(716) 669-2141
fax: (716) 669-9573
E-mail: spwtrctr@servtech.com

Yvonne Rand
Redwood Creek Dharma Center
1821 Shoreline Highway
Muir Beach, CA 94963
(415) 388-5572
E-mail: goats@igc.org

Bobby Rhodes
Kwan Um School of Zen
528 Pound Road
Cumberland, RI 02864
(401) 658-1176

Sharon Salzberg
Insight Meditation Society
1234 Pleasant Street
Barre, MA 01005
(617) 355-4378
E-mail: sharonsz@aol.com

Colleen Schmitz
California Vipassana Center
P.O. Box 1167
North Fork, CA 93643
(559) 877-4386
E-mail: info@mahavana.dhamma.
 org
Web site: www.mahavana.dhamma.
 org